NEW MEDIA DISCOURSES, CULTURE AND POLITICS AFTER THE ARAB SPRING

NEW MEDIA DISCOURSES, CULTURE AND POLITICS AFTER THE ARAB SPRING

Case Studies from Egypt and Beyond

Edited by
Aziz Douai and Eid Mohamed

I.B. TAURIS
LONDON • NEW YORK • OXFORD • NEW DELHI • SYDNEY

I.B. TAURIS
Bloomsbury Publishing Plc
50 Bedford Square, London, WC1B 3DP, UK
1385 Broadway, New York, NY 10018, USA
29 Earlsfort Terrace, Dublin 2, Ireland

BLOOMSBURY, I.B. TAURIS and the I.B. Tauris logo are trademarks of
Bloomsbury Publishing Plc

First published in Great Britain 2022
This paperback edition published 2023

Series design by Adriana Brioso
Cover image: A joyful man displays a laptop showing the Al Jazeera
news channel's coverage of the resignation of President Mubarak,
Cairo, Egypt, 2011. (© Guy Martin/Panos Pictures)

ISBN: HB: 978-0-7556-4050-8
         PB: 978-0-7556-4054-6
      ePDF: 978-0-7556-4051-5
     eBook: 978-0-7556-4052-2

Typeset by Integra Software Services Pvt. Ltd.

To find out more about our authors and books visit www.bloomsbury.com and
sign up for our newsletters.

CONTENTS

CONTRIBUTORS

Dr Eid Mohamed is Assistant Professor of Arab–US cultural politics at the Comparative Literature Program at Doha Institute for Graduate Studies. Mohamed taught at numerous institutions, including the George Washington University, University of Guelph, Wilfred Laurier University, Sheridan College and State University of New York at Binghamton. Mohamed's work is located at the crossroads of several areas of inquiry in US–Middle East studies, literary, media and cultural studies. His recent publications include a sole-authored book on the role of Egyptian cultural and literary producers in mediating critiques of the US power and how one can historicize the Egyptian responses to power as well as the hopes and despairs of the Obama presidency and the Arab Spring (*Arab Occidentalism*, I.B. Tauris, 2015; and a new paperback edition in 2017), a co-edited volume about the 2011 Egyptian uprising and its aftermath (*Egypt beyond Tahrir Square*, Indiana University Press, 2016) and a co-edited collection titled 'Arab Spring: Modernity, Identity and Change' (Palgrave, 2019) He has published more than twenty journal articles and book chapters and his work appears in *New Media and Society, International Journal of Cultural Studies, Diaspora: A Journal of Transnational Studies, Journal of Refugee Studies, Refuge: Canada's Journal on Refugees, Journal of Islamic and Muslim Studies* and many others.

Dr Aziz Douai (PhD in Mass Communications, Pennsylvania State University) is Professor of Journalism and the Dean of the Faculty of Graduate Studies and Research at the University of Regina and currently researches disruptive media technologies and the politics of global media. He has published more than fifty journal articles and book chapters dealing with Arab media and other global communication issues. Dr Douai is the author of *Arab Media and the Politics of Terrorism: Unbecoming News* (Peter Lang, 2020), and co-editor of *Mediated Identities and New Journalism in the Arab World: Mapping the "Arab Spring"* (Palgrave Macmillan, 2016) and *New Media Influence on Social and Political Change in Africa* (IGI Global, 2013).

Dr. Magdalena Karolak is Associate Professor of Humanities and Social Sciences at Zayed University, UAE. She received her PhD in Linguistics, MA in Political Science, MA in Latin American Studies and BA in French Language. Prior to working at ZU, Dr Karolak held Assistant Professor positions in Bahrain and Saudi Arabia. In 2014–15, she was an American Political Science Association MENA Fellow. Her research interests include transformations of societies in the MENA region and comparative linguistics. Dr. Karolak has published more than forty journal articles and book chapters on the shifting gender relations, social media, culture and identity, and political system transformations in the MENA countries. She is the author of three scholarly monographs.

Dr. Emad Mohamed is Senior Lecturer in Computational Linguistics & Translation Technology at the Research Group in Computational Linguistics, Research Institute in Information & Language Processing, University of Wolverhampton, West Midlands, England, UK. His research interests include Computational Linguistics, Machine Learning, Translation Technology, Computational Linguistics for the Digital Humanities, Cultural Analytics, Corpus Linguistics, and Arabic. He is especially interested in how computational linguistics can help better the understanding of the Humanities. He finished his PhD in Computational Linguistics at Indiana University in 2010, and he has experience in both the industry and academia. He previously held positions at Carnegie Mellon, UQAM, Nuance Communications and Indiana University.

Dr. Sahar Khamis is Associate Professor in the Department of Communication and Affiliate Professor of Women's Studies at the University of Maryland, College Park. She is an expert on Arab and Muslim media, and the former Head of the Mass Communication Department at Qatar University. She is a former Mellon Islamic Studies Initiative Visiting Professor at the University of Chicago in 2014 and a former Visiting Scholar at the Annenberg School for Communication at the University of Pennsylvania in 2015. She is the co-author of the books *Islam Dot Com: Contemporary Islamic Discourses in Cyberspace* (Palgrave Macmillan, 2009) and *Egyptian Revolution 2.0: Political Blogging, Civic Engagement and Citizen Journalism* (Palgrave Macmillan, 2013), and the co-editor of the book *Arab Women's Activism and Socio-Political Transformation: Unfinished Gendered Revolutions* (Palgrave Macmillan, 2018). She authored and co-authored numerous book chapters, journal articles and conference papers, and she has publications in English, Arabic, German, French and Italian. Dr. Khamis is a frequent international media commentator and analyst, public speaker, radio host and former human rights commissioner.

Dr. Ehab H. Gomaa is Assistant Professor in the Faculty of Arts at the Alexandria University, Egypt, where he has been a faculty member since 2003. Ehab holds PhD in mass communication from Alexandria University, Egypt, and MA in journalism and mass communication from the American University in Cairo. He came to new media and mass communication studies from a sociological background and is working now as Director of the Alexandria University General Center for career development. He is a Ford Fellow, Hiekal Foundation for Arab Journalism Fellow, and was a visitor journalist to Reuters Institute for the study of Journalism, Oxford University, UK. Ehab was a Fulbright visiting scholar to the University of Maryland, USA, and he is an alumnus of Edward R Murrow program for journalists. He has received numerous awards for his academic contributions in journalism and mass communication.

Dina Abdel-Mageed is a PhD candidate at the School of Culture and Communication, the University of Melbourne. She has professional experience in journalism and communication. She received a Master of Digital Communication and Culture and a Master of Arts in media studies (Research) from the University of Sydney. Her research interests include media and politics in the Middle East, social media, Islamophobia and media portrayal of Muslim minorities.

Dr. Grant Bollmer is Associate Professor of Media Studies at North Carolina State University, where he teaches in the Communication Department and the Communication, Rhetoric, and Digital Media (CRDM) PhD Program. He is the author of three books, *Inhuman Networks: Social Media and the Archaeology of Connection* (2016), *Theorizing Digital Cultures* (2018) and *Materialist Media Theory: An Introduction* (2019).

Dr. Mustafa Menshawy joined the Lancaster University's SEPAD (Sectarianism, Proxies and De-Sectarianisation) in 2021. His work focuses on Middle East Studies, politics of authoritarianism and strategic narratives. He is the author of *State, Memory, and Egypt's Victory in the 1973 War: Ruling by Discourse* (2017) and *Leaving the Muslim Brotherhood: Self, Society and the State* (2020). He wrote articles for *Third World Quarterly*, *Politics*, *Middle Eastern Studies* and *Religions*. Menshawy worked for the University of Westminster and the London School of Economics. A former BBC reporter (and a winner of Lorenzo Natali Prize), Menshawy regularly appears at media outlets such as the BBC, Sky News and Aljazeera. He currently conducts four projects related to 'The Meso-level of Sectarianisation: The Muslim Brotherhood as a Case Study', 'Discursive Battles of (De)sectarianisation in the Arab World', 'First Ladies of Authoritarianism: State, Power and Double Agency' and 'Sovereignty as Emotions in Middle East Politics'.

Azza El Masri is the North Africa, West Asia Program Associate at media-tech non-profit Meedan, working with independent media organizations, human rights organizations and journalism students to develop and support open-source investigations and fact-checking projects in the region. Her research examines Arab-language misinformation on encrypted messaging apps and tries to understand the effect of content moderation on Arab independent media and free speech online. She is a Fulbright Scholar and holds a Master's degree in Media and Communication Arts from Florida State University.

Dr. Safa Elnaili is Associate Professor of Arabic language and literature at the University of Alabama. Her research interests are Libyan literature, literary translation, the *Arabian Nights*, stylistics analysis and critical discourse analysis. Dr. Elnaili is currently pursuing an MFA in creative writing and literary translation at Vermont College of Fine Arts. She is devoted to translating Libyan literature and bringing it to the international readership.

Dr. Touria Khannous is Associate Professor in the Department of World Languages and Literatures and the International Studies Program at Louisiana State University. Her research interests include Film Studies, Black diaspora studies and Maghrib studies. She has published articles on Maghrebian literature and film, as well as a manuscript on African women's literature, film and internet discourse.

Contributors

Hasnaa Mokhtar is the Postdoctoral Associate at Rutgers University's Center for Women's Global Leadership. She is a scholar, researcher and activist, with expertise on the Arabian Gulf, focusing on narratives of Muslim survivors of gender-based violence. She holds a PhD from Clark University and her dissertation focused on narrative power and the invisible trauma of gendered violence in Kuwait. Hasnaa's writings have been published in mainstream media such as Fortune and Yahoo and in academic journals such as Feminist Review and Feminist Anthropology. Previously, Hasnaa served as Executive Director of the Center for Nonviolent Solutions in Worcester, MA, and more recently as Special Program Director at Peaceful Families Project. Hasnaa is passionate about life, personal growth, spirituality and everything in between.

ACKNOWLEDGEMENTS

This book project is made possible by the NPRP Grant NPRP9-225-5-024 from the Qatar National Research Fund (a member of Qatar Foundation), titled 'Transcultural Identities: Solidaristic Action and Contemporary Arab Social Movements'. The grant is led by Dr. Eid Mohamed and is based at the Doha Institute for Graduate Studies (DI).

Chapter 1

THE 'ARAB SPRING' WAVES: MEDIA, CULTURE AND SOCIAL PROTEST

Eid Mohamed and Aziz Douai

A perpetual culture of dissent and the Arab Spring

The interrogation of the Arab Spring uprisings and critical engagement with the contingent conditions from which they arose constitute the focal concerns of this edited volume issued ten years after the anniversaries of the Tunisian and Egyptian uprisings. Most of the studies in the volume focus on cases and issues emanating from the Egyptian experience; yet, their contributions are applicable to the region as they grapple with the perpetual culture of dissent in these Arab Spring waves. The promise of social and genuine change, while blindingly clear from the first calls in Arab streets, has painfully come crashing down. It has required a rethinking of the modes of political engagement and, as this volume aims, a cross-examination of how the arts and social media superstructures provide pivotal avenues for contesting political repression through culture.

Social change and revolutions across history, always born out of fundamental crises, surprise the world when they happen, and their aftermath usually seems unpredictable. The Arab Spring uprisings validate this tried and true – albeit seldom recalled – history lesson. The 2011 uprisings heralded a tumultuous period of cultural, political and social realignments in the region as citizens stormed the streets to demand democratic freedoms and inclusive forms of governance. The whole world watched in awe as dictators in Tunisia, Egypt and Libya were toppled, authoritarian governments, such as those of Morocco and Jordan, bowed to popular pressure and enacted constitutional reforms, and other recalcitrant regimes opted to double down and violently suppress protesters. The momentous nature of the events understandably shook the world, confounded world powers and leaders, and inspired popular demands for social justice and democracy in other parts of the world. The Arab Spring stirred hopes of change and empowerment among global social movements and activists, from the US-based Occupy Wall Street grassroots movement to ordinary African citizens marching in the streets of Luanda, Angola, and students in the Burkina Faso city of Koudougou (Harsch 2011).

Among world powers, however, the United States stood out for its incoherent and contradictory responses to the uprisings. Barack Obama sought to initially align the United States with Arab yearnings for democracy and dignity, as he asserted in early 2011:

> We have the chance to show that America values the dignity of the street vendor in Tunisia more than the raw power of the dictator … America must use all our influence to encourage reform in the region … we need to speak honestly about the principles that we believe in, with friend and foe alike.
>
> [Arab citizens'] shouts of human dignity are being heard across the region. And through the moral force of nonviolence, the people of the region have achieved more change in six months than terrorists have accomplished in decades.
>
> (paras. 23, 40, 17)

Obama's subsequent halting 'embrace' of Arab popular demands exposed deep fissures in the US foreign policy establishment as the limits of democracy promotion discourse became visible (Douai 2020). Two years later, tacit support for the overthrow of democratically elected Mohamed Morsi and the Egyptian military takeover, led by Abdel-Fattah el-Sisi, revealed a befuddled strategic vision and difficult geopolitical calculations that the Arab uprisings imposed on the US foreign policy establishment (*Al Jazeera* 2019).

With the relative exception of Tunisia, the promise of social and political change in the Arab Spring went unfulfilled or simply bogged down amidst violent strife and foreign intervention. Hopeful and peaceful calls for democracy in Syria quickly disintegrated as the Baathist Bashar al-Assad regime, his foreign allies and the Islamic State unleashed ruthless and devastating attacks against rebels and opponents seeking his ouster, a war that killed hundreds of thousands, displaced millions and ruined the country. As Phillips explained in an essay published in *The Atlantic* (2018), 'The regime used cynical and brutal tactics to maintain key backing at home, while abroad it had steadfast allies and reluctant and incompetent enemies' (para. 3). The brutal Syrian experience demonstrated the slim odds of success the Arab Spring uprisings and the dreams of democratization in the region faced: the Assad regime's ruthless deployment of barrel bombs to attack civilians in Aleppo and other rebel-held areas in 2016 and 2018 (Amnesty International 2018); the cynical use of the threat of terrorism by releasing from state prisons hundreds of radical extremists who went on to form and lead terror groups such as Ahrar as-Sham, Jaysh al-Islam, Jabhat al-Nusra and ISIS; a fractured opposition with no visible high-profile leadership; and global weakness countered by robust diplomatic support and military assistance from Iran and Russia (Phillips 2018).

Democracy did not evolve in post-Muammar Qaddafi Libya and, in fact, the country descended into 'perpetual chaos' (Chorin 2019) and unforgiving political deadlock. Armed factions and terror groups aligned with the Islamic State, among other militants, continued to destabilize and tear down the national fabric as they vied for control of the oil-rich country. Nearly a decade after the fall of the Qaddafi regime, efforts at national reconciliation and unity have faltered, as Field

Marshal Khalifa Haftar, a warlord leader of the east-based Libyan National Army, assaulted Tripoli (the nation's capital) and threatened to upend the rule of the UN-recognized Government of National Accord (Chorin 2019). Donald Trump endorsed strongman Haftar under the excuse of 'fighting terrorism and securing Libya's oil resources, and … a shared vision for Libya's transition to a stable, democratic political system' (Cook 2019, para. 1) and signalled US embrace of a likely dictator. With no end in sight to spiralling violence, a failed state in Libya could upend the peaceful and democratic promise of the Arab Spring even further by destabilizing Tunisia through the infiltration of militants, irregular (Sub-Saharan) immigrants seeking to cross the Mediterranean to Europe or other security and economic threats (Gramer and Jilani 2018).

New affordances face persistent failures

The various contributions in this volume inform our understanding of the geopolitical and cultural complexities and contexts of the Arab Spring uprisings. The conditions that gave birth to these upheavals have largely survived unscathed, with chaotic violence and democratic backsliding threatening fragile democratic institutions. The self-immolation of Mohammed Bouazizi, a fruit street vendor, on 17 December 2010, sparked massive public protests that toppled dictator Zin El-Abidin Bin Ali in Tunisia, appeared to be largely driven by a demand for dignity over pent-up political, social and economic frustrations. In the wider Arabic-speaking region, rampant corruption, economic stagnation, political repression and a clamping down on personal liberties relegated the region to the bottom of international rankings (Salih and Eldin 2013). A year before the uprisings, for instance, Transparency International (TI)'s Corruption Index rated the region poorly with 'a score of less than four on a scale from 0 to 10 where 0 means highly corrupt and 10 means very clean' (Hassan 2011, para. 1), noted a senior programme coordinator in TI's Middle East and North Africa department at the time. To put the issue in perspective, 'Transparency International (TI) defines corruption as the abuse of entrusted power for private gain' (TI 2021, p. 4). TI's definition 'encompasses corrupt practices in both the public and private sectors. The Corruption Perceptions Index (CPI) ranks countries according to the perception of corruption in the public sector' (TI 2021, p. 4). Commenting on the poor 2010 CPI ranking of Arab states, Hassan (2011) wondered: 'The message is clear, but will the new administrations in countries such as Egypt and Tunisia be able to tackle the problems of unaccountability, nepotism, wide-scale corruption and the ensuing economic injustice, which was a key cause of the uprisings?' (para. 2). Fast-forward eight years later, the answer to the above question would be a resounding 'no', with most Arab states lacking in good governance and accountability and, as TI's Fatafta (2018) observes, 'In a region stricken by violent conflicts and dictatorships, corruption remains endemic in the Arab states while assaults on freedom of expression, press freedoms and civil society continue to escalate' (para. 1).

Profound malaise and discontent continue to feed off tired tyrants and regimes, and the same failures and legitimate grievances plague the Arab Middle East as if history was doomed to repeat itself in an unceasing farce. No wonder Algerian and Sudanese citizens took to the streets with new vengeance in 2019 with slogans that strongly echoed those of the 2011 Arab Spring uprisings: democratic reforms, good governance, social justice – to wit, dignity. As Momani (2019, para. 3) observes:

> Their faces may differ, and their Arab dialects certainly do, but Algerian and Sudanese youth are united in their frustration with the lack of economic opportunity and advancement, rising costs of living, increased taxation, government corruption, cronyism, nepotism, inadequate public services, securitization of their daily lives and their leaders' failure to see past their own power-hungry ambitions to govern in a manner that is good for their countries.

The Second Wave of the Arab uprisings deposed the autocratic leader of Sudan, Omar al-Bashir, and forced an incapacitated Algerian president, Abdelaziz Bouteflika, not to seek another term and to resign instead (Krasna 2019). The Arab Spring 2.0, according to Momani (2019), faces steep challenges, not only from an increasingly reluctant international community but also from the learning curve of their armed forces that ostensibly respond to popular demands in an attempt to co-opt the protests. In both countries, protesters have sought to avoid the pitfalls of Syria, Libya and Egypt by insisting on the peaceful nature of their protests, being inclusive of various social and political actors and avoiding the tarnish of jihadism (Krasna 2019). Arab struggles have been and will always remain about fundamental rights and autonomy and date to a breakdown in the social contract between the governing elites and the people, even prior to 2011 (Hellyer 2019). Regardless of the eventual outcome of the Second Wave of Arab uprisings, the Arab region will not see an end to these eruptions of violence and protest in the foreseeable future. That is, 'until the peoples of the region live under governments that uphold their fundamental rights and allow them to feel a sense of ownership over and with those who rule' more springs are likely to come (para. 14).

The region's youth bulge and an ongoing information communication revolution exacerbate the crisis of Arab governance and calls for fundamental change. Given that more than half the population is under the age of twenty-five, some analysts argue that the young demographic composition of the Egyptian population and the region in general works as a force multiplier, along with unemployment and lack of economic opportunities, to create social unrest and political instability (LaGraffe 2012). Whereas some surveys and studies might suggest contemporary Arab youth to be generally less religious, more likely to be unemployed, urbanized and more likely to protest (Hoffman and Jamal 2012), the connectivity of these youth cohorts to global discourses of modernity and the use of new information communication technologies differentiate these youthful cohorts from previous generations. While we do not embrace facile, deterministic explanations of the role of social media and communication technologies in enabling social and political change, we recognize that the prevalence of social media, the high penetration of the internet and other mobile technologies have facilitated collective social action among this young generation.

Additionally, online activists in the Arab world use the vast array of communication tools to mobilize previously disengaged publics and elude state control repression. In Morocco, for example, online activists disseminated videos of the gruesome death of Mohcine Fikri, a fish street vendor in the northern region of Morocco known as Al-Rif, which eventually resulted in months of unrest and popular protests (called 'Hirak al-Rif') in 2016 and 2017 (Spadola 2017). Hirak activists deployed social media tools in the information battle against accusations of being separatists, capitalized on the organizational affordances of digital media technologies, shared videos of their protests and sought to circumvent traditional media. The decentralized nature of this web-powered grassroots activism enabled an anonymously led boycott campaign against high-priced staple goods and gas, market monopolization and manipulation. The French-owned dairy company Centrale Danone, one of the targeted corporations, took heavy losses and had to drop its prices as a result of the online consumer boycott (Ben Saga 2018).

The Arab uprisings have captured a unique moment in history where media and culture are shaping Arab publics' defiance of autocratic regimes and the quest for inclusive and democratic forms of governance. For example, cultural and artistic expression reflected these struggles during the Syrian uprising and defiance of Bashar al-Assad's Baathist regime. In fact, visual and literary output from the early days of the Syrian uprising recorded the cultural gestations, peaceful ideas and ideals, of a vibrant civil society yearning for freedom. As Creswell (2015) concluded in a piece about the visual art and literary work featured in the anthology *Syria Speaks* (2015, para. 7):

> The culture one finds here is pacifist, anti-sectarian, and feminist. The artists do not shy from slogans (sometimes that is the whole point) and so their political commitments are clear. Their posters, for example, call for civil disobedience and deplore the regime's choice to confront peaceful protesters with guns. Other works depict the results of this policy of repression *à l'outrance*: martyred children, political prisoners stuffed into cells, a rosary made of human heads. But this is to make the art sound more earnest and less pleasurable than it often is. The best work is blackly humorous, profane, or bluntly insulting – for instance, a stencil by Alaa Ghazal of Bashar al-Assad's face with the caption, 'Step here'.

The works of art and literature produced in the Syrian revolution bear much kinship with artistic and cultural expression in other Arab locales since 2011. The cultural expression of social and political protest fuses testimonial accounts about repression with yearnings for a better tomorrow that create what Salime (2015) has described as 'aesthetic citizenship'. The artistic expression of the uprisings transcends fear of and repression by the state, and seeks to hold the powerful to account, as rapper Hamada Ben Aoun (aka 'El-GeneralVoice') of Tunisia does in his 'Rais L'bled' ('Mr. President') video clip (Salime 2015, p. 138):

Rais L'bled ('Mr. President')
I am talking to you,
You are watching, misery everywhere
Those who can't afford a shelter
I represent them, I represent the people,
I represent those who spoke up,
And those stepped on
I speak to you with no fear.

Much like 'El-General' in Tunisia, rap artists El-Haqed ('The enraged)' and 'Muslim' in Morocco wove 'art, metaphor, image, and sharp lyrics together in a way that embeds politics in a new aesthetic genre' before Arab youth took to the streets in 2011 (Salime 2015, p. 138). Cultural and artistic expression provided new tools and momentum against autocracy and the politics of apathy/indifference (Salime 2015, p. 138). In summary, the cultural and technological shifts in the region mean that the stagnant status quo could no longer be tolerated, subjects will challenge the autocrat and a new social contract will have to be negotiated.

Talking about the Arab Spring: Narratives on the origins and future prospects

We are aware, as the curators of these diverse contributions, that the scholarship and commentary about the Arab uprisings have created fractured narratives and renewed questions about the nature of change that these tumultuous events were ushering in: social movements, gender equality and racialized identities, religious discourse or 'political Islam', the cultural and literary maelstrom and the information communication revolution scaffolding the Arab Spring, among other themes. It is instructive for a book about the Arab Spring uprisings to examine the nature of the scholarship it seeks to contribute to. We revisit some of the main books on the Arab uprisings since it is impossible to provide an exhaustive account of all published output on the Arab uprisings in this limited space. The list of published books in the Arab uprisings we look at includes both edited and single-authored volumes, as well as research-based monographs from both established and emerging scholars from the region and outside it. We discern three overarching and intertwined themes: (1) continuity and change in the Arab uprisings, (2) change in everyday life and (3) critique of dominant narratives about change in the region.

In a volume edited by Hudson, Iskander and Kirk, *Media Evolution on the Eve of the Arab Spring* (2016), the authors suggest that early scholarship on the Arab Spring was more to focus on new media as a driving force behind the uprisings instead of delving deep into on-the-ground narratives from the street, explaining the Arab Spring from below (perhaps Herrera's [2014] strong focus on the role of social media in the Egyptian Revolution stands as a good example of this wave). Their book shows evidence of the continuity we are witnessing in the Arab public sphere rather than any abrupt change in the 2010–11 moments of uprisings, arguing that there was a longer-term development of social and revolutionary movements which then culminated in the Arab Spring (Hudson et al. 2016). The ten years before 2011 could thus be viewed as a period of capacity building for media engagement in Egypt, for instance (Hudson et al. 2016, p. 6). The so-called Arab Spring was bound up in prolonged changes that had been occurring in social spheres, political culture and the development of new Arab media genres, for example, resulting in global repercussions and influencing the development of Arab media theory. This conclusion is compounded by various sorts of evidence from the Arab media sphere.

Moreover, Douai and Ben Moussa, in their edited collection entitled *Mediated Identities and New Journalism in the Arab World: Mapping the 'Arab Spring'* (2016), stress that notion of continuity over sudden change, and challenge media narratives of technological determinism. Their book also takes issue with the media narrative that the 2011 Egyptian Revolution was a social media revolution and instead asserts that technology was not the main wellspring of these uprisings. Instead, it delves deep into various socio-economic factors that played a vital role in that regard. Their collection not only criticizes technological determinism, but also suggests that a new media ecology has erupted in the MENA region, one which has paved the way for these revolutions to happen. Social media has been vital in delivering a message that came from the street – that is, the medium itself. Social media helps give shape to the messages and ideas on the street (Hudson et al. 2016, p. 4). Thus, this collection succeeds in going against so many other narratives that try to distract the moment of uprisings from its root elements, which are deeply integrated into people's lives and their social, economic, political and cultural conditions. The various authors in Douai and Moussa (2016) perceive the role of old and new media in the Arab Spring as integral to its development but also show awareness of the driving force behind these uprisings, as evident in what people have been experiencing in real life. As with the Hudson, Iskander and Kirk book, Douai and Moussa conclude that the revolution was not a sudden action that was determined only by media, and that it unveiled deeper connections with a heavy burden of social, political, cultural and economic problems.

The consistent attendance to these problems is also evident in a collection of essays by Sowers and Toensing, *Journey to Tahrir* (2012), which is based in part on research collected from the Middle East Research and Information Project, and published originally in various issues of the *Middle East Report*. The essays investigate the eighteen days before the toppling of Mubarak in Egypt and explore the Egyptian revolutionary popular culture and arts. What is unique about this work is that it puts that investigation of art and culture in Egypt within the social, political and historical context of the country. Including essays written before 2011 reveals an awareness of existing conditions that helped that moment of revolt to happen. It provides evidence of pre-existing conditions by highlighting the activist workers' movements that took place in Egypt long before Tahrir Square. The authors manage to present a narrative of continuous revolutionary spirit as reflected in the media, arts and cultural production in Egypt over the last three decades.

There is still an ongoing debate over what happened and if it can be termed a revolutionary act or an uprising, a debate our contributors are keenly aware of. This debate is based on the kind of change that occurred, the definitions of 'revolution' and 'uprising' and how to define 'regime' and whether it only refers to the toppling of a political regime or to a change in the sociopolitical context, as well as cultural and knowledge production. For example, Dabashi (2012) and Amar and Prashad (2013) term these movements 'revolutions'. Bayat (2017) and Gunning and Baron (2014), on the other hand, argue, in light of more historical contexts, that the term 'revolution' does not apply in the case of Egypt and other Arab Spring states. Activist-writer and blogger Cole also terms the Arab movements as 'revolutions'. He dedicates his book, *The New Arabs* (2014), to those who died before the end of the revolution and to contemporary political prisoners. Cole argues that the new generation Y is the reason for the revolutions because of their secularity, literacy and technological connectedness, and appears personally very invested in the eventual success of these movements. Dabashi, in his *Arab Spring: The End of Postcolonialism* (2012), stresses that the Arab uprisings, in their transnational spirit, drive us to analyse the Arab consciousness, or rather the transformation of it, against the 'mystified consciousness' (p. xvii) affixed to it by colonial powers. This transcendent spirit catalyses a quest for 'new metaphors' (p. xvii) beyond the world of sheer binarism that marks the condition of postcoloniality, 'the false dawn of nations liberated from the decades of European colonialism and the waning of the Ottoman Empire' (pp. 605–6) and its ideological formations and structures of domination. Under this Arab mode of defiance or protest, Dabashi's argument would go, national boundaries thaw and transnational connections reconfigure accordingly. Much like socialism, nationalism and Islamism are ideological formations inherited from colonial rule, which coalesce to produce the hegemonic centre–periphery illusion of the West and the Rest.

In the aftermath of the contemporary popular uprisings in the Arab world, existing modes of production have been thoroughly critiqued as perpetuating Eurocentric modes that sustain Western dominance through purist or exclusionary discourses of nationalism, pan-Islamism and pan-Arabism – outdated discourses that were thoroughly debunked as effete following the Arab nationalist revolts of the 1950s and 1960s. Seeking to replace these anachronistic paradigms of the past, the acephalous Arab revolutions are excavating new metaphors that could encapsulate the burgeoning spirit of revival and renewal. This transformative quest builds on an umbilical link between the 'national and the transnational', in what Dabashi terms as a 'politics of hope' (2012, p. 239) or for discovery of new geographies of liberation that is sufficiently radical to transcend colonial mapping, as crystallized in the expanding Tahrir Square(s) over vast geographic spaces, guided by limitless stretches of imagination. Similarly, Amar and Prashad cautiously think that what happened in Egypt can be described as a revolutionary movement. In *Dispatches from the Arab Spring: Understanding the Mew Middle East* (2013), they argue that Egypt's uprisings constitute a 'revolutionary dynamic' (p. 25). They discern in Morsi's short presidency a moving element for a political revolution, and that the social change that resulted from the uprisings also constituted a civic revolution

(p. 38). Recent events indicate that the nation has not been able to shake its militarism, cronyism and moralism. Amar and Prashad's attempt to split Egypt's movements into different types of revolution is useful here.

Other scholars who adopt a traditional definition of revolution as an act that should result in a complete change of the political regime argue that what happened in Egypt cannot be termed a revolution. Bayat (2017) offers a comparative and historical perspective of other movements in the 1970s, to argue that the Arab Spring was not actually a revolutionary movement. He contends that, since the deep state remained, and dependence on neoliberal economic policy after attempts at reform resulted in collapse of dreams for social reform, even though autocrats were deposed, no revolutionary success can be claimed. Bayat also argues that the Arab Spring did not witness the birth of intellectual visionaries. He concludes the Arab Spring did not produce revolutions, but instead, 'refolutions' – that is, a hybrid between reform and revolution (2017, p. 17). We find here a contradictory view to what has been proposed by Dabashi (2012) and Gunning and Baron (2014) with regard to the birth of new intellectual Arab modes of knowledge production.

Gunning and Baron, in *Why Occupy a Square* (2014), agree with Bayat's (2017) conclusion that these movements were not 'revolutions' in the traditional sense of the word, but they recognize an intellectual Arab awakening in the movements where Bayat does not. Also seeing continuity as opposed to abrupt revolution, Gunning and Barron (2014) argue that Egyptian social activism networks that were building over the previous decade were essential to the eighteen days of revolution that happened in 2011. The authors suggest the movement, although termed a revolution popularly, was more of a mass social movement that was able to move en masse because of crafted waves of social and political protests. These ranged from labour protest, feminist protest to religious activism; the mass movement of 25 January 2011 could not have happened without this ten-year history of activism. They also argue against the suggestion that this revolution was primarily a result of economic and political frustration, by using social movement theory – cross-class coalition was central to its success. They also effectively make use of social movement theory to analyse what occurred. This use of critical theory is interlaced with primary source evidence including interviews, witness narratives and a variety of documentary evidence. The appendices of this work are bursting with primary source data that has been effectively woven into the narrative. Scholarship that makes use of extensive primary source evidence, as well as more traditional definitions of revolution, tends to understand what occurred in Egypt in 2011 as Bayat's 'refolution', as collective uprisings, or as social mobilization that resulted in the ousting of Mubarak.

All of this can lead us to reconsider the Arab Spring and its role in reshaping the Arab world more precisely, in terms of conceptualized ideologies and, similarly, temps the role and function of both civil society and media institutions in redefining the role of media in a post-Arab Spring state. This volume will provide heretofore unimaginable access to the societal dimensions of the relationship of media and culture to the state, and they will bolster the case that putative threads of conservativism and repression in the Arab world are ultimately driven by ethnic and sectarian divisions. Moreover, the chapters herein raise crucial questions about the sources and origins of these divisions, taking into consideration a history of Western intervention and manipulation – covert and overt alike – designed to weaken Arab influence and empower imperialist aspirations in the region.

In the same vein, this volume examines culture and civil society as a site and vehicle of protest more broadly – that is, beyond the immediate scope of society and politics as such. In that context, the arts and social media prove pivotal avenues for contesting political repression through culture – particularly on issues germane to gender and sexuality. Thus, many researchers have been trapped by the surprising effects of the revolutions and have thus built biased timelines in order to explain them. There is first a fierce critique of how everything has been labelled as new, especially the media and their use, without taking into account the 'ecologies of the anti-authoritarian uprising – that is, the availabilities of different forms of communication to different actors involved in the revolutionary processes at different points in time' (Rinke and Röder 2011, p. 13). The same can be said for ideological changes and social movements. Islamists, for example, were not suddenly changed by the revolution but the specific context of transition that followed it allowed them to expose the post-Islamist transformations they were experiencing even before the toppling of dictators (Bayat 2013a).

Some authors explain that Western researchers have mainly been trying to commodify changes the Arab world has been experiencing for the past fifteen years. They have done so by defining a specific limited period of time/timeline they called the 'Arab Spring' as a way to keep control over the intelligibility of these changes. This '*temporal Othering* renders ambiguous processes intelligible, manageable, and ultimately securable under the rubric of democratization' (Hom 2016, p. 166). To counter this, a longitudinal approach is recommended, with a substantial focus on individuals' multiple relationships to the revolutionary process. This idea of unfolding the Arab Spring as a process is also found in the analysis of the ways that communication occurred 'with the interplay of the media available to different actors, the cultural contexts of protest communications, and the different stages of the lifetimes of such movements' (Rinke and Röder 2011, p. 1276). Still in the vein of focusing on parallel trajectories of change, others have underlined the importance of understanding State reformation (and the idea of the nation) efforts, according to varying contexts of change. The various attempts to redefine the State and their consequent contentious politics could well be considered as opportunities to reactivate 'latent identities, mobilize passive populations, and give rise to new ideologies and actors' (Saouli 2015, p. 316).

There is a growing consensus that agency and protests should also be looked at by understanding the continuity of relationships between individuals and their State, their communities, the public sphere, the police, the economy (Bogaert 2013), etc., that allowed/triggered/sustained them (Hinnebusch 2015). The heterogeneity of time frames at work in the aftermath of the uprisings also includes some reflections on continuing patterns inherited from colonialism, now under new forms (Rivetti 2015). Finally, as the brief review above shows, a number of clichéd temporalities that need to be debunked, including such labels as Arab

Spring/Islamic Winter, leaderless and spontaneous mobilizations, the Arab street, Facebook revolution and failed revolutions.

Arab culture and the dynamics of social change: Current contributions

In this edited book, we approach change in politics, identity, public spaces, etc., from below, to analyse and understand Arab culture dynamics and the continuing volatility after the Arab Spring uprisings. While protests are not dismissed and still considered as a major repertoire of change, researchers are more interested in the self-centred daily concerns that are pushing people to hope for change (through the streets, mobilizations, etc.) (Bayat 2013a). There is a greater attention to the corpus and material gathered by individuals themselves to express willingness (or fear) of change. As Khalil (2012, p. 63) explains:

> It is through their humor, satire, images and novels that we can get a sense of the discontent of youth that will inevitably lead the next revolution. The crowd re-articulates history as local, connected and malleable to the will and desire of political subjects, as opposed to the will of a corrupt dictator.

There is a lot also on how people are rewriting changes they have experienced through autofictions/biographies, *istishhad* ('martyrdom' or 'heroic death') narratives, etc.

The importance of localizing change does not escape our attention as co-editors and contributors. How people retranslate and understand the revolutionary 'grand schemes' (Schielke 2015, p. 13) in their daily lives and what kinds of anxieties and fears may arise from the discrepancy between the revolutions' promises and local experiences (Belakhdar et al. 2014). Overall, the idea that informal daily politics, like the relationship between online and offline activism (Zayani 2015), has given us more information about how change has occurred, has started to be widely shared since 2015–16. Moreover, it seems quite pertinent in this regard to refer to a conference convened by the Baker Institute's Center for the Middle East, called 'Divided societies, volatile states: The politics of identity post-Arab Spring' (2015), which highlighted the role of identity politics in 'reshaping the political and social landscape' of the Middle East (Baker Institute 2015, p. 3). The conference addressed sectarian, gendered, identitarian and nationalist tensions following the Arab Spring. Conceptualizing collective identity within the post-First World War modern state systems, informed by local, statist and transnational perspectives, the participants maintained that identity is a flexible construct that involved, not only individual or community aspects, but also external/transnational dimensions. Telhami, keynote speaker at the conference, acknowledged the role of Arab Spring uprisings in the disintegration of national identity; he attributed the current identity crisis more to an 'increased perceptions of a threat to Islamic identity following the 2003 invasion of Iraq' (Baker Institute 2015, p. 3). Highlighting the self/other reciprocity in the process of identity formation, Shibley maintained that 'people cannot define themselves in their relationship with us independently from what we do to them. It is an interactive relationship' (p. 4). He also noted a rising tendency among Arab citizens to maintain their 'Arab and Muslim', rather than their 'national', identities, with the exception of countries where sectarian tension looms large, as in such cases, the people opt for what Shibley called 'defensive identity selection' (p. 4).

In 'Modes of countering gender violence: Assessing the effectiveness of 'the Nude Revolution' in the MENA region', Magdalena Karolak (Chapter 2) examines the Nude Revolution and the effectiveness of radical feminist activism in the MENA region. Her research employed content and discourse analysis of social media contents created by two feminist activists, Aliaa Elmahdy from Egypt and Amina Sboui from Tunisia, and traditional media coverage of their activism. She concluded that the nude forms of feminist activism in the MENA region had little impact in generating social transformation as social audiences viewed such activism as 'negative deviance'.

In 'Do Egyptians still care about the Arab Spring? Computational cultural assessment of online and offline activism', Emad Mohamed and Eid Mohamed (Chapter 3) provide a quantitative and qualitative analysis of 120,000 news articles from the Egyptian newspaper *Almasry Alyoum* ('The Egyptian Today'), along with their social engagement indicators, to understand how much Egyptians still take an interest in the Arab Spring. Utilizing natural language processing and machine learning, the authors extracted quantitative data from the corpus of news articles which were then used to produce a ranking and a score for each article, employing forest regression analysis. The chapter presents a new method of studying media content and demonstrates that the revolution was not ranked as a priority topic in the newspaper studied.

In 'Cyberactivism and the (re)framing of identities and revolutionary narratives: A tale of two Egyptian political actors', Sahar Khamis and Ehab H. Gomaa (Chapter 4) explore how the Muslim Brotherhood and revolutionary youth – two major political actors in Egypt – engage in online and offline power struggles in the contemporary Egyptian political landscape. The chapter examines main identity frames used by these two actors to define themselves and the terms used by each group to reflect their identity frames by employing a content analysis of blog posts, online articles and press releases published from 2009 to 2016. The authors argue that both groups changed the frames they use to identify themselves before, during and after the revolution, under changing political contexts and shifting conditions.

In 'E-sheikhs: How online Islamic discourse can reproduce authoritarian power structures', Dina Abdel-Mageed (Chapter 5) examines Facebook content posted by prominent Sunni Muslim preachers between 2013 and 2016 to understand how Islamic discourse was used to justify the existing social order in the Arab world, and particularly in Egypt. The author employs critical discourse analysis to investigate the sociopolitical aspects of preacher discourses through the lens of public sphere theory. The chapter reveals that some prominent Muslim preachers reframe politics by presenting political opinions in a religious context via social media platforms. The chapter demonstrates that their media discourse help preserve the existing power structure and consolidates the hegemonic narratives of both the state and its Islamist rivals.

In 'The revolution of "pronouns": Shifts of power and resistance in Egypt's Muslim Brotherhood', Mustafa Menshawy (Chapter 6) analyses how former Muslim Brotherhood members disengaged from the group and how the post-2011 socio-politics facilitated their disengagement. Using a critical discourse analysis of autobiographies written by former Muslim Brotherhood members, published between 2011 and 2017, as well as transcribed interviews conducted with thirty-two other former members who announced their departure from the group within the same period, Menshawy discusses the shift in pronouns juxtaposing the 'I' with the 'we' to understand how they regain their 'I' and remodify their 'we', which narrates a shift in power and resistance in Egypt's Muslim Brotherhood.

In 'Hybridity and online public spheres after the Arab Spring: The case of Raseef22', Azza El Masri (Chapter 7) examined Raseef22, a pan-Arab website launched in 2013, as the voice of the Arab Spring. The chapter builds on Habermas's concept of the role of mass media in the public sphere and examines the internet as a space for deliberative democracy. The author conducted a qualitative content analysis of twelve Raseef22 articles to examine the nature of the public sphere emerging through the website. The chapter concludes that Raseef22 served as a platform for several counterpublics that focused on Arab uprisings.

In 'Promoting Libyan nationalism concepts via Facebook: A critical discourse analysis', Safa Elnaili (Chapter 8) examines how Islamists and nationalists, two major political orientations in Libya, discuss and promote nationalism on their Facebook pages. The author uses critical discourse analysis to demonstrate how nationalism is conceptualized in their posts. The study reveals that Libyan nationalism is based on negative concepts on such Facebook pages, and the discussions around nationalism are built on contradicting concepts such as treachery versus loyalty and inclusion versus seclusion.

In 'Marriage and politics in Hanan Abdallah's documentary *In the Shadow of a Man*', Touria Khannous (Chapter 9) provides a critique of Hanan Abdallah's documentary *In the Shadow of a Man* (2012). As Khannous describes, the film depicts the stories of four Egyptian women (Wafaa, Badreya, Suzanne and Shahinda) from a feminist perspective to reveal the social, political and economic struggles of women in Egyptian society. Khannous presents a detailed review of the film and argues that the film contributes to the efforts to promote the position of women in the politics of the new Egypt.

The final chapter, '#TechRevolt in the Arab Gulf: Gendered grassroots resistance or state violence?', Hasnaa Mokhtar (Chapter 10) revisits the Arab Gulf region and calls into question the prevailing Orientalist tropes about the region, and the pervasive 'Whitestream male gaze' – state-centric, top-down and gender-blind – that tend to erase people's lived experience and their resistance, including the minutia of gender, class struggle, racialized division of labour, ethnicity, tribal belonging, education, citizenship status, language, ability and family origin. Furthermore, the author uses the Saudi women's rights activist, Manal Al-Sharif, who was hailed for leading and becoming the public face of #Women2Drive movement, to deliver a nuanced and critical analysis of the relationship between Arab Gulf women's advocacy, organizing and activism, and the impact new media might or not have on their efforts.

Throughout this book, the authors unpack the complicated and multilayered interactions between media, culture and social protests prior to and in the aftermath of the Arab Spring. Our contributors reflected honestly on the moment of transformation that was embodied by the Arab Spring, and naturally there was at times great disagreement at others' shared views. Our goal was to bring Arab voices to the world in an English academic collection and to let researchers tell their story from their own perspectives. The book's diversity of views and approaches is a testament to the diversity of the Arab world today.

References

Al Jazeera. (2019). 'Egypt's Morsi: The final hours', *Al Jazeera World*, 19 March. Available at: https://www.aljazeera.com/program/al-jazeera-world/2019/3/19/egypts-morsi-the-final-hours [accessed 11 May 2021].

Amar, P. E. and Prashad, V. (2013). *Dispatches from the Arab Spring: Understanding the new Middle East*. New Delhi: Leftword Books.

Amnesty International. (2018). 'The circle of hell: Barrel bombs in Aleppo, Syria', 12 January. Available at: https://www.amnesty.org.uk/circlehellbarrel-bombs-aleppo-syria [accessed 11 May 2021].

Baker Institute. (2015). *Divided societies, volatile states: The politics of identity post-Arab Spring*. Conference report, Center for the Middle East. Houston, TX: Rice University. Available at: https://www.bakerinstitute.org/media/files/files/d66273ca/CME-Pub-DividedSocieties-060215.pdf [accessed 11 May 2021].

Bayat, A. (2013a). 'The Arab Spring and its surprises', *Development and Change*, 44(3), pp. 587–601.

Bayat, A. (2017). *Revolution without revolutionaries: Making sense of the Arab Spring*. Stanford CA: Stanford University Press.

Belakhdar, N., Eickhof, I., El Khawaga, A., El Khawaga, O., Hamada, A., Harders, C. and Sandri, S. (eds.). (2014). *Arab revolutions and beyond: Change and persistence*. Proceedings of the International Conference, Tunis, 12–13 November 2013, Working Paper No. 11. Berlin: Freie Universität Berlin, Center for North African and Middle Eastern Politics; Cairo: Faculty of Economics and Political Science. Available at: https://www.polsoz.fu-berlin.de/polwiss/forschung/international/vorderer-orient/publikation/working_papers/wp_11/WP11_Tunis_Conference_FINAL_web.pdf [accessed 30 May 2020].

Ben Saga, A. (2018). 'It's been a bumpy ride: A recap of the Moroccan boycott', *Morocco World News*, 22 May. Available at: https://www.moroccoworldnews.com/2018/05/246931/prices-economy-moroccan-boycott/ [accessed 11 May 2021].

Bogaert, K. (2013). 'Contextualizing the Arab revolts: The politics behind three decades of neoliberalism in the Arab world', *Middle East Critique*, 22(3), pp. 213–34.

Chorin, E. (2019). 'Libya's perpetual chaos', *Foreign Affairs*, 19 April. Available at: https://www.foreignaffairs.com/articles/libya/2019-04-19/libyas-perpetual-chaos [accessed 11 May 2021].

Cole, J. (2014). *The new Arabs: How the millennial generation is changing the Middle East.* New York: Simon and Schuster.

Cook, S. A. (2019). 'Loving dictators is as American as apple pie', *Foreign Policy*, 26 April. Available at: https://foreignpolicy.com/2019/04/26/loving-dictators-is-as-american-as-apple-pie/ [accessed 30 May 2020].

Creswell, R. (2015). 'Syria's lost spring', *The New York Review of Books*, 16 February. Available at: https://www.nybooks.com/daily/2015/02/16/syria-lost-spring/ [accessed 30 May 2020].

Dabashi, H. (2012). *The Arab Spring: The end of postcolonialism.* New York: Zed Books.

Douai, A. (2020). 'Democracy promotion 2.0: Barack Obama and the "Arab Spring" conundrum', in E. Mohamed and D. Fahmy (eds.) *Arab Spring: Critical political theory and radical practice*, pp. 99–117. Cham, Switzerland: Palgrave Macmillan. Available at: https://link.springer.com/chapter/10.1007%2F978-3-030-24758-4_6 [accessed 1 June 2021].

Douai, A. and Moussa, M.B. (2016). *Mediated identities and new journalism in the Arab World.* London: Palgrave Macmillan.

Fatafta, M. (2018). 'Rampant corruption in Arab States', *Transparency International News*, 21 February. Available at: https://www.transparency.org/news/feature/rampant_corruption_in_arab_states [accessed 30 May 2020].

Gramer, R. and Jilani, H. (2018). 'Libya an obstacle on Tunisia's path to stability'. *Foreign Policy*, 6 August. Available at: https://foreignpolicy.com/2018/08/06/libya-an-obstacle-on-tunisias-path-to-stability/ [accessed 29 May 2020].

Gunning, J. and Baron, I. Z. (2014). *Why occupy a square? People, protests and movements in the Egyptian revolution.* Oxford: Oxford University Press.

Harsch, E. (2011). '"Arab Spring" stirs African hopes and anxieties', *Africa Renewal*, August. Available at: https://www.un.org/africarenewal/magazine/august-2011/%E2%80%98arab-spring%E2%80%99-stirs-african-hopes-and-anxieties [accessed 29 May 2020].

Hassan, A. (2011). 'Corruption perceptions index 2011: After the Arab Spring', *Transparency International*, 30 November, Available at: http://blog.transparency.org/2011/11/30/corruption-perceptions-index-2011-corruption-and-the-arab-world/ [accessed 2 June 2020].

Hellyer, H. A. (2019). 'Until the Arab world enjoys fundamental rights, there will be many more springs to come', *The Globe and Mail*, 25 April. Available at: https://www.theglobeandmail.com/opinion/article-until-the-arab-world-enjoys-fundamental-rights-there-will-be-many/ [accessed 2 June 2020].

Herrera, L. (2014). *Revolution in the age of social media: The Egyptian popular insurrection and the Internet.* Brooklyn, NY: Verso.

Hinnebusch, R. (2015). 'Conclusion: Agency, context and emergent post-uprising regimes', *Democratization*, 22(2), pp. 358–74.

Hoffman, M. and Jamal, A. (2012). 'The youth and the Arab Spring: Cohort differences and similarities', *Middle East Law and Governance*, 4(1), pp. 168–88.

Hom, A. R. (2016). 'Angst springs eternal: Dangerous times and the dangers of timing the "Arab Spring"', *Security Dialogue*, 47(2), pp. 165–83.

Hudson, L., Iskandar, A. and Kirk, M. (eds.). (2016). *Media evolution on the eve of the Arab spring.* Cham, Switzerland: Palgrave Springer.

In the shadow of a man. (2012). *Directed by Hanan Abdallah.* England: Magic Works Production Company.

Khalil, A. (2012). 'The political crowd: Theorizing popular revolt in North Africa', *Contemporary Islam*, 6(1), pp. 45–65.

Krasna, J. (2019). 'The second wave?: The legacy of the "Arab Spring" of 2011', Available at: https://saisreview.sais.jhu.edu/the-second-wave/ [accessed 11 May 2021].

LaGraffe, D. (2012). 'The youth bulge in Egypt: An intersection of demographics, security, and the Arab Spring', *Journal of Strategic Security*, 5(2), pp. 65–80.

Lynch, M. (2014). 'Media, old and new', in M. Lynch (ed.) *The Arab uprisings explained: New contentious politics in the Middle East*, pp. 93–110. New York: Columbia University Press.

Middle East Research and Information Project. (n.d.). Available at: https://merip.org/ [accessed 11 May 2011].

Momani, B. (2019). 'Arab Spring 2.0: New protests, same failures that plague the Middle East', *The Globe and Mail*, 10 April. Available at: https://www.theglobeandmail.com/opinion/article-arab-spring-20-new-protests-same-failures-that-plague-the-middle/ [accessed 11 May 2021].

Obama, B. (2011). Remarks by the President on the Middle East and North Africa. 19 May 2011, The White House, Office of the Press Secretary. Available at: https://obamawhitehouse.archives.gov/the-press-office/2011/05/19/remarks-president-middle-east-and-north-africa [accessed 10 May 2021].

Phillips, C. (2018). 'The world abetted Assad's victory in Syria', *The Atlantic*, 4 August. Available at: https://www.theatlantic.com/international/archive/2018/08/assad-victory-syria/566522/ [accessed 11 May 2021].

Rinke, E. M. and Röder, M. (2011). 'The Arab Spring – Media ecologies, communication culture, and temporal-spatial unfolding: Three components in a communication model of the Egyptian regime change', *International Journal of Communication*, 5, pp. 1273–85. Available at: https://ijoc.org/index.php/ijoc/article/download/1173/603 [accessed 6 May 2021].

Rivetti, P. (2015). 'Continuity and change before and after the uprisings in Tunisia, Egypt and Morocco: Regime reconfiguration and policymaking in North Africa', *British Journal of Middle Eastern Studies*, 42(1), pp. 1–11.

Salih, K. and Eldin, O. (2013). 'The roots and causes of the 2011 Arab uprisings', *Arab Studies Quarterly*, 35(2), pp. 184–206. Available at: https://www.jstor.org/stable/pdf/10.13169/arabstudquar.35.2.0184.pdf?refreqid=excelsior%3A701991ece56d42a8d5a824ad3b34e8ba [accessed 11 May 2021].

Salime, Z. (2015). '"I Vote I Sing": The rise of aesthetic citizenship in Morocco', *International Journal of Middle East Studies*, 47(1), pp. 136–9.

Saouli, A. (2015). 'Back to the future: The Arab uprisings and state (re)formation in the Arab world', *Democratization*, 22(2), pp. 315–34.

Schielke, S. (2015). *Egypt in the future tense: Hope, frustration, and ambivalence before and after 2011*. Bloomington: Indiana University Press.

Sowers, J. and Toensing, C. (eds.). (2012). *The journey to Tahrir: Revolution, protest, and social change in Egypt*. London: Verso.

Spadola, E. (2017). 'Justice and/or development: The Rif protest movement and the neoliberal promise', *Third World Resurgence*, 326/327, pp. 60–3. Available at: https://www.twn.my/title2/resurgence/2017/326-327/world5.htm [accessed 11 May 2021].

Telhami, S. (2015). 'Keynote address: Identity selection in a changing Middle East', *Divided societies, volatile states: The politics of identity post-Arab Spring*. Rice University, 10 March. Houston, TX: Baker Institute for Public Policy.

Transparency International. (2010). *Corruption perceptions index 2010 Report.* Transparency International. Available at: https://images.transparencycdn.org/images/2010_CPI_EN.pdf [accessed 11 May 2011].

Transparency International. (2021). 'What is corruption?'. Available at: https://www. transparency.org/en/what-is-corruption# [accessed 11 May 2011].

Zayani, M. (2015). *Networked publics and digital contention: The politics of everyday life in Tunisia.* Oxford: Oxford University Press.

Chapter 2

MODES OF COUNTERING GENDER VIOLENCE: ASSESSING THE EFFECTIVENESS OF 'THE NUDE REVOLUTION' IN THE MENA REGION

Magdalena Karolak

Introduction

The transformations brought about by the Arab uprisings raised important questions with regard to human rights and relations between the society and the state in the Middle East and North Africa (MENA) region. Women's rights were not the focus of the protests, and women and men participated on an equal footing in order to bring changes in their countries. Yet, the uprisings inadvertently raised the issues of women and their role in Arab societies. On the one hand, in some countries female protesters experienced sexual harassment and physical abuse during demonstrations that were not prosecuted or even, as in the case of virginity tests in Egypt, encouraged and conducted by the authorities. On the other hand, the rise of Islamist parties during political transitions questioned women's position in society under previous secular regimes. In politics women also suffered a setback when electoral quotas for female candidates were abolished in Egypt in the post-Mubarak era. To counter such fears of gender discrimination and abuse, an Egyptian activist Aliaa Elmahdy (2011) posted her nude pictures online with a message 'my body is mine'. Other Arab female activists such as Amina Sboui (2013) from Tunisia followed what is known as the 'Nude Revolution' waged online and offline. These acts also marked an attempt at reclaiming and forging a new female identity in these patriarchal contexts where women's statuses, whether defined by state feminist agendas or Islamist programs have been used for purposes other than the advancement of women's rights and ultimately, are controlled solely by men. Elmahdy's and Sboui's public posts aimed at taking women outside of these politicized agendas and claiming their own agency in defining who they are as women.

The aim of this chapter is to find out the effectiveness of such radical feminist activism in the MENA region as a mode of countering patriarchal structures looking from the point of view of how these acts have been framed. Using theories on performativity, this chapter examines how such acts affect the perceptions of gender and sexuality, and how they relate to gender activism in the region and in the West. The analysis is based on the examples of the two most prominent activists, the above-mentioned Elmahdy from Egypt and Sboui from Tunisia. This chapter uses an eclectic method that includes content and discourse analysis applied to social media produced by the activists themselves and to media coverage of their activism in order to understand whether and to what extent the use of the body as means of resistance has a potential to transform social perceptions of gender in the MENA region. We conclude that such radical activism has had only a limited impact in engendering social change. Consequently, this chapter examines the possible reason why in the regional context of MENA, the Nude Revolution as exemplified by these two case studies was particularly inefficient to exert direct change in the target societies. While the Egyptian revolution ended with the return to authoritarianism and, as a result, state feminism that offers women small tokens in return for their support of the military takeover (Zaki 2015), Tunisia's reforms to the gender status progressed through the parliamentary means, albeit slowly, given the rise of Islamist voices (Zayat 2020). In both cases, the 'nude activism' did not yield an impact on the course of events. Both cases of activism are nonetheless of interest to study as they testify to the potential that individuals have to use the body as a site of resistance and liberation despite the consequences such actions may have in their personal lives.

Gendered identity

Identity is one of the most complex constructs as different approaches have led to the multiplication of its meanings, rendering the concept difficult to grasp (Brubaker and Cooper 2000). However, as Hall (1996) stated, identity is 'an idea … without which certain key questions cannot be thought at all' (p. 2). Many scholars argue that identity is a fluid construct that is constantly shaped and reshaped by our experiences and interactions as well as by the social context (Giddens 1991; Hall 1996; Stern 2008). Hall (1996, p. 4) pointed out, for instance, that identity is a narrative of self, which is constantly negotiated through one's everyday life and experience. Goffman (1959) introduced the idea of identity as performance. He argued that in social interactions we present ourselves to others in a way that conveys the way we want them to define us. In other words, we perform our identities through interactions that are context- and audience-bound. Performance includes voice, gesture, facial expression, bodily posture and actions. Simone de Beauvoir introduced the concept of the socially constructed gendered identity. She argued that 'one is not born but becomes a woman' (cited in Butler 1988, p. 519). Building on de Beauvoir's argument, Butler (1988, 1990) argued that becoming a woman involves constant negotiation and performance of identity. She further stressed that gender identity 'is in no way a stable identity or locus of agency from which various acts proceed; rather, it is an identity tenuously constituted in time – an identity instituted through a stylized repetition of acts' (Butler 1988, p. 519). Gender identity is a performative construct. Women, and men for that matter, learn to perform their gendered identity in accordance with cultural and societal expectations of the roles and identities associated with each gender. Based on the example of a drag, Butler (2004, p. 361) wrote that drag 'constitutes the mundane way in which genders are appropriated, theatricalized, worn, and done; it implies that all gendering is a kind of impersonation and approximation. If this is true, it seems, there is no original or primary gender that drag imitates, but gender is a kind of imitation for which there is no original; in fact it is a kind of imitation that produces the very notion of the original as an effect and consequence of the imitation itself.'

From this quote it is clear that concepts such as gender identity become social reality through the performance of the body. Hence, the performance defines the concept and not the other way around. As a result, concepts retain their fluidity and there is always a possibility of change. Indeed, Baumeister (1991) highlighted how nudity, hence a nude performance, has the potential of erasing social roles and promoting equality: 'Just the act of removing one's clothes can help strip away symbolic identity and work roles, allowing one to become merely a body' (p. 28). In this manner, an individual gets rid of 'all the grand, complex, abstract, wide-ranging definitions of self and become just a body again' (p. 12). Furthermore, Jones (2010) suggested that nudity may challenge the established order 'because it denies the naturalization of that order and reveals the potential for alternatives that become visible when social roles and bureaucracy are "stripped off"' (p. 256). Although he mentions that this potential exists in a limited way, he shows, however, citing Souweine, that protesters using nudity are able to step out of 'the artificial sanction of prescribed social relations and demonstrate that the individual has the potential to rise above any system of social control merely by rejecting its premises' (p. 256). Rather than being merely an object subjected to social control and discipline, the body holds the potential of becoming a site of resistance (Rasmussen and Brown 2005), social subversiveness and self-empowerment (Davis 1995).

The body in the public sphere: An overview

The degree of social acceptance of public nudity has witnessed various changes throughout human history. In the Western world, the ancient Greek civilization pioneered public nudity in many contexts, but their Roman successors had already a more complex approach with regard to it. Mores have evolved further over time, with the introduction of Christianity and clothing becoming a must. In this perspective, public nudity could pose a threat to the social norms and could thus, constitute a form of protest against the established order. The story of Lady Godiva, whether true or not, is one of the earliest accounts of such uses of public nudity for social change. In modern times, the uses of nudity have proliferated. Some aspire to appropriate it as a form of protest, for instance, PETA campaigners, environmental activists, cyclists, pacifists, FEMEN. Nudity as a form of protest plays multiple functions. On the one hand, some activists stress that they choose to use it to highlight vulnerability of humans, animals or the environment (Alaimo 2010) or to exercise their right to nudity such as the Top Free Seven. Lunceford (2012) assessed that nudity, in case of PETA protests, allows the activists to become more animalistic and play animal roles in protests. In addition, it equates humans and animals and allows the activists to build a common identity. Nudity is, however, also a form of media attention grabbing, which is why it raises questions about the objectification of women. Indeed, the use of the naked body and its reception are problematic, and nudity may convey multiple meanings. It often displays gendered and racial readings. For instance, the sexualized female body has acquired a commercial value and is a common feature of the advertisement industry, where images of partially or fully naked women woo customers, especially male, to buy various products (Gill 2009). The naked female body sells, and the heterosexual male gaze is paramount in the West. Such uses of the body in advertising have gained a social acceptance, while a woman breastfeeding in public may not be fully accepted in public spaces. Nudity exposes thus complex issues of objectification, the power to decide when nudity is accepted as well as the aesthetics of nudity. Gill points out a recent shift in the advertising industry that has begun to show females as autonomous and free agents; yet these representations disavow any notion of cultural and political influence as they link free choice to consumerism, and present rigid standards of female beauty (p. 106). Gill further asserts that these representations objectify women even further as they have evolved into a 'self-policing narcissistic gaze [through which] male gaze is internalized to form a new disciplinary regime' (p. 107). Thus, under what seems to be empowerment and free choice, sexualization of women is presented as self-chosen and pleasurable, rendering any critique more difficult. The uses of nudity in protests to advance social change are equally problematic as they become embedded within these prevailing norms. As noted by Einwohner et al. (2000), 'Movements that draw on feminine stereotypes face a double bind that hampers their success' (p. 679). This is because images of the protests, even in issues that are not related to gender, convey cultural constructions of masculinity and femininity and may be subject to manipulation. But these concerns are especially salient in the case of female body and nudity being used in protests in order to promote change of women's status in society. The most vivid examples of such activism are SlutWalk and FEMEN.

FEMEN is a group of activists established in Ukraine in 2008 and operating from its French headquarters (France 24 2013). It aims at protecting women's rights by fighting patriarchy around the world in its three forms, namely sexual exploitation, dictatorship and religion, by means of topless protests, referred to by the group as 'sextremism'. The group has staged multiple protests over the years with topless activists displaying painted slogans over their bodies and has challenged public figures, among others, Vladimir Putin. The group is open about the use of sextremism to grab media attention to their cause. The effectiveness of such strategies is, nonetheless, subject to various criticisms. Jensen (2014, p: 5) pointed out, for instance, that, in order to convey their message and to collect funds, FEMEN uses the sexualized female body; as a result, it acts against its own agenda of subverting patriarchy. It is also highlighted by the fact that, in order to grab media attention, the activists have to fit into the established standards of beauty. While the activists do not agree with such accusations, claiming that patriarchy always sought to control the female body and nudity and, hence, female liberations would occur through liberation of the female body, questions abound. O'Keefe (2014, p. 14) argued that linking nudity to liberation is problematic at least, as it generalizes female experiences with nudity, the meanings of nudity and does not penetrate beyond the obvious element that constitutes the female body. This is also the case of the critiques addressed to SlutWalk (Dines 2010; O'Keefe 2014). The latter are a series of demonstrations organized in various parts of the world to protest against blaming women's attire for sexual violence, especially rape, in urban areas (Carr 2018, p. 24). Women gather in such protests wearing often skimpy clothes that would fit in the label 'slut'. The aim is to advance a change of social perception of women, sexual violence and the meaning of consent and blame in instances of sexual violence. O'Keefe (2014) pointed out, however, that, as with FEMEN, SlutWalk reproduces patriarchal norms as they fail to challenge the male gaze and the established standards of female beauty; and it fails to even question the label 'slut', which is deeply rooted in patriarchal terms. Indeed, the participants dressed as sluts fulfil male sexual fantasies rather than challenging them or challenging the ways in which a woman can be sexual. Female sexuality thus becomes equated with 'being a slut' and that limits the possibilities for female self-expression supporting ultimately the already-established patriarchal norms. Gill (cited in O'Keefe 2014, p. 9) highlighted the fact that such constructions 'must also be understood as authentically owned by the women who produce them'. This is not the case with SlutWalk, which reproduces the patriarchal label. It is also important to question the appropriation of such events by celebrities. Amber Rose organizes the yearly SlutWalk in Los Angeles since 2015 (@slutwalk_la), but the event has consistently failed to question the labels stemming from the male gaze, which, apart from 'slut', include 'stripper', 'hoe' and 'gold digger'. In addition, in 2017 Rose promoted the event by posting full frontal nudity pictures of herself on social media with the label 'bring back the bush'.[1] The explicit photo – that could easily feature in a men's magazine – while not the first nude of Amber Rose circulated online, is yet again another example of fulfilling male sexual fantasies rather than questioning the male gaze. Her photograph, following Bourdieu's distinction of obscenity and art (1984), would be considered obscenity as 'nakedness fails to be symbolic' (Nead 2001, p. 119). Besides the fact that the celebrity is bi-racial and thus may bring a more diverse female public to the cause, it could be also argued that such photos and events may serve her own self-promotion rather than to advance the improvement of female status in society. Furthermore, O'Keefe (2011) stressed that the response to SlutWalk among the male public reveals inconsistencies between the aim of the event, a preoccupation with female status in society, and the outcomes – sexualized readings of the female bodies by men. All in all, FEMEN and SlutWalk nevertheless raise important questions about the female body being at the centre of struggle and its potential as a site of resistance.

The female body is even more in the centre of struggle in Muslim societies. The policing of women's actions and women's bodies is paramount, as it serves to uphold the families' honour – as exemplified by an Arab proverb 'honor rides on the skirts of women'. Consequently, women are held 'more responsible for upholding family honor than men' (Shoup 2009, p. 177). An act considered inappropriate when committed by a woman will bring dishonour to all her family members, especially to her male kin. In addition, the female body has been used in various nationalistic projects in Arab countries where the 'purity' of women is equated with purity of the nation (Timmerman 2000, p. 18). In these discourses, the female body is used as a means of preserving local culture and heritage and fighting against Westernization and Western colonialism. Not surprising, since in the past Western colonial nations have attempted to use Muslim women as a means of advancing their Western agendas (Fanon 1965). In Arab societies, traditionally, the private and public spheres are separate, with the latter reserved for men and the former for women. As a result, the MENA region, for most, is characterized by an unequal female participation in the public sphere. Recent analyses highlight substantial advancements of female empowerment in certain areas, which can 'compare favorably with those of other regions' (World Bank 2004, p. 1). Moreover, patterns of female empowerment in MENA are in sharp contrast with the experiences observed elsewhere. Indeed, 'women's gains in health and education in other parts of the world have been matched by gains in economic and political participation to a much greater degree than has been the case in the Arab states' (United Nations 2007).[2] Not only traditions but also the legal systems in most Arab countries, exemplified in the existing family law codes or the verbal interpretations of the shari'a, support the patriarchal readings of gender roles. In addition, they often make it difficult to prosecute gender and sexual violence, female genital mutilation or other practices aimed at policing female bodies. Nudity, whether male or female, is against Muslim principles, yet due to the reasons explained above, it is the female body that remains in constant focus rather than the male body. Furthermore, tradition often obliges Muslim women more or less strictly to don the veil, covering the hair or, in some cases, covering the whole face.

In Muslim countries, partial or full nudity may have dire consequences for the perpetrator, who would face not only the legal system but also the judgement of the religious establishment, or the unwritten norms of the society, which could lead to public shaming and even the application of mob justice. In these circumstances, the fight over the female body presents multiple challenges. Policing of female bodies not only represents the male gaze but may also easily become the means for discrediting a Muslim activist by other Muslim women. Since in many countries the social norms have in recent decades increasingly stressed donning of the veil as an obligatory practice for a Muslim woman, Muslim activists without the head cover may be easily discredited as being Westernized (Spiegel 2010, p. 231). Such judgements based on a woman's looks will challenge their activism and authority overall. Activism using the female body in such contexts may be thus more challenging than in the West. That is why it is even more important to analyse the recent activism of Muslim women who use their bodies as a means of contesting these established norms.

The Arab uprisings raised important questions with regard to human rights and the relations between society and political structures. Women's rights were not the focus of the protests, yet the uprisings inadvertently raised the issues of women and their role in Arab societies. To counter fears of gender discrimination and abuse, an Egyptian activist, Aliaa Elmahdy, posted her nude pictures online with a message 'my body is mine' in 2011. She inspired a fellow activist, Amina Sboui in Tunisia, and received online support from women around the world – but also violent threats in her home country. Posting of the images by Elmahdy and Sboui on social media caused wide exposure of their activism that no doubt surpassed their own expectations. The use of new technologies and new media is not coincidental. Considering the realities of Arab women, the internet can provide a space where women can express their voices globally. It can also provide access to information that might be obstructed by cultural, political and local barriers. It can offer opportunities of networking that are not viable otherwise (Wheeler 2004). Moreover, cyberspace provides spaces of identity articulation and negotiation that were not available before through traditional media.

The issues at stake are very high as they not only touch upon the patriarchal structures of the society supported by the legal systems but also on participation in the public sphere, religious interpretations of the role of women and deeply rooted social traditions. In order to understand to what extent the use of the body as a site of resistance holds to potentially transform social perceptions of gender in the MENA region, an eclectic method was applied to the data. The researcher gathered data online through the analysis of web pages created by female activists, past interviews and news reports related to their activism. The analysis uncovers the aims of the activism, the methods used and the perceptions of the activism itself.

Methodology

For data collection, the researcher used social media pertaining to both activists, namely Facebook, Twitter and blog posts,[3] and the responses to their posts on social media as well as coverage of their activism in international English-speaking press. Data was collected between January 2011 and December 2018. The coverage of Elmahdy's and Sboui's activism in the West included major news channel's such as BBC, CNN, the *New York Times* and ABC News. A total of thirty-five articles were found as a result of a search performed on Google with names of the activists as keywords. Some of the articles included personal interviews. The material was subsequently studied using content and discourse analysis.

Researchers often choose to apply content analysis, an unobtrusive method, to online content (D'Enbeau 2011; El-Nawawy and Khamis 2010; Russell 2005). Content analysis is well suited for retrieving frames from any written, verbal or visual form of communication (Cole 1988). Given its wide scope of application, it was deemed an appropriate method to begin this study. In the process of inductive content analysis, categories or concepts were obtained to describe the studied phenomenon. Secondly, in order to understand 'the meaning of social reality for actors' (Hardy et al. 2004, p. 19), critical discourse analysis (CDA) was applied. It stresses that social reality is constructed through meaningful interaction and it strives to examine how that reality has been produced. In addition, these discourses or 'interrelated bodies of texts' (p. 20) bring new ideas, objects and practices to life. It is important to note that CDA is subjective in its approach: 'Discourse analysis does not look for truth but rather at who claims to have truth, and at how these claims are justified in terms of expressed and implicit narratives of authority' (Carver 2002, p. 52). The data analysis follows the chronology of the postings. The data was organized in this manner to show the evolution of the activists' personal journeys and challenges as well as to provide a comparative perspective.

Data analysis and discussion

The two examples of activism chosen for this research ought to be placed within the context of events occurring in Egypt and Tunisia as they were a response to the political developments at that time. Elmahdy (2011), the first activist to use nude forms of activism in the MENA region, established her blog 'Diary of a Rebel' in October 2011. Her nude photo posting preceded the parliamentary elections held between November 2011 and January 2012. The period after the fall of Mubarak regime leading up to the elections brought a division within Egyptian society with the rise of the Muslim Brotherhood, which promoted a return to conservative values, including, among others, changes in the status of Egyptian women. Elmahdy posted her nude picture with a manifesto:

> Put on trial the artists' models who posed nude for art schools until the early 70s, hide the art books and destroy the nude statues of antiquity, then undress and stand before a mirror and burn your bodies that you despise to forever rid yourselves of your sexual hangups before you direct your humiliation and chauvinism and dare to try to deny me my freedom of expression.
>
> (quoted in Jones 2011)

Her black and white picture in stockings and red accented shoes and flower hairpin is no doubt an echo of the models she mentions in her manifesto, but it is also a cry against the restrictions she faced at home, imposed by her parents. Furthermore, Elmahdy used this very same photograph to compose a tryptic with symbolic blockages placed on different body parts that she explained as follows:

> I have the right to live freely in any place. I feel happy and self satisfied when I feel that I'm really free. The yellow rectangles on my eyes, mouth and sex organ resemble the censoring of our knowledge, expression and sexuality.
>
> (ANI, 2011)

Through that statement Elmahdy pointed out at the restrictions to the body that affect women equally in these areas.

Subsequently, Elmahdy established an Egyptian branch of FEMEN in December 2012. Nonetheless, she had to continue her activism from abroad in response to new challenges from the evolving Egyptian political scene. In between, she was forced to seek asylum in Sweden due to an attempted kidnapping and threats she received. The division in Egyptian society surrounding the drafting of the constitution, which was heavily influenced by Muslim Brotherhood (MB) ideas, pushed Elmahdy to stage a protest together with FEMEN activists in front of the Egyptian Embassy in Stockholm in December 2012. She stood naked with a slogan painted across her chest 'Sharia is not a constitution', while her two FEMEN colleagues donned anti-religion and anti-Islam slogans: 'Religion is slavery', 'No Islamism, yes secularism', 'No religion' and 'Apocalypse by Mursi' (Harrington 2016). The staged performance had Elmahdy as the centre of attention between two other activists. She was the only activist fully exposing her nudity as the other two covered their crotches with a copy of the Torah and the Koran, respectively. Elmahdy's fears were surely confirmed when the MB condemned and rejected the UN document to 'end violence against women' in 2013, stating that 'these [i.e. steps to end violence against women as highlighted in the UN document] are destructive tools meant to undermine the family as an important institution; they would subvert the entire society, and drag it to pre-Islamic ignorance' (The Muslim Brotherhood 2013, para. 14).

In March 2013, Sboui became the first Tunisian woman to post online a half-nude photo of herself with the inscription 'my body is mine and not the source of anybody's honor'.[4] Similarly to Elmahdy, she was responding to the pressures of the Tunisian political scene, with the rise of radical Islamist groups, such as Ansar Al-Shariah. She also, initially, adhered to FEMEN. Yet, subsequently, Sboui's and Elmahdy's activism began to differ. Following the incarceration of Sboui, FEMEN staged topless protests calling for 'topless jihad' at the Paris Grand Mosque in support for her that included a parody of a prayer and burning a flag with 'Tawhid' written on it (an inscription meaning 'oneness of God'), which Sboui criticized. As a result, she resigned from the group but in 2013 posted more topless selfies with the inscription 'we don't need your democracy',[5] a reference to Islamist parties in Tunisia. Elmahdy, on the other hand, remained a member of FEMEN. She supported the campaign encouraging the voluntary unveiling for Muslim women. In addition, her subsequent activism has more recently included a topless performance at a cultural centre during a day promoting understanding of Islam, hence in her own perception – promotion of the practice of veiling. On 8 March 2016, she stood during the event with an inscription 'hijab is sexism not anti-racism'. She wrote further:

I met countless women who were forced or pressured to wear hijab, who wanted to take it off but feared incarceration, beatings and/or social rejection. My best friend was locked and tortured in a mental institution after she took off the hijab she was coerced to wear as a child, and was only considered sane enough to be let out when she wore it again against her will, […] and countless other women who were locked up, beaten, had 'virginity'-tests, had their hairs cut and had their books torn up, for resisting the obligation to veil.[6]

Sboui, however, distanced herself from FEMEN due to the perceived offense they caused to the Muslim community and to the encroachment on other people's freedom to be believers. She also disappeared from the media headlines, continuing her education in France and, upon her return to Tunisia, sought a less radical role as a feminist magazine editor. Elmahdy, while remaining abroad, continued her activism, motivated by current events. In 2014, she posted a nude photograph of herself menstruating on the flag of ISIS, while a woman partially covered with abaya and hijab is seen defecating on it.[7]

The activism of Elmahdy and Sboui shows similarities, but ultimately their paths diverged. To begin with, both resorted to posting a nude picture online that spread quickly through the networks nationally and internationally and drew mostly condemnation from their fellow countrymen. It is clear that the reception of a nude performance depends on the social norms established. In the Western context, nude protests have had an already long history of existence and have been used to highlight a variety of issues, but in the MENA region, protests using naked bodies in this way are a first of their kind. As a result, while in the West they drew media attention, especially given the country of origin of the activists, they were inscribed in a long line of similar protest activism; in the MENA region they sent shockwaves throughout the society. A person who publicly exposes their naked body is considered either mentally ill or somebody who does not respect themselves. As a result, they require psychiatric treatment or, in the second case, does not deserve the respect of others. What is even more disturbing for conservative segments of society is that nudity is a breach of Islamic principles; hence, it offends the religious establishment and the individual feelings of believers. In addition, in the West there is a more or less well-established distinction between art and pornography. Artwork does not promote lust, or in other works objectifies its subjects, as noted by Sontag (2009): 'This notion of the annihilation of the subject we have perhaps the only serious criterion for distinguishing between erotic literature or films or paintings which are art and those which (for want of a better word) one has to call pornography' (p. 26). Pornography does exactly the opposite. From that perspective, Elmahdy's and Sboui's images are not pornographic. They do not aim at promoting lust but to convey a politically charged message. Yet, a reading from a Middle Eastern perspective could only be pornography as the division does not exist in public spaces. Nonetheless, both suggested that pornography would not have offended that many people; what offended was the use of their bodies to convey a message:

There are a lot of Arab women who do pornographic movies and who get naked in movies and nobody says anything to them. When we did it all the people started criticising us. We are doing this for good reasons. We are not doing this is a sexy way but to tell the world that the body you spend all your life either pushing me to hide it or to show it for sex, I'm using it for a political message.

(Namazi 2014)

Indeed, Jensen (2014, p. 112) noted that, even in the West, 'the hybrid between politics and sexuality continues to provoke. We are used to the commercialization of naked bodies and sexuality, and we are used to controversial politics, but combining them we have a new potential in political, yet bodily activism.' This potential remains highly controversial in the MENA region. It is not a surprise that Elmahdy's performance was condemned by all sides on the Egyptian political scene and activists denied any links to her in order not to discredit their own social activism (Mourad 2014). Rather than being seen as an icon of the revolution and a champion of female rights, she was sidelined as an uncomfortable by-product and even a damaging element to the protests. This is a striking contrast with the 'girl in blue bra', whose partial exposure and violence that she had experienced were forced upon her. Elmahdy's exposure, on the other hand, was self-inflicted. Indeed, Sutton (2007, p. 145) stresses the fact that

> a woman with scant clothing, a woman with clothing deemed – indecent, a woman who chooses to assert her sexuality, or a woman who resorts to sexuality as a means of survival, may be judged as morally suspect and therefore – deserving to be physically punished, raped, or murdered. While this kind of violence occurs regardless of women's sexual demeanor or appearance, a woman's unclothed body can be readily invoked to justify violence against her. – She asked for it may be easily attached to a naked woman. Thus, in certain contexts, women's naked protest may entail particular risks, especially in a solo performance.

Both Elmahdy and Sboui received various threats from not only social media users but also from religious figures, calling for their deaths. After an attempted kidnapping, Elmahdy was forced into exile. Sboui, on the other hand, returned to Tunisia; however, she withdrew her affiliation with FEMEN and from subsequent nude performances, as of 2018. This may well have been to guarantee her safety in her home country. In light of the above, it is clear that both activists displayed a great deal of courage to use the nude strategy for political protest. But overall, they were unable to gather a large following willing to use the same strategies in their home countries or to start a meaningful debate within society on the status of women, as other activists sought to distance themselves from their performances.

It is important to question why the scope of the Nude Revolution was overall limited in the MENA region. To begin with, it is clear that the nude performances became a form of personal liberation for both activists. As Elmahdy wrote in her blog (subsequently removed), the pictures were 'screams against a society of violence, racism, sexism, sexual harassment and hypocrisy'. She provided detailed accounts on how she was repressed at home with regard to her personal freedom, such as movement, wearing the clothes she chose to wear, the restrictions on talking about certain subjects such as menstruation, the severe corporal punishments she received from her parents, as well as the double standards with regard to the treatment of different genders she observed daily in Egypt. In the same vein as SlutWalk she stated: 'Even if we "girls" are naked, nobody has the right to attack us or harass us' (subsequently removed). The photos she posted online were an act of defiance against her family and the society around her. Her actions have become a personal liberation but in order to exercise her freedom she had to flee Egypt. The liberation of her body was not only spiritual but had to become a physical act of her body leaving the country, most probably for good. Similarly, Sboui's performance constituted an act of exercising her personal freedom. From that perspective, personal liberation may inspire others to self-liberate. And through a nude performance, the erasing of social roles and promoting equality might be achieved. Yet, in the MENA region, the outcome was limited. The support for both activists came from many individuals but most of them were located outside of the region, as was shown on Elmahdy's blog pages. Würger (2013, para. 27) noted that her photograph 'only became an icon because the West made it into one'. Once circulated in international media, Elmahdy acquired the status of a rebel who was defying Egyptian cultural norms and her society, risking her life to liberate her body. This mediation through the Western lens is, however, problematic from the point of view of MENA activists. Ahmed (1992) pointed out that Western domination is often justified on the basis of the noble mission of modernizing Arab societies and rescuing Arab women by making them reject their culture and adopting Western values. Elmahdy's and Sboui's stories thus fit these most Orientalist portrayals of Arab/Muslim women, who are oppressed and need liberation and saving. This could be the reason why they received such wide coverage in the Western media. Yet, back home they would be perceived as agents of Westernization and implied colonialism, which may explain why political parties and other activists particularly in Egypt made firm statement that they did not associate with them. It is a stark difference with the girl in blue bra, whose forced ordeal galvanized further protests in Egypt that 'intended not only to restore the honor of young women who were dragged and beaten in Tahrir but also to redress the imbalance created within the patriarchal system that in principle should uphold the protection of females by males' (Hafez 2014, p. 4). Sboui's performance received a more nuanced reception, with some supporting but others also starkly condemning her act for its potential to undermine efforts to promote women's rights further by encouraging Islamists to hijack the outcomes of the revolution. While the understanding of her goals did exist, the method she used was deemed problematic. All in all, the use of nudity as means of resistance was limited in Egypt and Tunisia. Had there been many more cases, the outcomes could have been different. Nonetheless, the use of shocking imagery and nudity did not appeal to the masses and single activists using such strategies may be easily dismissed.[8]

Furthermore, the activism of Elmahdy and Sboui exposed a cleavage between the understanding of liberalism in the West, founded in the complete separation of church and state,[9] and in parts of the MENA region, especially in Egypt. Elmahdy expressed her disbelief at the statement of a liberal April 6th Movement during the Arab Spring protests:

> What shocked me is April 6th's statement clarifying that Aliaa Magda Elmahdy is not part of their organization and how they don't accept 'atheism'. Where is the democracy and liberalism they preach to the world? They only feed what the public wants to hear for their political ambitions.

(quoted in Fahmy 2011)

From this quote, it is obvious that even some liberals in the MENA region were for most part not secular in the Western understanding of the word. Indeed, the Middle East has not experienced a separation of religion and state like the one that occurred in the West. The connection between Islam and state is especially visible in the area of family matters, which are governed by laws (or in cases when they are not codified, by interpretation of a judge) based on religion, which do not uphold equality between genders. On the contrary, they support different readings of gender roles and place different obligations upon men and women within the family sphere.

While in the aftermath of the revolution grassroots efforts and women's organizations have focused on the problems of harassment and empowerment, the political movements in Egypt that are male-led did not question the family laws specifically[10] or the lack of laws protecting women from various types of violence, which could have been a matter of political opportunism. Nonetheless, the brutality experienced by women during the Arab Spring protest did not lead to a broad pressure in the Egyptian society and did not translate to political programs in the 2011–12 elections. The victory of Islamic parties in the Egyptian parliamentary elections of 2011–12 is an indication of the public opinion that is conservative in nature and does not seek major changes in this sphere. The return to authoritarianism brought some form of an official acknowledgement of the extent of the problem (Zaki 2015) as well as the passing of an anti-sexual harassment law in 2014. The latter was criticized for not being comprehensive and falling short of the intended outcomes (El-Rifae 2014), the lack of which was visible in the results of a Reuters study that in 2017 ranked Cairo as being the worst city for women's safety (France 24, 2017), after New Delhi, Karachi and Kinshasa, among major large cities worldwide. From a comparative perspective, Tunisia, which is considered the most advanced country in the MENA region with regard to women's rights, passed important amendments to women's status after the 2011 revolution. The new constitution guarantees equality of men and women, while a law passed in 2017 criminalizes all forms of violence against women, be it physical, moral, sexual, psychological or economic. This law sets a precedent in the MENA region, given its broad scope of application. The Tunisian case is, however, an outlier in the Arab world. The legacy of secularism under Bourguiba and the passing of the Personal Status Code in 1956 have left a mark on Tunisia, along with the existence of an important secular–nationalist current countering the Islamists.[11] The former, while present also in Egypt, is nowadays a minor political force in comparison to the popularity of Islamist parties. Thus, Tunisia started the reforms of women's status from a different level of legal premises and national sentiment with regard to women's rights. Nonetheless, the question of equality between men and women in inheritance marked a sharp end to the steady progress of women's status with the new president voicing opposition to the amendment in 2020, citing the Koran as the basis. Yet, Tunisia presents a very different set of characteristics that are not easily comparable to other countries in the Arab world, such as Egypt.[12] Ultimately, these differences may help explain why Sboui was able to return to Tunisia after residing in Europe, while Elmahdy continues to live in Sweden.

Conclusion

This research provides an analysis of the Nude Revolution in the MENA region. It follows the activism of Aliaa Elmahdy from Egypt and Amina Sboui from Tunisia. In their assessment of deviant behaviour, Wolf and Zuckerman (2012) analysed deviant heroes whom they define as altruistic individuals trying to change oppressive social norms even if that involves personal risks. Depending on the social context, deviant heroism can be viewed positively, leading to deviant admiration, in case the social audience views the norms as unjust or, on the contrary, as negative deviance, when the social audience views the norms as reasonable. In the MENA region, the activism of Elmahdy and Sboui has been so far overwhelmingly viewed as negative deviance, while it has been viewed positively in the West. Through the overview of the tactics applied and the responses to the activism of the two women, this chapter has analysed why the Nude Revolution did not have a significant impact in the region. It points out, among others, the differences in the perceptions of nudity, the understanding of secularism and the fears of Westernization. Nonetheless, it also shows that nude activism provided a personal liberation forum for the two activists, and possibly, for some others who follow and embrace this tactic. Ultimately, it also points to the personal risks of such activism in the MENA region.

All in all, researchers questioned the effectiveness of nude activism globally. O'Keefe (2014, p. 5) pointed out that movements such as FEMEN or SlutWalk fall into the trap of using the language and labels of the dominant and replicate the existing social norms, falling short to subvert them:

> Their protests embrace heteronormative, hegemonically masculine ideals of women and sexuality through performance in an attempt to challenge societal norms. The endeavors of SlutWalk to reclaim 'slut' and FEMEN to 'take back' women's breasts succumb to the doublebind, however, as their failure to inject mockery and irony into their approach means it is commonly read as repetitive of such norms rather than subversive.

Some of the nude performances by Elmahdy also fell into this trap as, rather than subverting the discourse, they rejected it directly with means deemed offensive in the MENA region. It is, among others, the case of anti-ISIS performance that Muslims felt to be offensive as it desecrated the *shahada* ('declaration of faith') written on the ISIS flag. While such performance reflected Elmahdy's perception of current events, it could not appeal to the majority of the inhabitants in the region.

Jensen (2014, p. 114) noted that the reason for activists choosing radical tactics could be more symbolic:

> Perhaps it is when activists do not believe they can start by changing the system that they turn to their bodies and the sexual embodiments of politics as a focal point of resistance – and it is this starting point which makes up the foundation for a trend in contemporary activism, where the ideal future seems unattainable

on a linear scale, but can be invoked as a presence as, and through, certain engagements of the body.

The activism of Elmahdy and Sboui could not directly impact the social norms in their home countries, but it offered them a unique form of resistance in the MENA region and a form of personal liberation through the body performance and the forging of a new identity for both individuals. These two cases also present a difference with regard to the countries of origin of the activists.

Notes

1   The original post, deleted by Twitter due to its nudity, has been preserved elsewhere (see Donahue 2017).
2   This UN source is no longer available.
3   Most of the material analysed has been so far removed due to new rules on posting nudity – and controversial imagery in general – on social media.
4   Source for quote has since been removed.
5   The photo, since deleted, was reposted; see Huffpost Maghreb (2013).
6   Elmahdy's manifesto is available on the FEMEN official blog (FEMEN 2016, para. 5).
7   The photos, deleted since, were reposted (Steinhauer 2014).
8   Three European FEMEN activists protested topless in Tunis in 2013 to support Elmahdy. They were arrested and deported after a month spent in jail (BBC 2013).
9   Such uncompromising positions are sometimes referred to as 'absolutist secularism' (Scott 2007, p.181).
10 For instance, the liberal Free Egyptians Party did not call for removing Article 2 of the constitution that states the Islamic Sharia principles are the main source of legislation. Interestingly, women's representation in social democratic or socialist parties was found to be higher after the revolution than in liberal parties, irrespective of when the party was formed (OECD 2018, p.17). Women's parties formed in 2011 called for advanced reforms of women's status but did not succeed in the elections.
11 The most important political parties are the Islamist party 'Ennahda' and secular parties such as 'Nidaa Tounes', and, since 2019, its splinter groups and other nationalist currents.
12 FEMEN and SlutWalk messages found some response in the Maghrib countries with forms of local appropriation of methods such as the use of national dress (Salime 2014).

References

@slutwalk_la (Amber Rose SlutWalk). (2015) [Twitter]. Available at: https://twitter.com/slutwalk_la?lang=en [accessed 3 November 2017].
Ahmed, L. (1992). *Women and gender in Islam: Historical roots of a modern debate.* New Haven, CT: Yale University Press.
Alaimo, S. (2010). 'The naked word: The trans-corporeal ethics of the protesting body', *Women & Performance: A Journal of Feminist Theory*, 20(1), pp. 15–36.

Asian News International (ANI). (2011). 'Egyptian artist defies Islamic extremism by posting nude self-photos on web', *Yahoo News*, 16 November. Available at: https://in.news.yahoo.com/egyptian-artist-defies-islamic-extremism-posting-nude-self-121205250.html [accessed 12 September 2017].

Baumeister, R. (1991). *Escaping the self: Alcoholism, spirituality, masochism, and other flights from the burden of selfhood*. New York: Basic Books.

BBC. (2013). 'Tunisia frees Femen topless protest activists', 27 June. Available at: https://www.bbc.com/news/world-africa-23075871 [accessed 3 March 2017].

Bourdieu, P. (1984). *Distinction: A social critique of the judgement of taste*. Cambridge, MA: Harvard University Press.

Brubaker, R. and Cooper, F. (2000). 'Beyond identity', *Theory and Society*, 29, pp. 1–47.

Butler, J. (1988). 'Performative acts and gender constitution: An essay in phenomenology and feminist theory', *Theatre Journal*, 40(4), pp. 519–31.

Butler, J. (1990). *Gender trouble: Feminism and the subversion of identity*. London: Routledge.

Butler, J. (2004). 'Imitation and gender insubordination', in S. Salih and J. Butler (eds.) *The Judith Butler reader*, pp. 119–37. Malden, MA: Blackwell.

Carr, J. L. (2018). 'The SlutWalk movement: A study in transnational feminist activism', *Journal of Feminist Scholarship*, 4(4), pp. 24–38.

Carver, T. (2002). 'Discourse analysis and the "linguistic turn"', *European Political Science*, 2(1), pp. 50–3.

Cole, F. L. (1988). 'Content analysis: process and application', *Clinical Nurse Specialist*, 2(1), pp. 53–7.

Davis, K. (1995). *Reshaping the female body: The dilemma of cosmetic surgery*. New York: Routledge.

D'Enbeau, S. (2011). 'Transnational feminist advocacy online: Identity (re)creation through diversity, transparency, and co-construction', *Women's Studies in Communication*, 34(1), pp. 64–83.

Dines, G. (2010). *Pornland: How porn has hijacked our sexuality*. Boston, MA: Beacon Press.

Donahue, R. (2017). 'Amber Rose posted this NSFW Photo to her Instagram – and Instagram deleted it', *Allure*, 10 June. Available at: https://www.allure.com/story/amber-rose-nsfw-instagram-photo-deleted [accessed 15 December 2019].

Einwohner, R.L., Hollander, J.A. and Olson, T. (2000). 'Engendering social movements: Cultural images and movement dynamics', *Gender & Society*, 14(5), pp. 679–99.

Elmahdy, A. (2011) [Blog]. 'Nude art', 23 October, 12:30PM. Available at: http://arebelsdiary.blogspot.com/2011/ [accessed 1 February 2013]. See also: Facebook (https://www.facebook.com/aliaaelmahdy) and Twitter (@aliaaelmahdy).

El-Nawawy, M. and Khamis, S. (2010). 'Collective identity in the virtual Islamic public sphere: Contemporary discourses in two Islamic websites', *International Communication Gazette*, 72(3), pp. 229–50.

El-Rifae, Y. (2014). 'Egypt's sexual harassment law: An insufficient measure to end sexual violence', *Middle East Institute*, 17 July. Available at: https://www.mei.edu/publications/egypts-sexual-harassment-law-insufficient-measure-end-sexual-violence [accessed 18 December 2020].

Fahmy, M. F. (2011). 'Egyptian blogger Aliaa Elmahdy: Why I posed naked', 20 November. Available at: http://edition.cnn.com/2011/11/19/world/meast/nude-blogger-aliaa-magda-elmahdy/index.html [accessed 14 January 2012].

Fanon, F. (1965). *A dying colonialism*. New York: Grove Press.

FEMEN. (2016) [Blog]. 'Hijab is sexism, not anti-racism', 8 March. Available at: https://femen.org/hijab-is-sexism-not-anti-racism/ [accessed 23 January 2017].

France 24. (2013). 'Femen: Modern amazons, radical actions', 1 November. Available at: https://www.france24.com/en/20131101-reporters-femen-modern-amazons-radical-actions-topless-protests-breasts-ukraine-russia-feminists [accessed 13 May 2016]. See also: https://www.facebook.com/pg/femenmovement/about/?ref=page_internal

France 24. (2017). 'Cairo named world's "most dangerous" city for women', 16 October. Available at: https://www.france24.com/en/20171016-cairo-deemed-worlds-worst-city-women [accessed 2 December 2019].

Giddens, A. (1991). *Modernity and self-identity: Self and society in the late modern age.* Stanford, CA: Stanford University Press.

Gill, R. (2009). 'Supersexualize me!: Advertising and the "midriffs"', in F. Attwood (ed.) *Mainstreaming sex*, pp. 93–110. London: I.B.Tauris.

Goffman, E. (1959). *The presentation of self in everyday life.* Garden City, NJ: Doubleday.

Hafez, S. (2014). 'Bodies that protest: The girl in the blue bra, sexuality, and state violence in revolutionary Egypt', *Journal of Women in Culture and Society*, 40(1), pp. 20–8.

Hall, S. (1996). 'Introduction: Who needs identity?', in S. Hall and P. du Gay (eds.) *Questions of cultural identity*, pp. 1–17. London: Sage.

Hardy, C., Harley, B. and Phillips, N. (2004). 'Discourse analysis and content analysis: Two solitudes?', *Qualitative Methods*, 2(1), pp. 19–22.

Harrington, H. (2016). 'Site-specific protest dance: Women in the Middle East', *The Dancer-Citizen*, 2. Available at: http://dancercitizen.org/issue-2/heather-harrington/ [accessed 15 May 2017].

Huffpost, Maghreb. (2013). 'La Femen tunisienne Amina Sboui publie une nouvelle photo choc', 15 August. Available at: https://www.huffingtonpost.fr/2013/08/15/femen-tunisienne-amina-sboui-publie-nouvelle-photo-choc-international-_n_3760897.html [accessed 13 May 2017].

Jensen, M.B. (2014). *The body theatre: An analysis of FEMEN's feminist activism.* Master's Thesis. Roskilde University, Institute of Culture and Identity, Denmark.

Jones, M.T. (2010). 'Mediated exhibitionism: The naked body in performance and virtual space', *Sexuality & Culture*, 14, pp. 253–69.

Jones, N. (2011). 'The revolution stripped bare', *New Statesman*, 21 November. Available at: https://www.newstatesman.com/blogs/nelson-jones/2011/11/naked-revolution-egypt-women [accessed 5 May 2015].

Lunceford, B. (2012). *Naked politics: Nudity, political action, and the rhetoric of the body.* Lanham, MD: Lexington Books.

Mourad, S. (2014). 'The naked body of Alia[a]: Gender, citizenship, and the Egyptian body politic', *Journal of Communication Inquiry*, 38(1), pp. 62–78.

Namazi, M. (2014). 'This is my body; I will do whatever I want with it', Interview with Amina Sboui and Aliaa Magda Elmahdy. Fitnah Movement, 28 December. Available at: http://fitnah.org/fitnah_articles_english/interview_%20with_Amina_and_Aliaa.html [accessed 15 July 2017].

Nead, L. (2001). *The female nude: Art, obscenity, and sexuality.* New York: Routledge.

O'Keefe, T. (2011). 'Flaunting our way to freedom? SlutWalks, gendered protest and feminist futures', *New Agendas in Social Movements*, National University of Ireland, Maynooth, Ireland, 26 November.

O'Keefe, T. (2014). 'My body is my manifesto! SlutWalk, FEMEN and femmenist protest', *Feminist Review*, 107, pp. 1–19.

Organisation for Economic Development (OECD). (2018). *Women's political participation in Egypt: Barriers, opportunities and gender sensitivity of select political institutions.*

OECD-MENA Governance Programme. Available at: https://www.oecd.org/mena/governance/womens-political-participation-in-egypt.pdf [accessed 15 December 2020].

Rasmussen, C. and Brown, M. (2005). 'The body politic as spatial metaphor', *Citizenship Studies*, 9(5), pp. 469–84. Available at: https://www.tandfonline.com/doi/abs/10.1080/13621020500301254 [accessed 22 December 2020].

Russell, A. (2005). 'Myth and the Zapatista movement: Exploring a network identity', *New Media & Society*, 7(4), pp. 559–77.

Salime, Z. (2014). 'New feminism as personal revolutions: Microrebellious bodies', *Signs*, 40(1), pp. 14–20.

Sboui, A. (2013) [Facebook]. 8 March. Available at: https://www.facebook.com/profile.php?d=100004452976431 [accessed 2 January 2015].

Scott, J.W. (2007). *Politics of the veil*. Princeton, NJ: Princeton University Press.

Shoup, J.A. (2009). 'Gender and gender relations', in S. Maisel and J.A. Shoup (eds.) *Saudi Arabia and the Gulf States today: An encyclopedia of life in the Arab States*, pp. 177–8. London: Greenwood Press.

Sontag, S. (2009). *Against interpretation, and other essays*. London: Penguin Books.

Spiegel, A. (2010). *Contested public spheres: Female activism and identity politics in Malaysia*. Wiesbaden, Germany: Springer Verlag für Sozialwissenschaften.

Steinhauer, J. (2014). 'Feminist activists bleed and defecate on Islamic State Flag #NSFW', *Hyperallergic*, 27 August. Available at: https://hyperallergic.com/145768/feminist-activists-bleed-and-shit-on-islamic-state-flag-nsfw/ [accessed 15 November 2017]

Stern, S. (2008). *Instant identity: Adolescent girls and the world of instant messaging*. New York: Peter Lang.

Sutton, B. (2007). 'Naked protest: Memories of bodies and resistance at the world social forum', *Journal of International Women's Studies*, 8(3), pp. 139–48.

The Muslim Brotherhood. (2013). 'Muslim Brotherhood statement denouncing UN Women declaration for violating sharia principles', *Ikhwanweb*, 14 March. Available at: https://www.ikhwanweb.com/article.php?id=30731 [accessed 17 November 2016].

Timmerman, C. (2000). 'Muslim women and nationalism: The power of the image', *Current Sociology*, 48(4), pp. 15–27.

United Nations. (2007). Gender equality – Part Three Political and economic participation. *ESCWA – Center for Women Newsletter*, 2(13).

Wheeler, D.L. (2004). 'Blessings and curses: Women and the internet revolution in the Arab World', in N. Sakr (ed.) *Women and media in the Middle East: Power through self-expression*, pp. 138–61. London: I.B. Tauris.

Wolf, B. and Zuckerman, P. (2012). 'Deviant heroes: Nonconformists as agents of justice and social change', *Deviant Behaviour*, 33(8), pp. 639–54.

World Bank. (2004). *Gender and development in the Middle East and North Africa: Women and the public sphere*. Available at: http://go.worldbank.org/ENRPGWBY40 [accessed 5 February 2011].

Wurger, T. (2013). 'From icon to exile: The price of a nude photo in Egypt'. Available at: https://abcnews.go.com/International/icon-exile-price-nude-photo-egypt/story?id=21287268 [accessed 3 May 2021].

Zaki, H.A. (2015). 'El-Sissi's Women? Shifting gender discourses and the limits of state feminism', *Egypte/Monde arabe*, 13, pp. 39–53. Available at: https://journals.openedition.org/ema/3503 [accessed 13 December 2020].

Zayat, I. (2020). 'Tunisia marks long struggle for women's rights', *The Arab Weekly*, 15 August. Avalable at: https://thearabweekly.com/tunisia-marks-long-struggle-womens-rights [accessed 18 December].

Chapter 3

DO EGYPTIANS STILL CARE ABOUT THE ARAB SPRING? COMPUTATIONAL CULTURAL ASSESSMENT OF ONLINE AND OFFLINE ACTIVISM

Emad Mohamed and Eid Mohamed

Introduction

This chapter analyses change and continuities in a post-Arab Spring era, with a focus on the Egyptian case, through a preliminary framework of analysis of our understanding of and approach to social, cultural and political change/transformation, and continuities, hopes and frustrations in Egypt, and by corollary in the Arab world, for the past thirty years. What mainly came out of it is that scholars should focus on change in a multilayered way to avoid the clichés carried by the analysis of 'brutal' change after the revolutionary 'awakening' or its consequent authoritarian 'stagnation'. The main problem with this approach is that it only considers change in terms of rupture, transition, modernity and tradition. Considering change as a multi-influential, multi-scaled long-term process may help us analyse the visible and invisible transformations of Arab identities and social realities in a finer way.

One interesting methodological approach would be to comprehend change through the analysis of the changing use, reception and circulation of specific media and news stories (i.e. our research material). Here it can be a good segue into how the Egyptian revolution sparked a change. Some scholars argue that, in fulfilment of the process of change, there was a failure to complete a democratic transition because of the coup. Others argue that there was a change in the way Egyptians defied the laws set in place by the Mubarak regime, which restricted Egyptians from these forms of expression, and that this defiance constituted a major gain of the 2011 uprising. While there is no readily available information on how these changes apply today under the Sisi regime, it does not mean that such changes are not occurring. For a long time, under the repression of the Mubarak regime, activists remained underground. It was only after the fall of Mubarak that their activism came out into the public sphere.

There are several scales of analysis we can use to understand change in the Egyptian case: individual or collective, daily or historical (at the national level) and local or global. We can superimpose these levels (and media such as literature, personal biographies) on one another in order to understand how past social narratives are constructed differently in the present. How Egyptians reconstruct and understand the past (not only their role as individuals, but also their perception of notions, such as the West, the Arabs, the revolution, etc.) to redefine their present agency could be one of the main research questions of this article.

The approach we employ in this research is both quantitative and qualitative. At the quantitative level, the chapter uses tools and algorithms from computational linguistics and data mining to extract useful information from the corpus from the Egyptian newspaper *Almasry Alyoum* (The Egyptian Today). This information is then used build a regression model that can be used for both explanation and prediction. The qualitative side of the analysis makes use of this quantitative analysis to gain, and provide, meaningful insights that can be used in the historical and sociopolitical aspect of the project. Choosing *Almasry Alyoum* is based on its being a successful independent newspaper which is able to challenge taboos, criticize the regime's performance and at the same time maintain professional standards of journalism in terms of accuracy, objectivity and credibility.

Below are the most interesting themes found in the post-2011 Arab Spring literature that we reflect upon.

A critique of how the Arab Spring had not been predicted

Many scholars note that overstatement of the robustness and stability of Arab authoritarianism led to a culturalist myth of Arab fatality or exceptionalism. This view has been shaped by researchers who took a holistic approach to the question of Arab people's agency and then their inability to have predicted the revolt. This is the main critique we find in the literature when talking about how to assess the post-Arab Spring change in Egypt. Some macro causal approaches, though, explain that change is simply not predictable, since it depends on 'elite mis-assessments of the situation' or their anticipation of contestation through ad-hoc reforms (Volpi 2013, p.969). The critique is based on the lack of attention to the salience of a cross-border Arab identity (Gause 2011) and an intense focus solely on regime change (Kohstall 2016), obstacles to democratization (Schwedler 2015) and organized/institutionalized social movements as the main actors of transformation (Morjé and Walters 2014). Again, we outline that some authors (Gause 2011; Kohstall, 2016; Volpi 2013) label the revolutions as failures because there was no regime change, or in some cases there were illegitimate regime changes. This is another point that is in accordance with the examined literature that points to lack of regime change as the sole cause of decline in the state of the country.

Indeed, neither the revolution itself nor its trajectory and current outcome were predictable. Such predictions are difficult if not impossible to make. Some researchers have been trapped by the surprise effect of the revolutions and built biased timelines in order to explain them. One critique that can be found in these works is describing the use of media as something 'new' without taking into account the 'ecologies of the anti-authoritarian uprising – that is, the availabilities of different forms of communication to different actors involved in the revolutionary processes at different points in time' (Rinke and Röder 2011).

The same can be said about analysing ideological changes and social movements. Islamists, for example, were not suddenly changed by the revolution but by the specific context of transition that followed. It allowed them to expose the post-Islamist transformations they were experiencing even before the toppling of dictators (Bayat 2013b). Some authors explain that Western researchers have been trying to commodify changes experienced in the Arab world for the past fifteen years. They have done so by defining a specific, limited period of time – a timeline – they called 'Arab Spring' as a way to keep control over the intelligibility of these changes. This 'temporal Othering' renders ambiguous processes intelligible, manageable and ultimately securable under the rubric of democratization (Hom 2016). A longitudinal approach is recommended with a focus on individuals' diverse relationships to the revolutionary process.

This idea of unfolding the Arab Spring as a process is also found in the analysis of the ways communication occurred 'with the interplay of the media available to different actors, the cultural contexts of protest communications, and the different stages of the lifetimes of such movements' (Rinke and Röder 2011, p. 1276). Still in the vein of focusing on parallel trajectories of change, others have underlined the importance of understanding state reformation efforts (and the idea of the nation) according to varying contexts of change. The various attempts to redefine the state and its consequent contentious politics could well be considered as opportunities to reactivate 'latent identities, mobilize passive populations, and give rise to new ideologies and actors' (Saouli 2015, p. 316). Although some suggest that 'new technologies and social media which, capitalizing on past mobilizations, have been a new and relevant feature in the protests and which may change future mobilization patterns for good' (Lynch 2014, p. 6), there is a growing consensus that agency and protests should also be looked at by understanding the continuity of relationships between individuals and their state, their communities, the public sphere, the police, the economy, etc. (Bogaert 2013), that allowed, triggered and sustained them (Hinnebusch 2015). The heterogeneity of timeframes at work in the aftermath of the uprisings also includes some reflections on continuing patterns inherited from colonialism (under new forms) (Rivetti 2015). Finally, cliché temporalities that need to be debunked include labels such as 'Arab Spring'/'Islamic Winter', 'leaderless and spontaneous mobilizations', 'the Arab street', 'Facebook revolution' and 'failed revolutions'.

The literature on how to comprehend change in post-Arab Spring has also revealed deep fractures and frustrations between Western and local Arab scholars. Of course, some are quite superficial. But the question of why some discourses are heard more than others and what consequences this de facto hegemony may have on the way they see, trust or distrust each other (and also the impact this division may have on the actors of Arab change themselves) seems to be a really interesting question. There are two main critiques emanating from the Arab world:

1. The behaviours of some Western researchers who focused in an opportunistic way on fashionable countries. Suddenly, a large number of writers were researching Egypt or Tunisia and writing about these countries without having visited them even once, and they interacted with local researchers as native informers (Abaza 2017) with no plan of building a common knowledge.
2. The flood of publications from US universities and think tanks has contributed to orientating research on the Arab Spring and influencing perceptions of change that are linked to specific topics, such as the victory or failure of Islamist parties, neutralization or return of the military (75 per cent of the scholarly production comes from outside the Arab World) (Maghlouth et al. 2015).

Feasible alternative: An exploration of everyday social change

Unfortunately, the coup on 3 July 2013 in Egypt has changed the scene of activism so much that it relatively impedes what we are proposing here about change and the expression of the willingness for change. This is not to say that there is no research available since the literature we surveyed highlights the significance or the impact of the revolution – in anxieties, perceptions, hopes and dreams – on local communities and daily life. But the historical distance from that event goes against our investigation of evidence for the change we want to map out, not because it is not or was not there, but because we have a reversal of events that took place after the coup; whatever change happened has been forced into hiding – not removed, we believe, but hidden. Added to this are the restrictive measures adopted by the counter-revolutionary forces either to alienate and oppress revolutionary figures and movements or to suppress and manipulate revolutionary processes and incentives. Examples of these restrictive measures include, without being limited to, print media, state-/self-imposed censorship and state-controlled internet trolls. However, we do not think that there is no form of online activism taking place; there has to be. Considering the fearlessness and defiance that were evident under the former regime, we believe that it is hidden and underground. Unfortunately, there is insufficient research to back this up since the available research does not study this; it just stops at reporting repression. Here, it is about an academic approach to change (in politics, identity, public spaces, etc.) from below. While protests are not dismissed and are still considered a major repertoire of change, researchers are more interested in the self-centred daily concerns that are pushing people to hope for change (through the streets, mobilizations, etc.) (Bayat 2013b).

The corpus and material gathered by individuals themselves has shown greater interest in expressing willingness (or fear) of change:

> It is through their humor, satire, images and novels that we can get a sense of the discontent of youth that might lead the next revolution. The crowd re-articulates history as local, connected and malleable to the will and desire of political subjects, as opposed to the will of a corrupt dictator.
>
> (Khalil 2012, p. 63)

There also is a lot on how people are rewriting changes they have experienced through autofictions and biographies, including, for example, Tahrir Monlogues (Tahrir Monologues 2012).

An interesting idea is the importance of localizing change: how people retranslate and understand the revolutionary 'grand schemes' (Schielke 2015, p. 13) in their daily lives and what kind of anxieties and fears may arise from the discrepancy between the revolutions' promises and local experiences (Belakhdar et al. 2014; Rivetti 2015). Overall, the idea that informal daily politics, like the relationship between online and offline activism (Zayani 2015), gave us more information about how change occurred and how it has started to be widely shared since 2015–16.

Data and methods

In spite of the fact that it is really hard to monitor and analyse formal daily activities, there is an option of using a proxy to understand how people in countries of the Arab region interacted with the news of the day. Instead of analysing people's reactions and actions directly, we measure how much they interacted with media. For this purpose, we analysed a corpus of 169,000 news articles from newspapers. We focus the discussion on the number of times these articles were shared on Facebook to measure people's interest. Our working hypothesis is that people share only that which they feel strongly about. Sharing does not, however, mean that the sharers share the same views as the writers. Sharers may pass along those ideas because they strongly object to them. By analysing people's sharing patterns and interest, we hope to gain some insight into the mindset of the people of the region at a specific point in time.

Data

According to the web-intelligence website Similarweb.com, the website of the Egyptian newspaper *Al-Masry Al-Youm* (Almasryalyoum.com) ranks 2,699th on the list of the top visited websites in the world. It is also the 23rd most visited website in Egypt and, in the category of news and media, *Al-Masry Al-Youm* ranks 389th, which makes it one of the most important venues for news and political commentary in the Arab world in general and in Egypt in particular. Most of the traffic for the website comes from Egypt (69 per cent), followed by Saudi Arabia (7 per cent), the United States (3 per cent), the United Arab Emirates (3 per cent) and Kuwait (1.38 per cent).

Methods

To answer the questions posed in this chapter, we adopt a quantitative approach and supplement it with qualitative analysis. We use a pipeline of natural language

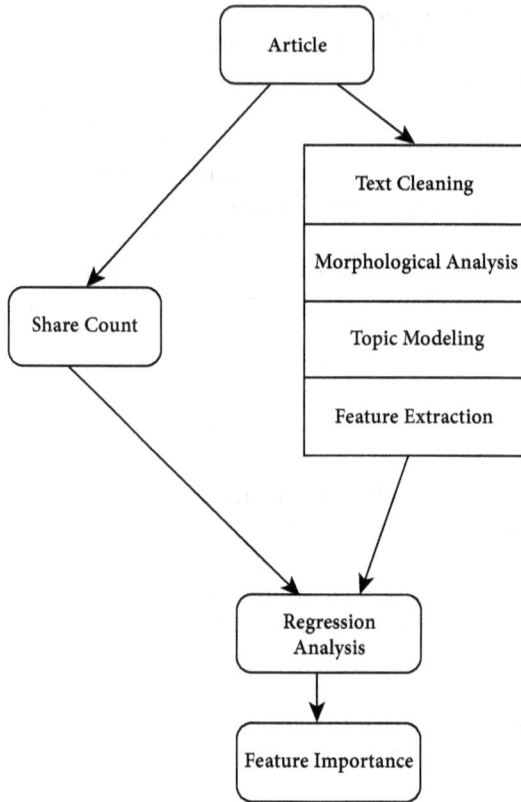

Figure 2.1 A flowchart of the research pipeline showing the processes a document goes through until feature importances are extracted.

processing and machine learning. The pipeline is outlined in Figure 2.1 and comprises the following steps:

Every article in our corpus undergoes the analysis pipeline outlined in the flowchart above. Each one of these steps deserves some consideration.

Text cleaning

The corpus we use, Almasryalyoum.com, is a website in html. In order to work with the data from the website, we extract the text from the html, making sure the encoding is uniform. This is probably the easiest kind of textual processing. This step also includes minimal processing, such as separating punctuation from text and separating numerical from alphabetical characters. This step is absolutely necessary, because any information-extraction task depends on plain text, and the form in which webpages naturally occur has many tags, comments and metadata that are not conducive to the kind of research we do.

Morphological analysis

Arabic is a morphologically complex language. While in many languages a word can be defined as a whitespace-delimited unit, such units in Arabic are far more complex. The word *wllmSryyn* ('as and for the Egyptians') comprises four units: the conjunction *w* ('and'), the preposition *l* ('to'/'for'), the definite article *Al* in its assimilated form and the noun *mSryyin* ('Egyptians'), which is itself made up of the adjective *mSry* ('Egyptian') and the genitive sound plural masculine marker *-yn*.

For morphological analysis, we use the memory-based segmenter and tagger developed by Mohamed (2012). Given a sentence such as:

وأعلن الرئيس مبادرته في المؤتمر المشترك مع الرئيس الأمريكي

The morphological analyser produces the output listed in Table 2.1.:

The purpose of morphological analysis is twofold: (1) mapping different forms of the same word together and (2) disambiguation. Mapping different forms of the same lemma can be exemplified by the word *ktAb* ('book'), which can appear in so many different forms: *kitAby* ('my book'), *Alkutub* ('the books') and the plural *kutub*. It does not make much sense to treat these as different words; hence the importance of mapping.

Disambiguation is usually a result of part-of-speech (POS) tagging, a process by which a grammatical category is assigned to each word/lemma/token. For example, the Arabic word علي can be either a proper noun (the name 'Ali') or the preposition على plus the first person singular pronoun ي, in which case it means 'on me'. The combination of morphological segmentation and POS tagging achieves this disambiguation.

As depicted in Figure 2.2, the word *wllmSryyn* has two levels of morphological analysis. At the second level, the token *mSryyn* can be divided into two

Table 2.1 The morphological analysis (segmentation + part of speech tagging) for one Arabic sentence.

Form	Analysis
وأعلن	wa/CONJ+AElan/PV
الرئيس	Al/DET+r}ys/NOUN
مبادرته	mbAdrp/NOUN+h/POSS_3MS
في	fy/PREP
المؤتمر	Al/DET+m}tmr/NOUN
المشترك	Al/DET+m$trk/ADJ
مع	mE/PREP
الرئيس	Al/DET/r}ts/NOUN
الأمريكي	Al/DET+>mryky/ADJ

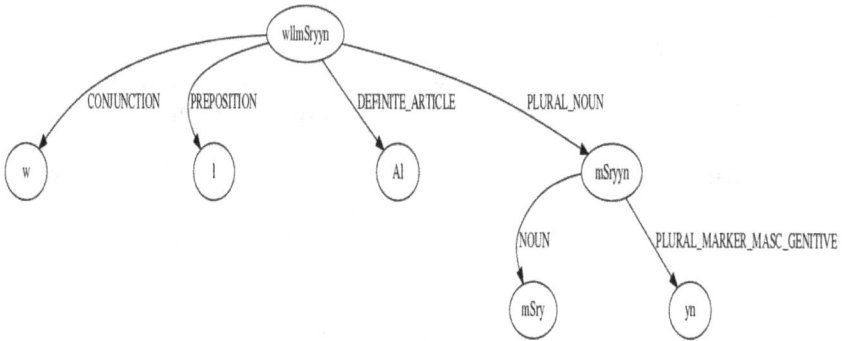

Figure 2.2 The morphological analysis of the Arabic word *wllmSryyn* ('and for the Egyptians').

segments: a noun and a suffix. Since this suffix is inflectional, we have decided, in our scheme of segmentation, not to split it off. We end up with the word having four segments, with the lexical unit being *mSryyn*. This level of segmentation is suitable for topic modelling since it reduces the vocabulary and at the same time maintains interpretability.

Topic modelling

Topic modelling is a statistical model that clusters documents into topics and is widely used in the humanities. It is capable of discovering the thematic structure of a large corpus, and it assumes that each document may contain a number of topics (Steyvers and Griffiths 2007). This is very important for our purposes, since an article that talks about both elections and torture in prisons may easily be assigned two topics. Usually, the researcher determines the number of topics wanted and the software arranges the documents according to the most prominent topics. The choice of number of topics is a question of trial and error and basically depends on finding the most topics with the least noise. Topic modelling is especially good when dealing with large bodies of text. With thousands of documents, it is usually unfeasible to go through them manually. Topic modelling analyses those documents and assigns clusters of words to them (we call these clusters 'topics'). A document may be associated with several topics with varying probabilities. For this study, we use the MALLET topic-modelling toolkit (McCallum 2002) because it is open source and easy to use.

We use the topic modelling output for three purposes: (1) obtaining a topic classification for all the topics in the corps; (2) ranking the most important topics according to the *Al-Masry Al-Youm* website, which gives us an idea about what the newspaper focuses on as well as what it neglects; and (3) the topics produced by the topic modelling algorithm are fed into the random forest regressor as independent variables while the number of shares per document is the dependent variable. The objective here is to rank the importance of the topics as viewed by the newspaper readership and followers. The whole setting allows us to compare the interests of the editorial staff with those of the readership. We can then pick any topic covered in the newspaper and see how it ranks among the netizens of social media as compared to how much focus the editors give to it. For the purpose of this analysis, we will focus only on those topics related to the Arab Spring.

Feature extraction

We measure the importance to the readership by the number of shares a document has. A document that is shared more is considered to be more important (and vice versa). Shares represent active engagement with the document, unlike readings or views, which are more passive. Reactions can also be active engagements, but they are not as indicative of importance as shares are. Comments can also be considered active engagement, but comments are only active at the personal level. A commenter wants to express her opinion, but a sharer wants others to express their opinions as well. If it is true that a Facebook user has an average of 400 friends, shares can also tell us much about the reach of the article shared, which cannot be accounted for by other modes of engagement.

The choice of shares over comments, the only two measures available in our datasets, can also be justified by looking at the data. In our dataset, people seem to be more keen on sharing than on commenting. The average number of shares per document is 364.19, with a standard deviation of 1,510, a minimum of 0 and a maximum of 66,696. The median number of shares per document is 3, which shows a skewed distribution. Obviously, there are some documents with a large number of shares, while 50 per cent are shared less than three times each. A third quartile of 82 makes the picture clearer.

When it comes to comments, the average number of comments per document is 0.34, with a standard deviation of 2.93, a minimum of 0 and a maximum of 428. Also, 90 per cent of the documents in the corpus do not have any comments associated with them, while only 27 per cent of the documents have not been shared at least once. For these reasons combined, we have decided to use the share count rather than the comment count as our indicator of topic importance.

While share count tells us much about how significant an article is, it tells us nothing about how essential it is to the editorial board of the newspaper in question. However, this significance can be inferred from the topic(s) of the article. If the topics rank highly in the topic modelling stage, this may indicate that the article expresses an important topic. This is vital since, by combining these two metrics, we can compare the interest of readership to the interest of the editorial board. Such a finding can be central not only for research purposes but also for commercial applications, since we can use this to tell the editorial board what topics readers are interested in, thus making them focus more on what the readers know is important and not what the editorial boards think will grab the readers' attention.

Regression analysis

Random forests is a machine-learning algorithm that can be used for both classification and regression. It is capable of handling large numbers of variables, even when the information in each variable is limited, without being prone to over-fitting. Random forests are known to have high accuracy and to be 'relatively robust to outliers and noise' (Breiman 2001, p. 10). We have found random forests to be superior to ordinary least squares (OLS) multiple regression since we have tried several algorithms for the purpose of analysing the data for this chapter. One favourable feature of random forests is that they rank the independent variables in terms of their importance to the regression/classification model. To be specific to the problem at hand, random forests are capable of telling us which factors are most associated with sharing. Given a topic-classification scheme of the newswire articles (e.g. politics, religion, January 25th Revolution), random forests produce a ranking and a score for each. This is indispensable for our purposes since this is exactly what we are looking to achieve. While there are several implementations available, we have used the scikit-learn implementation (RandomForestRegressor) for analysis in this chapter for its ease of use and programmability.

Results

Preliminary statistics

We use a corpus from the Egyptian newspaper *Al-Masry Al-Youm*. The corpus covers the period from 1 June 2016 to 31 May 2017, and is thus a full year of coverage. The corpus comprises 169,026 documents, where a document is any published item (e.g. news item, opinion piece, interview). The number of items per month in the corpus over this period is as follows: 14,944 (June 2016), 13,862 (July 2016), 14,625 (August 2016), 13,589 (September 2016), 14,891 (October 2016), 14,260 (November 2016), 13,489 (December 2016), 14,525 (January 2017), 12,787 (February 2017), 13,310 (March 2017), 14,804 (April 2017) and 13,940 (May 2017). In terms of word count, the one-year corpus has 41,260,327 words, not including punctuation, with an average of 246.11 words per document.

Topic Model Topics

We have decided to use forty topics for topic modelling, which is an easy number to handle. We have also tried up to 100 topics, and found that we gain more fine-tuned details by increasing the number of topics, and that 40 is a good approximation and valid generalization. The following are the forty topics suggested by MALLET, sorted in descending order of importance in the corpus. The more important topic appears first:

It should be noted that the order in which these topics appear reflects how important they are to the editors of *Al-Masry Al-Youm*. We can see also that the focus is mainly local and that international news takes a back seat, which is expected in a newspaper whose title translates to 'The Egyptian Today'. This, of course, does not mean a binary classification between local and international news, since many news items are essentially both. What this tells us is that, across

Table 2.2 T# = Topic Number, MR = MALLET Rank, RG = Importance in Regression Model

T#	MR	RG	Description	T#	MR	RG	Description
29	1	3	The Problems facing Egypt	8	21	12	Theft and other crimes
34	2	6	The news of the Parliament	23	22	22	Health and hospitals
36	3	10	Local news from different districts	30	23	26	Europe, refugees, elections
32	4	13	Projects for boosting the economy	11	24	4	Food supplies: wheat, sugar and meat
25	5	8	The relations between Egypt and the other Arab countries	19	25	24	Tourism
33	6	1	Media coverage of President Al-Sisi	16	26	39	ISIS
18	7	14	Conduct of the people of Egypt	38	27	17	Egyptian ports
0	8	21	Police, incident and explosions: most probably foreign news	2	28	9	Military operations in Sinai
5	9	2	Family and marital issues	6	29	27	China, North Korea, Iran and Nuclear programmes
3	10	34	Women and children	26	30	7	Movies, TV series and songs
14	11	18	Education and universities	27	31	30	Agriculture, Nile, irrigation
37	12	23	Utilities and roads	17	32	20	Azhar, Mosques and fighting terrorism
7	13	28	US elections	31	33	32	Church, explosions and terrorism
4	14	36	Culture, arts and festivals	28	34	25	Sports news
12	15	15	Crime and accident news	22	35	37	European football: Barcelona, Manchester United, Bundesliga
24	16	5	Banks and the stock exchange	35	36	35	African football
9	17	19	Traffic	20	37	29	diet and sleep
10	18	16	January 25th Revolution, political parties, the Egyptian army and the Muslim Brotherhood	1	38	33	Cars, internet and technology
21	19	31	Ahli and Zamalek	15	39	40	Brazil Olympic Games
39	20	11	Criminal courts, possibly related to the Muslim Brotherhood	13	40	38	The Israeli occupation of Palestinian territories, Hamas and the West Bank

the entire corpus, there is more focus on the local part of the story, and a piece of international news may derive its influence on the local news.

Out of forty topics, the January 25th Revolution and its related news ranks 18th, which is somewhat in the middle. It is not priority news, but it is not in the bottom either.

Topic association

The focus of this article is the Arab Spring in Egypt, which is Topic 10 in Table 2.2, but a topic that hardly comes in isolation. When a writer mentions the January 25th Revolution, even when the revolution is the main focus of the article, she usually relates this topic to other relevant ones. She may talk about the detainees, violations of human rights, the economic situation in Egypt, among other topics. Since we have summarized the whole corpus into forty topics, we will now see which of these topics co-occurs with the revolution topic in the same document. For the sake of brevity, we have excluded any topic whose contribution to the document is less than 10 per cent. This guarantees that topics mentioned in passing are not given as much importance as those constituting an integral part of the document.

Table 2.3 lists the top ten topics associated with the Arab Spring. The ten topics together make up 70 per cent of all the topics associated with the Arab Spring in Egypt. The most important associated topic is Topic 29, the problems and challenges facing Egypt. Topic 29 alone represents 16.4 per cent of topic associations and, being negative in nature, tints the Arab Spring topic with a negative tone.

Table 2.3 Topic associations: The top ten topics associated with Topic 10

Topic		Frequency	Percentage	Cum%	EditorRank	PeopleRank
29	Problems of Egypt	3665	16.4107	16.4107	1	3
18	Conduct of the people of Egypt	3204	14.3465	30.7572	7	14
34	Parliament	1414	6.3314	37.0886	2	6
5	Art, science and revolution	1377	6.1658	43.2544	9	2
7	US elections	1369	6.1299	49.3843	13	28
25	Egypt and other Arab countries relations	1185	5.306	54.6904	5	8
33	Media coverage of President Al-Sisi	1083	4.8493	59.5397	6	1
16	ISIS	858	3.8418	63.3815	26	39
4	Culture, arts and festivals	848	3.7971	67.1786	14	36
30	Europe and the refugees	768	3.4389	70.6175	23	36

The second most related topic is Topic 18, which is mainly about the people of Egypt, talking primarily about the characteristics of the people and what they have been through. This connects smoothly with Topic 29, and we have the triangle of revolution, people and problems.

Less important associated topics follow. First, we have Topic 34: the Parliament. The general sentiments in the documents about the Parliament seem to be negative ones, basically claiming that this is not the kind of assembly one elects after a revolution.

While it makes sense to look at the cluster of topics representing the Arab Spring in terms of their ranked importance, this is not the only way to examine them. One important aspect is the difference in interest between editors and readers. The editors may think some topic is important while the readership views it otherwise, and vice versa. It thus benefits our analysis to examine the losers and winners as topics move from their static status on the website and their shareability on social media.

The biggest winner is Topic 5 (family and marital issues). While the topic ranks ninth in terms of editor interest, it is the second most shareable topic in its category and thus earns seven ranks in the move. The next biggest winner is Topic 33 (Sisi and the media), which wins five ranks as it moves up from rank six to rank one. These two topics are the only winners. All the other topics lose rank as they move from the website to social network.

The biggest loser is Topic 4 (culture, arts and festivals). While this is the 14th most covered topic on the website, sharers do not seem to care much about it, since it ranks 36th out of forty on the sharing scale, thus losing twenty-two ranks. The second biggest loser is Topic 7 (the US elections and President Trump). US elections and Trump's presidency seem to be a favoured topic for the editors, ranking 13th out of forty, but readers do not find it worth much sharing on social media, and it thus loses fifteen places and ranks 28th.

Below we will talk briefly about the top five of these topics:

Topic 29: Problems of Egypt

Topic 29 has the basic theme of 'Egypt is in crisis', with politics being the term of focus on all the crises facing Egypt: how young people are treated, detained in police custody and denied their rights and equal share of opportunities; the Muslim Brotherhood; the Egyptian parliament seen as unrepresentative of the people; the faltering economy; Egypt's rank in education and university ranking; Israel and Trump; the water crisis; the worsening conditions of tourism; automobile prices; religious discourse; and crises in the cinema industry and football. Some little focus is also paid to the conditions of the health sector in Egypt.

Topic 18: The deteriorating social demeanour in Egypt

Topic 18 can be summarized as 'how the conduct and social demeanour of the people of Egypt has changed for the worse'. In this broad topic, we find several examples: how young people do not show enough respect to the elderly, how the streets of Egypt are filled with garbage because people do not clean up after themselves, how many people are on a mission to find fault with the government instead of doing the right things themselves, Egypt's cultural degeneration, religious fanatics and many other social phenomena that may indicate that Egypt is headed in the wrong direction. All this relates to the January 25th Revolution, either in terms of causation or correlation.

Topic 34: The Egyptian Parliament, elections and decrees

Topic 34 has to do with every elected body that makes resolutions. In this topic, we find discussions of several parliamentary bills and laws; decrees by the president of Egypt that will have to be ratified by the Parliament; the Parliament and the nomination of a new president for the State Council, the highest administrative court in Egypt; and even news about the elections in several professional syndicates in Egypt. The main theme is elections and resolutions, a topic that ties in well with the January 25th Revolution.

Topic 5: Art, science and the revolution

Topic 5 discusses the relationships between art, science and the revolution. We find, for example, an interview with the Egyptian pop singer Amina, who declares that she will not sing in Qatar because Qatar is against the June 30th Revolution; an article discussing the relationship between art, football and politics; the TV series *Mamoun and Associates*, which is a political satire and parody of the Mubarak regime; a discussion of the benefits of scientific revolutions and the harms of political ones; and many other themes related to how the political sphere in Egypt has affected art, sport and science.

Topic 7: US elections

Although we call this topic US elections, the truth is that it is about elections around the world in general, with the United States having the lion's share of coverage. We have pieces on the French elections and racism, the attempted military coup in Turkey and even the Korean elections. The largest part is concerned with Obama and Trump and compares their policies towards the Middle East in general and Egypt in particular.

Regression analysis

The first thing to be noticed is that R^2 is quite high, with a score of 0.86, which means that this may have a high predictive power. In other words, the model encompassing the thematic topics is a good predictor of sharing activity. If we know what topics a certain document contains, then we have a good idea of how many shares it will get. Since we have forty topics, and each document is usually made up of several of these, with varying contributions, one needs to know which of these topics may trigger the sharing instinct. One good thing about random forest regressors is that they are able to rank the factors contributing to the sharing, assigning each factor its relative importance.

Conclusion

We have presented a new method of studying media, and while qualitative study is important, we have chosen to have a quantitative basis on top of which qualitative analyses can be realized. In the same vein, Bennett and Segerberg (2011, p. 21) stress the role that digital media technologies play in intertwining individualized and collective forms of protest, and how 'personalized communication technologies ... enable a large number of people to become linked to and recognized by a large number of others'. This individualized/collectivized protester figure has become a powerful actor in the sociopolitical scene, where Tahrir Square serves as an ideal example that encompasses both individual and collective participation and engagement, as well as local, national and even transnational causes.

Three lessons can be learned from this study. First, quantitative studies, especially ones that make use of large corpora, natural language processing and machine learning, are capable of producing results that are on par with, or even more insightful than, the ones produced by traditional methods. Second, digital humanities methods can be useful not only for the kind of analysis produced here but also in giving feedback to content creators. We have seen that regression analysis has shown that the editors' interests are in full agreement with those of the audience targeted by the editorial board. Editors can make use of this information to improve their content creation and writer selection processes. While we have not included the writer/editor/correspondent in this study, such a process is trivial and can tell us which writers attract a wider readership. Third, with the help of the analysis provided above, we are now in a better position to answer the question we started with: Do Egyptians still care about the Arab Spring? While this is a yes/no question, we prefer to give the more nuanced answer available through topic rankings as they relate to the Arab Spring. Both the editors of *Al-Masry Al-Youm* and the readership agree that the revolution is not a priority topic: the editors rank it 18th while the readership ranks it 16th. More important to the people are what may be described as the ramifications of the January 25th Revolution, especially what may be termed the problems facing Egyptians.

This study invites further research on the diverse tracks of the developments of these topics over time, perhaps at fixed intervals to see how time can affect the process. Also, the focus on Egypt, justified enough as a representative case study in the Arab world, allows for casting a wider net to include other Arab countries as well. Our regression models may also include other factors, such as the writers and the time of publication.

References

Abaza, M. (2017). 'Academic tourists sightseeing the Arab Spring', *Jadaliyya*, 27 September. Available at: www.jadaliyya.com/pages/index/2767/academic-tourists-sight-seeing-the-arab-spring [accessed 1 September 2018].

Bayat, A. (2013b). *Life as politics: How ordinary people change the Middle East*. Stanford, CA: Stanford University Press.

Belakhdar, N., Eickhof, I., El Khawaga, A., El Khawaga, O., Hamada, A., Harders, C. and Sandri, S. (eds.). (2014). *Arab revolutions and beyond: Change and persistence*, Proceedings of the international conference, Tunis, 12–13 November 2013, Working Paper No. 11. Berlin: Center for North African and Middle Eastern Politics, and Cairo: Faculty of Economics and Political Science. Available at: https://www.polsoz.fu-berlin.de/polwiss/forschung/international/vorderer-orient/publikation/working_papers/wp_11/WP11_Tunis_Conference_FINAL_web.pdf [accessed 11 January 2020].

Bennett, W. (2012). 'The personalization of politics: Political identity, social media, and changing patterns of participation', *The Annals of the American Academy of Political and Social Science*, 644, pp. 20–39. Available at: http://www.jstor.org/stable/23316140 [accessed 4 May 2021].

Bennett, W.L. and Segerberg, A. (2011). 'Digital media and the personalization of collective action', *Information, Communication & Society*, 14(6), pp. 770–99.

Bogaert, K. (2013). 'Contextualizing the Arab revolts: The politics behind three decades of neoliberalism in the Arab World', *Middle East Critique*, 22(3), pp. 213–34.

Breiman, L. (2001). 'Random forests', *Machine Learning*, 45(1), pp. 5–32.

Gause, G. III. (2011). 'Why Middle East Studies missed the Arab Spring: The myth of authoritarian stability', *Foreign Affairs*, 90(4), pp. 81–90.

Hinnebusch, R. (2015). 'Conclusion: Agency, context and emergent post-uprising regimes', *Democratization*, 22(2), pp. 358–74.

Hom, A.R. (2016). 'Angst springs eternal: Dangerous times and the dangers of timing the "Arab Spring"', *Security Dialogue*, 47(2), pp. 165–83.

Khalil, A. (2012). 'The political crowd: Theorizing popular revolt in North Africa', *Contemporary Islam*, 6(1), pp. 45–65.

Kohstall, F. (2016). *Beyond regime change: Middle East Studies and academic cooperation in the wake of the Arab uprisings*. Arab-German Young Academy (AGYA) – Transformation Group Working Paper No. 5. Berlin: Arab-German Young Academy of Sciences and Humanities. Available at: http://agya.info/fileadmin/user_upload/Working_Groups-images/Transformation/WPS_Academia_in_Transformation/Paper_5_Middle_East_Studies_in_the_Wake_of_the_Arab_Uprisings_Kohstall.pdf [accessed 12 May 2021].

Lynch, M. (2014). 'Media, old and new', in M. Lynch (ed.), *The Arab uprisings explained: New contentious politics in the Middle East*, pp. 93–110. New York: Columbia University Press.

Maghlouth, N. Arvanitis, R., Cointet, J. and Hanaf, S. (2015). 'Who frames the debate on the Arab Uprisings? Analysis of Arabic, English, and French academic scholarship', *International Sociology*, 30(4), pp. 418–41.

McCallum, A.K. (2002). 'MALLET: Machine learning for language toolkit'. Available at: http://mallet.cs.umass.edu.

Mohamed, E. (2012). Morphological Segmentation and Part of Speech tagging for Religious Arabic. Proceedings of the Fourth Workshop on Computational Approaches to Arabic Script-based Languages (CAASL4). San Diego, California, USA.

Morjé, M.H. and Walters, M.R. (2014). 'Explaining the unexpected: Political science and the surprises of 1989 and 2011', *Perspectives on Politics*, 12(2), pp. 394–408.

Rinke, E.M. and Röder, M. (2011). 'The Arab Spring – Media ecologies, communication culture, and temporal-spatial unfolding: Three components in a communication model of the Egyptian regime change', *International Journal of Communication*, 5, pp. 1273–85. Available at: https://ijoc.org/index.php/ijoc/article/download/1173/603 [accessed 6 May 2021].

Rivetti, P. (2015). 'Continuity and change before and after the uprisings in Tunisia, Egypt and Morocco: Regime reconfiguration and policymaking in North Africa', *British Journal of Middle Eastern Studies*, 42, pp. 1–11.

Saouli, A. (2015). 'Back to the future: The Arab uprisings and state (re)formation in the Arab world', *Democratization*, 22(2), pp. 315–34.

Schielke, S. (2015). *Egypt in the future tense: Hope, frustration, and ambivalence before and after 2011*. Bloomington: Indiana University Press.

Schwedler, J. (2015). 'Comparative politics and the Arab uprisings', *Middle East Law and Governance*, 7(1), pp. 141–52.

Steyvers, M. and Griffiths, T. (2007). 'Probabilistic topic models', *Handbook of latent semantic analysis*, 427(7), pp. 424–40.

Tahrir Monologues. (2012). 'Tahrir monologues: The idea', 12 May. Available at: www.youtube.com/watch?v=JtyhaPi3tsk [accessed 10 December 2017].

Volpi, F. (2013). 'Explaining (and re-explaining) political change in the Middle East during the Arab Spring: Trajectories of democratization and of authoritarianism in the Maghreb', *Democratization*, 20(6), pp. 969–90.

Zayani, M. (2015). *Networked publics and digital contention: The politics of everyday life in Tunisia*. Oxford: Oxford University Press.

Chapter 4

CYBERACTIVISM AND THE (RE)FRAMING OF IDENTITIES AND REVOLUTIONARY NARRATIVES: A TALE OF TWO EGYPTIAN POLITICAL ACTORS

Sahar Khamis and Ehab H. Gomaa

Introduction

Ten years after the eruption of the 2011 Arab Spring uprisings, remarkable changes have been sweeping both the political and media landscapes in this vibrant and volatile region, as the tug of war between autocratic regimes and their opponents and critics continues, taking on new forms and drifting in new directions. A key dimension in these ongoing push-and-pull struggles, and a significant toolkit which is constantly deployed in them, is cyberactivism (Howard 2011). In this chapter, we examine the contributions of two oppositional Egyptian communities, namely the Muslim Brotherhood (MB) and the young revolutionaries, to this ongoing struggle in their home country, analysing how they utilize a wide array of tools furnished by new communication technologies to disrupt, expose and resist the regime's official strategies, tactics and narratives over different phases, and how the framing(s) of their own identities, narratives and counter-narratives have been constantly shifting and evolving, through these complex and intertwined phenomena.

Using a comparative analysis framework, we contrast the framing – and (re)framing – of these actors' and political players' activism(s), identities and discourses to unpack broad and complex dynamics of resistance to authoritarianism, and to shed light on their varied implications. We argue that the differing tactics which each of these groups employs are grounded in varied contexts, and thus encourage disparate political, and discursive, outcomes. In conducting this comparison, we seek to unpack the complexities of overly simplistic understandings of Arab anti-authoritarianism and the role of internet technologies in activism that have unfolded across the Arab world in the last decade, by contextualizing them in the post-Arab Spring's shifting political and mediated environments.

However, before embarking on this journey, we have to first provide some background on the Egyptian political scene and the most important actors and players in it, in order to better understand the shifts and changes which have been taking place in Egypt, before, during and after the Egyptian revolution of 2011 – and their multiple implications.

Egypt suffered from dictatorship, autocracy and authoritarianism under successive regimes, since its declaration as a republic in 1952. Nasser, Sadat and Mubarak, who all came from a military background, exhibited varying degrees and forms of autocratic rule, with shrinking and stretching margins of freedom. A historic, peaceful revolution erupted in Egypt in 2011 to oust Egypt's ruler, Hosni Mubarak, and end his thirty years of dictatorship and autocracy. The revolution was characterized by bottom-up grassroots mobilization, youth leadership and the central role of cyberactivism in aiding popular revolt (Khamis and Vaughn 2011a).

The political scene changed in Egypt with the fall of Mubarak in 2011, after Egypt's historic revolution, with different political players and civil society activists emerging and rising to power. Different Islamist political groups merged and gathered under different political parties; non-religious political parties were also empowered; and more liberal, independent political figures entered the political scene. The young revolutionaries made different decisions, as some of them joined newly established political parties, others tried to establish their own political parties, while many of them decided to remain independent, as unaffiliated activists.

The active Islamists political forces in Egypt tried their best to fill the power vacuum after Mubarak's resignation and the transfer of authority to the Supreme Council of the Armed Forces (SCAF). *Al-Ikhwan Al-Muslimun* ('The Muslim Brotherhood') is the largest and oldest Islamist group in Egypt, which was established in 1928.

Although most of the previous literature on the (MB) has studied this group from the inside, in an effort to analyse and better understand the history, internal dynamics and organizational structure of this movement, as well as its hierarchy, ideology and positionality in society (Al-Anani 2016; Kandil 2014; Lia and Al Banna 1998; Mitchell 1969), some recent studies have started to pay closer attention to the importance of studying this group from the outside, with a special emphasis on those who decided to exit this group, and the reasons behind their decisions to disengage from it (Al-Awadi 2013; Menshawy 2020, 2021). Other studies have recently tackled the MB's articulation of their shifting identifies in general, and their revolutionary rhetoric in particular, through online platforms, such as *Ikhwanweb* (El-Nawawy and Elmasry 2018).

The MB has been largely a persecuted and banned group for a long time, under successive Egyptian governments. Its short-lived golden moment of public and political participation came after the ousting of Mubarak in January 2011, and lasted only until the ousting in June 2013 of President Mohamed Morsi, who came from the ranks of the brotherhood, after which it returned to being a banned group. The MB announced establishing a political party on 30 April 2011, and received their official license on 6 June 2011, months after the 25 January 2011 revolution took place. They called their newly established party 'The Freedom and Justice Party' (*France 24* 2011).

The *Al-Wasat* party, which was founded in 1996 but failed to receive its legal license until one week after the ousting of Mubarak, is another Islamist party. The party leader, Abou Ela Mady, mentioned that the political party is independent and ideologically different from the MB. The *Masr Al- Qaweya* ('Strong Egypt') party was established officially in November 2012 by the former MB leading figure and former presidential candidate Abdel Moneim Aboul Foutouh. Similarly, the Islamist group *Al-Gamaa' Al-Islamiyya* established its own political party *El Benna Wel Tanmya* ('Construction and Development Party') and enrolled in the political process (El Nahass 2015).

Liberal political forces also changed dramatically after the 2011 uprising. They started to establish political parties and to recruit youth, scholars, businessmen and elites to their parties. *Al-Masreyeen Al-Ahrar* ('The Free Egyptians') is a liberal party which was established in 2011 by the famous Egyptian businessman Naguib Sawiras. The party started a political coalition with the MB in the elections of 2011–12. After 25 January 2011, the *Al-Tagammu* party ('The National Progressive Unionist Party') became a strong opponent to the MB and to Mohamed Morsi, and acted as a main pillar in the 30 June rebellion against him. *Al-Tahaluf El Shabi El Ishtiraki* ('The Popular Socialist Alliance Party') was established in the aftermath of the 25 January revolution by several members who had resigned from the *Al-Tagammu* party. The party joined the coalition called 'The Revolution Continues' during the 2011–12 elections, along with other youth parties from the revolutionary camp. The *Al-Masri Al-Democrati Alegtemaii party* ('The Egyptian Social Democratic Party') was established in 2011 and embraced the principles and demands of the 2011 revolution. It enrolled in the 2011–12 elections and won nineteen seats months after its establishment. The party joined the 30 June protests and enrolled in the 2015 parliamentarian elections (Dunne and Hamzawy 2017; El Nahass 2015).

Unlike the MB, which represents one single, unified and largely homogenous group, the activists and young revolutionaries cannot be classified easily, due to their eclectic nature, diverse ideological orientations and different political affiliations. Some of them decided to join newly established political parties. Others decided to remain as members of social and political groups, such as the April 6th movement, which had been established in 2008, in the wake of the massive strike by workers in the *El-Mahala* industrial city in northern Egypt. This movement was one of the many different groups that called for the 25 January 2011 revolution, and one of the main pillars behind its success, along with the *Kefaya* movement, which means 'enough' in Arabic. Many of the young revolutionaries, however, decided to remain independent, as activists who were simply fighting for freedom, liberties and social justice, without being affiliated with any particular party or group (Abdalla 2013).

On 30 June 2013, the protests against President Mohamed Morsi marked the one-year anniversary of his inauguration as president. Millions of protesters across Egypt took to the streets and demanded his immediate resignation (Kingsley 2013). Reasons included accusations that he was increasingly authoritarian and pushing through an Islamist agenda, without regard to secular opponents or the rule of law. That was followed by the Egyptian Armed Forces issuing a forty-eight-hour ultimatum that gave the country's political parties until 3 July 2013 to meet the demands of the Egyptian people (Weaver et al. 2013). The Egyptian military also threatened to intervene if the dispute was not resolved by then.

In a late-night television address, Morsi declared that he would defend the legitimacy of his elected office with his life, emphasizing that there is no substitute to legitimacy, as he vowed not to resign. He accused supporters of former president Hosni Mubarak of exploiting the wave of protests to topple the government and to fight democracy, and he criticized the military for taking sides in this crisis.

On 3 July 2013, the Egyptian military announced the end of Mohamed Morsi's presidency, the suspension of the constitution and the holding of a new presidential election soon, an act which has been described by some as a military coup, by others as a popular uprising and by a third group as a popularly backed coup.

The military appointed Chief Justice Adly Mansour as interim president and charged him with forming a transitional technocratic government. Morsi was initially put under house arrest, and later on jailed, and MB leaders were arrested. The announcement was followed by demonstrations and clashes between supporters and opponents throughout Egypt; as well as the issuance of statements by the Grand Sheikh of Al Azhar Ahmed el-Tayeb, the Coptic Pope Tawadros II, as well as opposition leader Mohamed ElBaradei.

Following Morsi's ouster, pro-Morsi supporters gathered in Cairo in two places. Rabaa Al-Adawiya Square became as famous and symbolic as Tahrir Square in Cairo due to the thousands of protesters who resisted for more than two months. The Rabaa Al-Adawiya Mosque is one of the most famous mosques in Cairo, located on the northern edge of the Nasr City district in eastern Cairo. It was named after the eighth-century Sufi saint, Rabaa Al-Adawiya. As she was the fourth daughter in the family, the Arabic adjective *Rabaa* (meaning 'fourth') was chosen as her name. This provides an explanation for the 'four fingers' symbol that became widely used by the supporters of Morsi and the MB, and others who shared their vision and sympathized with their position, to remind people of the 14 August 2013 Egyptian security forces crackdown to disperse pro-Morsi sit-ins in Rabaa Al-Adawiya and Nahda Squares in Cairo and Giza, respectively, which has been described by some as a brutal massacre, and by others as a necessary operation.

A new presidential election in Egypt took place between 26 and 28 May 2014. There were only two candidates: former defence minister Abdel-Fattah Al-Sisi and the socialist candidate, Hamdeen Sabahi. Al-Sisi was elected with 97 per cent of the vote (Saleh and Kalin 2014), in what has been described by some as a farcical election, resembling Mubarak's landslide victories of 99 per cent in previous polls – and by others as a legitimate election.

As this background picture reveals, Egypt has witnessed a lot of controversies around the very nature of the Egyptian state: whether it should be secular or religious, the role and responsibilities of the president, the role of the army in the political scene and the relation between religion and politics, among other things. All of the political actors in the modern Egyptian political scene used both traditional media and new media to polish their mediated images (Gamson et al. 1992), broaden their outreach, strengthen their impact and aid their multiple forms of activism (Khamis 2020). In doing so, they were also asserting and framing their distinctive political identities and revolutionary narratives, while framing counter-narratives about 'Others', i.e., their opponents, and those who do not share their positions and visions.

Research questions

This chapter aims to answer two main research questions:

1. Q 1: What were the main identity frames used by the MB and the young revolutionaries to define themselves and their roles, before, during and after the Egyptian revolution of 2011, specifically during the period between 2009 and 2016?
2. Q 2: How did this identity framing phenomenon shape the dominant terms used by each group to define itself and its opponents, and how did this change before, during and after the Egyptian revolution of 2011, specifically during the period between 2009 and 2016?

Conceptual framework

This study revisits and explores the applicability of the concept of 'framing' (De Vreese 2005; Entman 1993; Goffman 1974; Hunt et al. 1994; Williams 2007), as it applies to the (re)construction, and (re)articulation, of the identities of different political actors and players in the contemporary Egyptian political scene (Khamis 2020).

Goffman (1974) defines the frame as a 'schemata of interpretation that provides a Context for understanding information and enables us to locate, perceive, identify and Label' (as cited in Hallahan 1999, p. 211). Entman said that, through this framing process, other aspects of perceived reality are basically grounded or ignored (Entman 1993). Frames are important, as they help audiences to locate, perceive, identify and label the information around them (Goffamn 1984).

It could be said that all the political players in the Egyptian political scene used this framing process to influence the shaping of public opinion (Page et al. 1987) and everyday reality for ordinary Egyptians. Through the use of social media, satellite television channels, public speeches and other means of communication, albeit in different ways and to varying degrees, the political players mentioned above attempted to frame their identities, and to frame public issues, by focusing on particular aspects of a perceived reality to enhance their salience, assert their legitimacy and broaden their popularity, outreach and base of support.

Through these efforts, political players also engaged in another, interrelated phenomenon called 'identity framing', which refers to the various ways by which people view themselves in the context of specific conflicts. It also allows us to think about how individuals who are part of a larger group are influenced by their affiliation with, and participation in, that group (Gardner 2003).

The concept of identity framing is important because it allows us to analyse how individuals' identities and group affiliations influence how they view and respond to conflict. According to Gardner (2003), because identity describes who we are as a person, we tend to protect those things (beliefs, values, group affiliations) that help create our sense of self. When individuals' identities are threatened or challenged through conflict, they respond in ways that reinforce their allegiance to these affiliations. In a nutshell, identity frames exclude information and perspectives that do not align with, or perhaps contradict, features of an individual's core identity (Gardner 2003).

Sociological and psychological studies explored the concept of framing analysis long before mass communication studies came to it. The 'concept of frame' itself can be traced back to 1974, in the work of Goffman, who defined frames as principles that organize and govern any social event. Thus, the concept of framing helps us to better understand how people tend to organize and categorize things cognitively. This explains, for example, how and why journalists choose what to cover, as well as how to cover it (Akhavan-Majid and Ramaprasad 2000).

Saleem (2007) says that framing is an analytical technique which was developed by social psychologists, like Goffman (1974) and Gitlin (1980, p. 131), to explain how the media define issues to the public. Gitlin (1980, cited in Park 2003, p. 148) defined frames as 'persistent patterns of cognition, presentation, selection, emphasis and exclusion by which symbol-handlers routinely organize discourse, whether verbal or visual'.

Entman (1993) also contends that these frames are located within the minds of individuals, since they are 'mentally stored clusters of ideas that guide individuals' processing of information' (cited in Duncan 2007, p. 27). Both Iyengar (1991) and Entman (1993) agree that frames function to define problems, diagnose causes, make moral judgements and suggest remedies.

Further theorization efforts about framing included Pan and Kosicki's (1993) model for explaining the framing process, which consists of syntactical structure, thematic structure and rhetorical structure, as well as Bostick's (2005) model, which focuses on the four basic dimensions for frame analysis, namely the topics, the framing mechanisms, the cognitive attributes and the affective attributes.

Research methodology

Content analysis

The research method used in this study is quantitative content analysis. Kerlinger (2000) defines content analysis as 'a method of studying and analysing communication in a systematic, objective and quantitative manner for measuring variables' (cited in Wimmer and Dominick 2006, p. 141). The rationale behind the selection of content analysis is the fact that it is one of the most heavily used methods of data collection and data analysis in framing studies (Busher 2006; Dulcan 2006).

Content analysis sample

Muslim Brotherhood sample

Before 2011 the MB dominated the professional syndicates and student associations in Egypt and was famous for its network of social services in neighbourhoods and villages, despite its banned status. In the 2000 parliamentary elections, the MB won seventeen parliamentary seats, and again in 2005, it won eighty-eight seats (20 per cent of the total seats, compared to only fourteen seats for the legally approved opposition parties). Therefore, it was able to form the largest opposition bloc, despite the arrest of hundreds of its members and despite its classification as a banned group. During these years the MB had one official online portal. For the purpose of this study, a simple random sample of fifty press releases was collected from this official website: http://www.ikhwanonline.com

Following the 2011 revolution that overthrew Hosni Mubarak, the MB was legalized for the first time and emerged as the most powerful and most cohesive political movement in Egypt. Its newly formed political party, The Freedom and Justice Party, won two referendums, and gained far more seats than any other party in the 2011–12 parliamentary election, while its candidate, Mohamed Morsi, won the 2012 presidential elections. A simple random sample of fifty press releases was collected through the same website to cover this period.

Within a short time, however, public opposition grew against President Morsi. By April 2013, Egypt had become increasingly divided between President Mohamed Morsi and his Islamist allies on one hand, and a more liberal opposition camp on the other. Opponents accused Morsi and the MB of trying to monopolize power, while Morsi's allies accused the opposition of trying to destabilize the country, to derail the democratic process and to undermine the elected leadership.

Following the ouster of Morsi from power in 2013, the MB returned again to being a banned group. On 15 April 2014, an Egyptian court banned current and former members of the MB from running in the presidential and parliamentary elections. Many of the group's members were arrested, and their properties and assets confiscated by the government.

In 2015, a split took place inside the MB's ranks between the old guard, who were afraid that resorting to violence could mean the ultimate annihilation of the Brotherhood, on one hand, and a younger, new leadership, who believed in the importance of continuing to fiercely fight the regime, on the other hand (Hashem 2016).

On 24 January 2015, Mohamed Montaser was appointed as the official MB spokesman, overseeing the following new websites:

1. http://www.ikhwanonline.net
2. http://www.alikhwanonline.com
3. http://ikhwanonline.info/

One hundred and fifty press releases issued by MB spokesman Mohamed Montaser (all came from the website http://ikhwanonline.info/). Fifty other press releases were included in the sample and were issued by Talat Fahmy, who was appointed as the MB spokesman on 5 July 2016 (all came from the website http://www.ikhwanonline.com).

Table 3.1 Content analysis sample: Size and distribution of the Muslim Brotherhood sample

	2009–11		2011–13		2013–16				
	N	%	N	%			N	%	N
Muslim Brotherhood Sample	50	14.2	50	14.2	Mohamed Montaser	150	42.8	350	100
					Talat Fahmy	50	14.2		

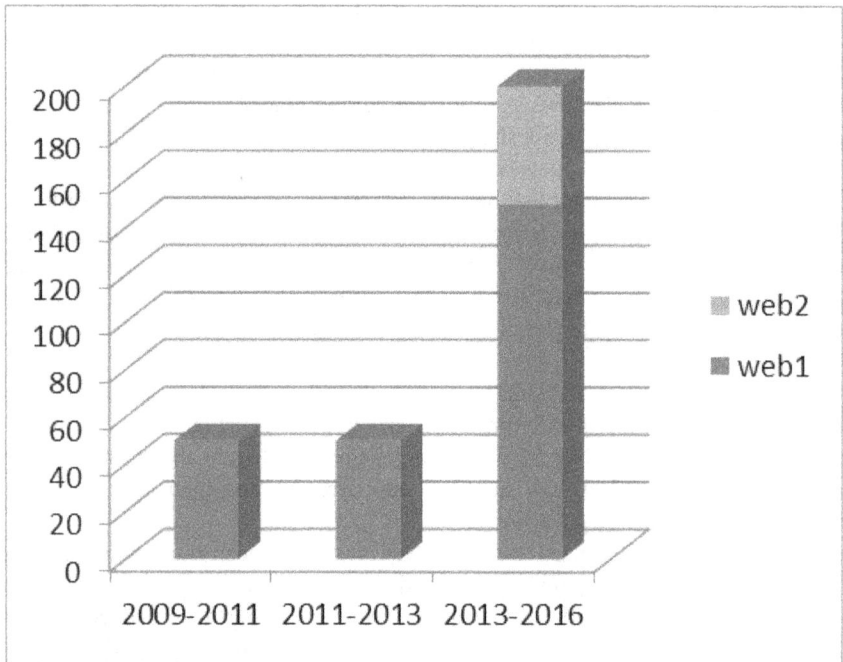

Figure 3.1 Muslim Brotherhood sample.

The activists and revolutionaries sample

The content analysis sample of the media content published by the young revolutionaries consisted of 350 blog posts and articles in the period between 2009 and 2016. This sample was divided among three key figures in the Egyptian political scene, who belong to this category of young revolutionaries, and who are all bloggers: Wael Abbas, Alaa Abdel-Fattah and Nawara Negm.

Although we cannot claim that these three activists are representative of the young Egyptian revolutionaries, we selected them based on their wide outreach and sweeping popularity, as well as their prominence and significance in the Egyptian political blogosphere (El-Nawawy and Khamis 2013), even though one of them is currently in jail: Alaa Abdel-Fattah. Also, even though the three of them eventually stopped blogging, they still express their views on ongoing political affairs, albeit through other platforms and with less frequency. We also included a female activist for the sake of gender diversity.

Wael Abbas was born in 1974 in Egypt, He is an internationally renowned Egyptian journalist, blogger and human rights activist, who blogs at 'Misr Digital'. Some of his posts include reporting on an incident of mob harassment of women in Cairo, and uploading several videos exposing police brutality. He was actively involved in the 25 January 2011 revolution, and then he became an opponent of the MB, during Morsi's rule in 2012, He was also against the government's violent crackdown on protesters at the sit-ins in 2013. Later on, he also voiced some criticisms of President Al-Sisi's rule (Brassinga 2013). Ultimately, Wael's political views resulted in his arrest on 23 May 2018, and he was released from jail on 11 December 2018 (Front Line Defenders 2018).

Alaa Abdel-Fattah was born in 1981. He is an Egyptian blogger, a software developer and a political activist. He has been active in developing Arabic-language versions of important software programs and platforms. He was also involved in the 25 January 2011 revolution, and then he was against the MB during Morsi's brief term as president in 2012. He has also criticized Al-Sisi, Egypt's current president. Alaa paid a high price for his activism. He was imprisoned in Egypt for organizing a political protest without official authorization, though he was released on bail on 23 March 2014. He was arrested again and also released on bail on 15 September 2014. He was subsequently sentenced to a month in jail in absentia. Later on, he received a five-year jail sentence in February 2015 (BBC Arabic 2015). After he was released from jail on probation for only six months in 2019, he was arrested again, and is currently behind bars (BBC 2019).

Nawara Negm was born in Cairo in 1973. She is an Egyptian journalist, blogger and human rights activist. She is the daughter of the late famous leftist poet, Ahmed Fouad Negm, and the Islamist thinker and journalist Safinaz Kazem. She obtained her BA in English Language from the Faculty of Arts at Ain Shams University (Cairo) and worked for the Egyptian Nile Television Network (NTN) as a translator and news editor (El-Nawawy and Khamis 2013).

Negm contributed a weekly Sunday column to the *Al Wafd* newspaper, and later on joined the *Al-Dustour* daily newspaper, contributing to its electronic version.

In 2006, Negm inaugurated her predominantly political blog, called *Gabhet El Tahyees El Shaabeya*, which could be imperfectly translated as 'The Popular Front of Sarcasm'. Among her most well-known contributions to the electronic edition of *Al-Dustour* newspaper is an Arabic translation in December 2010 of selected Wikileaks documents concerning Egypt and some other Arab countries. During the 25 January 2011 revolution, Negm was actively present in Tahrir Square in Cairo, and volunteered as a spokesperson for the revolution, reporting her observations and comments to the media, mainly Al Jazeera TV (El-Nawawy and Khamis 2013).

Alaa Abdel-Fattah's blog, Manal & Alaa, stopped in October 2013; Nawara Negm stopped blogging in July 2014 and stopped tweeting in December 2015; and Wael Abbas temporarily stopped blogging in March 2015.

Therefore, we collected the sample for the period from 2009 to 2013 from their personal blogs:

Wael Abbas	http://misrdigital.blogspirit.com
Alaa Abdel-Fattah	http://manalaa.net/
Nawara Negm	http://tahyyes.blogspot.com/

However, for the period from 2013 to 2016, the sample was selected from other online portals:

1. Wael Abbas has been writing opinion articles in *Huna Sotak*, which could be translated as 'Your Voice Is Here'. It is an online Arabic portal for RNW Netherlands Media, an organization for social change, which works with young people aged 15–30 years old, and has three core themes: democracy and good governance, sexual health, and human rights and international justice. https://hunasotak.com/user/16501
2. Alaa Abdel-Fattah used to write for *Mada Masr*, which can be roughly translated in English as 'Egypt's Scope'. It is an Egypt-based media organization focused on producing intelligent and engaging journalism and, more generally, re-examining the role of the media in informing the public and reconstructing the scope of journalism. https://www.madamasr.com/
3. Nawara Negm has been writing very few articles, compared to her previous contributions, occasionally posting to diverse portals like e3lam.org and *Al Tahrir* newspaper. http://almogaz.com/nawara-negm

The content analysis sample was divided amongst these three key figures in the Egyptian political scene as follows: 150 blog posts and opinion columns written by Wael Abbas, 50 blog posts and opinion columns written by Alaa Abdel-Fattah, and 150 blog posts and opinion columns written by Nawara Negm.

Pilot study

The researchers conducted a pilot study on 100 posts to make sure that all the coding categories were applicable to the sample and were also exhaustive and exclusive.

Table 3.2 Content analysis sample: Size and distribution of the young revolutionaries sample

		2009–11		2011–13		2013–16			
		N	%	N	%	N	%	N	%
Young Revolutionaries Sample	Nawara Negm	50	33.3	50	33.3	50	33.3	150	100
	Alaa Abdel-Fattah	7	14	30	60	13	26	50	100
	Wael Abbas	50	33.3	50	33.3	50	33.3	150	100
	Total	107	30	130	38	113	32	350	100

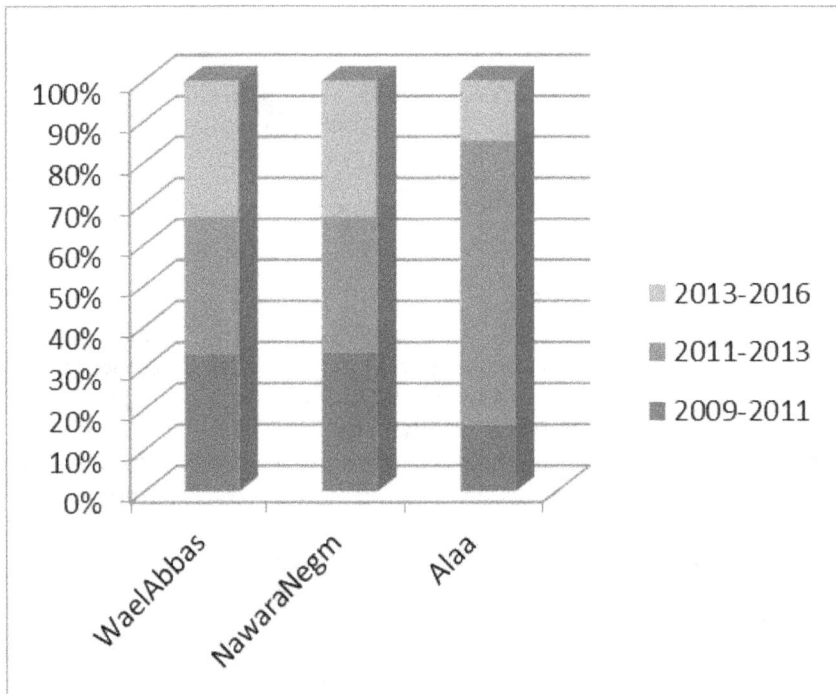

Figure 3.2 The activists and revolutionaries sample.

Unit of analysis

The unit of analysis in this study was the press release, the opinion column and the blog post.

Content analysis categories

1. Identity frames
2. Terms used to reflect these identity frames

Research findings

Q 1: What were the identity frames used by each group to define itself?

Table 3.3 Identity frames used by the activists sample

	2009–10			2011–13			2013–16		
	Activists	Blogger	Human Rights Advocate	Revolutionary	Political Activist	Change Agent	Writer	Social Justice Activist	Other
Nawara Negm	10	30	10	10	10	30	15	2	3
Alaa Abdel-Fattah	2	3	2	5	15	10	10	2	1
Wael Abbas	3	40	7	10	5	35	40	5	5
Total	15	73	19	25	30	75	65	9	9
		107			130			83	

The study's findings revealed that, between 2009 and 2010, the three activists mainly framed their identities as 'bloggers' first. In second place, they framed their identities as 'human rights activists' in 17 per cent of the posts. Finally, they framed their identities as 'activists' in only 15 per cent of the posts. However, the dominant identity frame in the period between 2011 and 2013 was 'change agents' (57 per cent), followed by the frame 'political activists' (23 per cent), then the

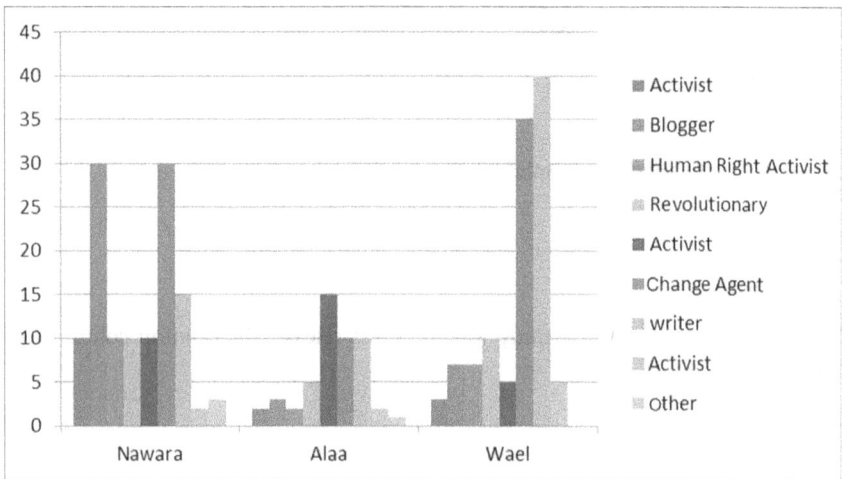

Figure 3.3 Identity frames shifts from 2009 to 2016: Activists sample.

Table 3.4 Identity frames used by the MB sample

	2009–10		2011–13		2013–16
	Advocates of Islam	Reformist	Revolutionaries	Advocates of Renaissance	Protectors of Legitimacy
MB Sample	60%	40%	30%	70%	100%

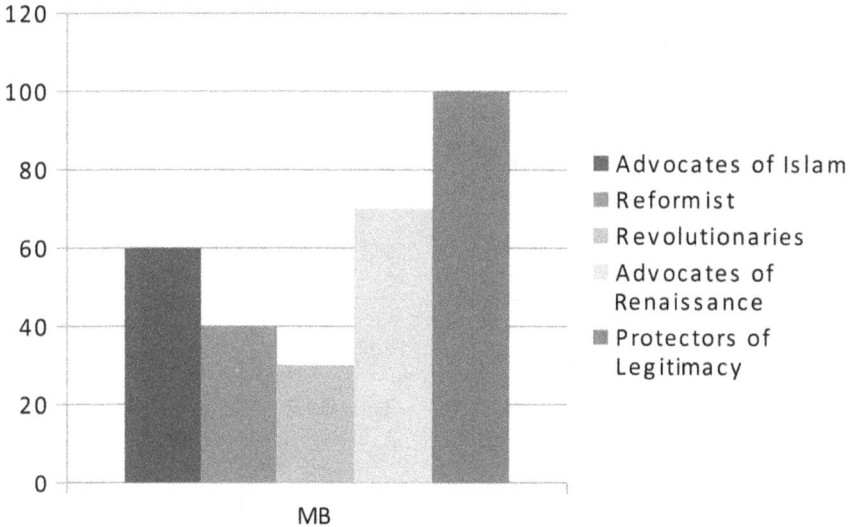

Figure 3.4 Identity frames used by the MB sample.

identity frame 'revolutionaries' (19 per cent). The dominant frame for the period between 2013 and 2016 was 'writers' (78 per cent of the sample posts during this period), followed by the identity frame 'social justice activists' (10.8 per cent).

The study showed that 60 per cent of the posts framed the MB identity as 'advocates of Islam' in the period between 2009 and 2011, followed by the identity frame of the 'reformists' (40 per cent). However, 70 per cent of the posts framed the MB identity as 'advocates of renaissance' in the period from 2011 to 2013, followed by the identity frame 'revolutionaries' (30 per cent). Finally, the dominant frame for the period between 2013 and 2016 was that of 'protectors of legitimacy' (100 per cent of the sampled posts during this period).

Q 2: Which terms were used to reflect their identity frames?
The study showed that 56 per cent of the posts in the activists' sample used the term 'the revolution' in the period between 2009 and 2011. It was the most commonly used term during that period, followed by the term 'freedom' (24 per cent), then 'social justice' (20 per cent). However, the dominant term used in the period between 2011 and 2013 was the 'continuity of the revolution' (60

Table 3.5 Terms used by the activists sample

		2009–10			2011–13			2013–16		
		Revolution	Social justice	Freedom	Hope	Continuity of Revolution	Defeat	Failure	Despair	Helplessness
Young Revolutionaries Sample	Nawara Negm	25	15	10	30	20	15	10	10	15
	Alaa Abdel-Fattah	5	1	1	10	15	7	1	1	4
	Wael Abbas	30	5	15	10	40	40	7	2	1
	Total	60	21	26	50	75	62	18	13	20
			107			125			113		

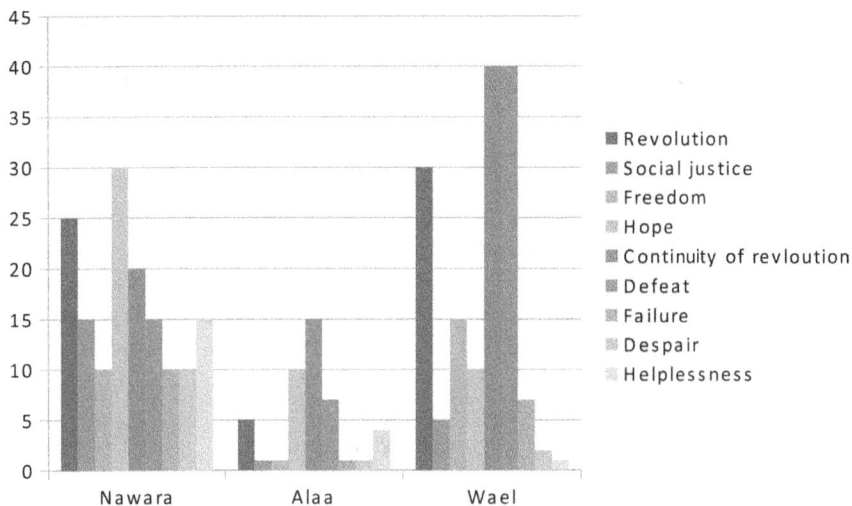

Figure 3.5 Terms used by the activists sample.

Table 3.6 Terms used by the MB sample.

| | 2009–11 | | 2011–13 | | | 2013–16 | |
	Religious Dawa	Reform	Revolution	Renaissance	Legitimacy	Rabaa Massacre	Others
MB Sample	55%	45%	35%	65%	50%	40%	10%

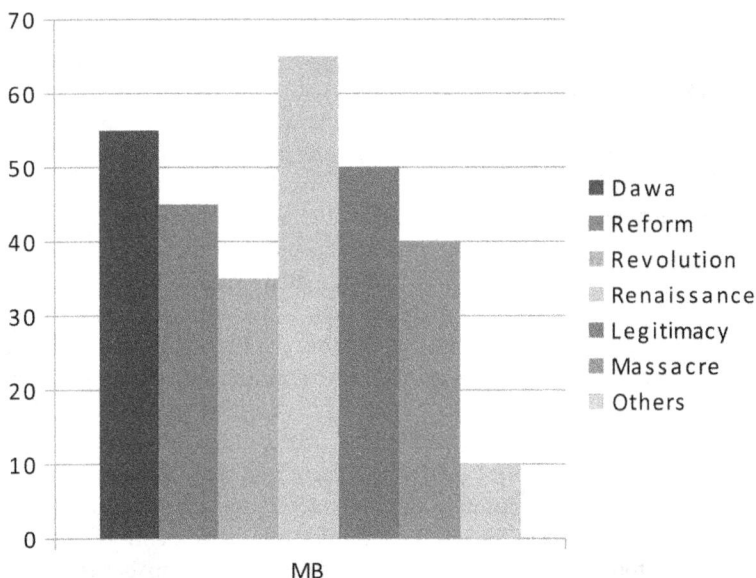

Figure 3.6 Terms used by the MB sample.

per cent), followed by the term 'hope' (40 per cent). The dominant term used during the period between 2013 and 2016 was 'defeat' (55 per cent), followed by 'helplessness' (18 per cent), then 'failure' (16 per cent) and, finally, the term 'despair' (11 per cent).

As for the MB sample, the study found that 55 per cent of the posts used the term 'religious *dawa*' (propagation of faith) in the period between 2009 and 2011, followed by the term 'reform' (45 per cent). However, 65 per cent of the posts used the term 'renaissance', followed by the term 'revolution' (35 per cent) in the period between 2011 and 2013. Finally, the dominant term used during the period between 2013 and 2016 was 'legitimacy' (50 per cent), followed by the term 'massacre' (40 per cent) and then other terms such as *Al Kasas* ('revenge' and 'punishment').

Discussion of research results

The Muslim Brotherhood

In order to better understand the identity frames highlighted by the MB over different phases, before, during and after the Egyptian revolution, we need to shed more light on some of their multiple, evolving roles during these phases. During Mubarak's era, the MB began fully participating in politics through elections, despite their banned status as a group. They usually got around this obstacle by running as independent candidates. Over the next three decades, the MB continued engaging in electoral politics and winning seats in syndicates and the People's Assembly. This gradual participation in elections helped shape the image of the MB as a viable opposition force to be reckoned with, rather than simply organizers of charity projects and providers of social services (El Nahass 2015). The first successful step that the MB took in this regard was taking over the unions and professional syndicates, which provide a wide range of useful services to their members, such as pensions, loans and subsidized health insurance.

By being very successful in this venture, they were eventually able to control many of the unions, such as the student unions in different universities, as well many of the syndicates, such as the doctors' syndicate. This proved to be very helpful to the evolution of the MB because it expanded their base of grassroots support and granted them access to considerable power. This, in turn, proved to be of double benefit. On the one hand, it furthered their image as an opposition force to the regime and, on the other, it solidified their image as a social force that could offer goods and services at subsidized prices that the Egyptian government could not offer, which is of special importance in an economically challenged country like Egypt.

This best explains the dominant identity frames put forward by the MB in the period between 2009 and 2011, and which were reflected in their publications, through articles, opinion columns and press releases, as 'advocates of Islam' and 'reformists' simultaneously. The connection between both identity frames could be best understood through the MB's constant slogan 'Islam is the Solution', which grounds all their activities, including their social welfare services, within an Islamist framework.

The MB tried during this period to convince Mubarak's regime that they were *not* the enemy, and that they did not pose a threat to authority; rather they were simply 'reformists'. That was very clear when the late Mahdi Akef, the *Murshed* ('counselor') of the MB, declared that the MB was not against a new presidency term for Mubarak. He was even more clear in an interview with the Middle East *AlSharq Al Awsat* newspaper on 12 May 2005, in which he said: 'We are not revolutionary people. We have no interest in the fall of the Mubarak regime. The MB have never been revolutionaries and the term "revolution" is not in our literature' (*AlSharq Al Awsat* 2005).

The Mubarak regime, just like Sadat's, tolerated the charitable activities carried out by the MB. This was made possible because the MB framed their activities as being part of religious *dawa* ('propagation of faith'), which was one of the dominant terms used by them, as revealed in this study, and they managed to keep working for years, within this framework, without crossing the regime's 'red lines'.

The MB kept using terms like 'reform' to assure the regime that they did not have any political ambition, were not interested in taking over the government in Egypt, and did not cross the red lines set by the regime in their discourse. These red lines were considered anything that threatened the authority of the regime. But what the regime did not anticipate was the strength of the charitable activities carried out by the MB, and the strong impact they would have in solidifying the MB's position, increasing its popularity and widening its outreach, by gaining more supporters. This also highlights the growing gap which was developing between the regime and the people, which the MB took full advantage of.

When Egypt's historic revolution erupted in 2011, they were the ones who started using the term 'revolution', and, for the very first time in their history, the MB framed its identity as 'revolutionaries' who protected the revolution in Tahrir square. They emphasized that without their large numbers and sacrifices, their organizational efforts and their wide outreach, which succeeded to mobilize at least a million people and bring them to Tahrir Square, Mubarak's National Democratic Party members and their thugs would have been able to easily crush the revolution. Interestingly enough, although they had never framed themselves as 'revolutionaries' before, and certainly were not the driving force behind igniting the flames of the 2011 revolution, the MB was, nevertheless, quick to jump on the revolutionary bandwagon and to take credit for its success.

Starting in 2012, while running for elections in the parliament and for the presidency, the MB used the term 'renaissance' more than any other word, to highlight the significance of their role in development and nation-building, in the post-revolutionary era. This could be best contextualized within their short-lived golden moment when they were not only freed from the burden of being treated as a banned group, which they suffered from for many decades, but were also successful in getting someone from their own ranks elected to the highest office in Egypt. A very significant achievement, despite its short duration of only one year.

Morsi's ouster from office, terminating his presidency in 2013, was vehemently opposed by members of the MB and their supporters, leading to the birth of new identity frames. This act, which some Egyptians described as a 'popular uprising' or even 'Egypt's second revolution', was described by the MB as *Inkilab* ('a military coup') against Egypt's first democratically elected president ever, a position which was shared not only by the group's supporters but also by some independent thinkers, writers, artists and human rights advocates.

This explains why the dominant terms used during the period between 2013 and 2016 by the MB centred around 'legitimacy', which could be best understood in light of President Morsi's decision to defend the legitimacy of his elected office, as he vowed not to resign. 'Legitimacy' was used heavily in the MB discourse, usually accompanied by the term 'coup', to describe what had happened in Egypt in 2013. This, in turn, explains the dominant identity frame used by the MB to describe themselves during this period, which was 'protectors of legitimacy'.

Also, notably, when the Egyptian security forces forcibly dispersed pro-Morsi sit-ins at the Rabaa Al-Adawiya and Nahda Squares in Cairo and Giza, resulting in many causalities, the death of hundreds of people and the injury of several thousands, another important term emerged in the MB's discourse, namely 'massacre', which was often accompanied by other terms such as 'punishment' and *Al Kasas* ('revenge'), especially among the younger generations within the MB.

The Activists and Young Revolutionaries

The Egyptian revolution of 2011 has often been described as a 'leaderless revolution' (Khamis and Vaughn 2011a, para. 65). This term, however, obscures the leadership, activism and heroism of many young people who played pivotal roles to aid the success of this revolution, albeit through diffused, bottom-up grassroots mobilization, rather than through top-down, centralized authority.

These activists were mostly young, upper-middle class, highly educated, urban elite and technologically savvy. They mostly employed new communication tools, such as social media, to rally support for the mass protests leading up to the 25 January 2011 revolution (Khamis and Vaughn 2011a). One good example was the Google executive, Wael Ghoniem, who encouraged people to assemble at Tahrir Square. He was the creator of the iconic Facebook page 'We are all Khaled Said', named after a young activist who paid for his online activism with his life, a result of police brutality, and who became a key, driving force behind igniting the 2011 revolution (Khamis and Vaughn 2011b).

Beside actively using social networking sites such as Twitter and Facebook to mobilize the masses, to galvanize support from those who share their views and to raise awareness about corruption and repression in their own countries to a national and an international audience, a number of these young activists, like the ones covered in this study, also discovered the power of blogging (Drezner and Farrell 2008).

By creating their own blogs, many of these young people were able to make their voices heard both inside and outside their home country, expose the wrongdoings and malpractices of the government, open platforms for effective brainstorming around ongoing issues, and, by doing so, pave the way for revolutionary change and transformation (El-Nawawy and Khamis 2013). This explains why the activists covered in this study framed their identity as 'bloggers', above everything else, in the period between 2009 and 2011.

The dominant identity frame among the young activists studied here, however, shifted in the period following the revolution of 2011 and before Morsi's removal in 2013 to reflect their new, evolving roles as 'change agents' and 'revolutionaries'. Acknowledging, and maybe even celebrating, their new roles as not just 'bloggers' but also 'activists' and 'agents of change', they started to heavily use new terms such as 'freedom', 'social justice' and 'hope', reflecting a general atmosphere of optimism, which was shared by many Egyptians during this period. Activist and blogger Alaa Abdel-Fattah explained in an interview with *AlMasry Al Youm* on 24 January 2016, 'Before the January 25 revolution, I never tackled the theme of hope' (*AlMasry Al Youm* 2016).

After the initial success of the 2011 revolution, which resulted in removing President Mubarak from office, and during the transitional period under the Supreme Council of the Armed Forces (SCAF), as well as during Mohamed Morsi's one year in office, these young activists emphasized the importance of the continuity of the revolution, as a main theme. Thus, reminding everyone of the need to keep pressure on whoever was in power, be it SCAF or Morsi, since removing a dictator from office is easy, but figuring out what to do next is not. A lesson which was learned the hard way in Egypt's case.

Following Morsi's departure and the violent dispersing of the pro-Morsi sit-ins in Rabaa Al-Adawiya and Nahda Squares in Cairo and Giza, a whole new discourse started to emerge among the young activists under consideration here, reflecting the serious challenges posed in this new phase. These challenges included deep division, fragmentation and polarization among the Egyptian people; a worsening economic crisis; the reinstating of emergency rule; the loss of trust in the effectiveness of the democratic process; and the loss of many hard-earned freedoms, such as freedom of expression and media freedom. This led many of the young revolutionary activists, including the ones covered in this study, to conclude that the 2011 revolution had failed to achieve its goals.

Therefore, some of the dominant terms which they frequently used in the period between 2013 and 2016 were 'defeat', 'helplessness' and 'despair', which reflected a general atmosphere of pessimism, frustration and disappointment, which is very different from the positive atmosphere which had prevailed after Mubarak was forced to step down in 2011.

This was reflected in some of these activists' writings, comments and interviews. For example, Nawara Negm wrote a post in January 2014 clearly stating that she simply could not lie to the Egyptian people, and that she must admit that the 2011 revolution had failed, and she did not see any hope (Negm 2014). Similarly, Wael Abbas in a post on the website *Huna Sotak* in 2016 said: 'Overall, I'm sure that the whole planet is collapsing' (Abbas 2016).

The one who seemed most negatively affected by the new situation, and rightly so, was Alaa Abdel-Fattah, who has been arrested several times, and is currently in prison again. He lamented the loss of his freedom on several occasions, explaining how his imprisonment deprives him of his ability to participate and to contribute to public life. In his interview with *AlMasry Al Youm* newspaper on 24 January 2016, on the fifth anniversary of the 25 January 2011 revolution, he said: 'I lost hope … I regret staying in Egypt' (*AlMasry Al Youm* 2016). A sad sentiment, which, unfortunately, has been echoed by many other young activists.

Interpretation of key findings

The results of this study clearly reveal how the Egyptian political actors examined here – the MB and the selected young activists and revolutionaries – framed their identities across different phases and under changing political contexts and shifting conditions, which, in turn, resulted in the birth of new, shifting identity frames, in a cyclical, ongoing and interconnected phenomenon.

This is indicative of the fact that the ongoing power struggle between the different actors in the contemporary Egyptian political scene is both accompanied, and framed, by a parallel rhetorical tug of war. The push-and-pull mechanisms characterizing this tug of war were evident in every group's efforts to credit itself, while discrediting 'Others'. By doing so, they were crafting both narratives about the 'self' and counter-narratives about the 'Other', while equally crafting narratives and counter-narratives about the revolution at the same time.

Whether they framed their identities as reformists or revolutionaries, allies of the state or opponents of the state, protectors of the homeland or protectors of legitimacy, defenders of human rights or defenders of social order, agents of change or advocates of stability – their aim, in every case, was to create a distinctive identity position that emphasized their uniqueness and set them apart from 'Others'.

These identity frames were reflective of a number of complex factors, including (but not limited to) the following. First, the individuals' understanding of their own core beliefs and values, such as freedom and equality, and their own sense of self, accordingly, as Gardner (2003) points out. Since most people often see themselves as advocates of a set of values and interests, they usually frame their position towards conflicts based on how they perceive the different alternatives, and whether they may advance one or more of their set of interests or not (Gardner 2003).

Second, beside the individuals' self-conception, there is also group loyalty and group affiliation. The more central the challenge is to one's sense of self, the more oppositional one is likely to act, and the more likely to cling to their group or cohort as well. Typical responses to threats to identity include ignoring information and perspectives that threaten the core identity, reinforcing affiliations with like-minded individuals and groups and negatively characterizing outsiders (Kaufman et al. 2003). We can argue that, in some cases, we can witness all of the above reactions simultaneously.

Third, there has been an amalgamation of underlying social, political, economic and cultural factors impacting how these acts of identity framing, and reframing, were taking place. These include the underlying modes of communication through which mediated messages are being framed and exchanged, in addition to demographic variables, such as age, gender and generation, which also affect the identity framing process and its articulation and expression. We can argue that all of these factors both mirror and mould, or reflect and shape, the ongoing, dynamic process of identity formation and identity framing, as witnessed in this study.

By engaging in all of these complex, ongoing dynamics, it could be said that these Egyptian political actors went beyond simply 'framing' their identity positions, to a more advanced level, that is: 'reframing' their identities. According to Kaufman et al. (2003), this complex process of reframing involves a number of processes, including reconciliation, negotiation, or joint problem solving, and the explicit management of frames, which may lead to important shifts in both the frames themselves and their impact on different dynamics.

However, the two parallel and equally complex processes of identity framing and reframing, which have been witnessed here, did not culminate in conflict management or conflict resolution (Drake and Donohue 1996), as suggested by Kaufman et al. (2003) and others. Rather, it could be argued that they contributed to the escalation of ongoing conflicts, by highlighting the distinctions between the 'Self' and the 'Other' and, thus, widening the gaps, escalating the tensions and deepening the polarization which Egyptian society is currently suffering from, by producing irreconcilable narratives and counter-narratives and clashing identity positions.

Some of the chapters in this volume clearly tackle the ongoing shifts and transitions in the post-Arab Spring political and mediated landscapes in a number of interesting ways that are relevant to this chapter's findings. For example, Elnaili (2021) addresses how Islamists and Nationalists, two major political players in the Libyan political landscape, design, address and frame the concept of 'nationalism' on their Facebook pages, and how, in the process of doing so, the concept of Libyan nationalism is reconstructed, (re)envisioned and rearticulated through binary opposites, such as inclusion versus seclusion and treachery versus loyalty, to mention only a few examples.

In line with the findings of this study, Elnaili (2021) concludes that political ideologies and affiliations shape the utilization of social media content, and are simultaneously shaped by it, since 'most Facebook pages feed their followers with political ideologies to form nationalistic sentiments according to their own political views. Unfortunately, such political opinions are based on associating betrayal with the opposite side and loyalty with their own political party' (P. 153[Ch.7, ms pg 15]). In other words, the process of 'Othering' is reinforced through social media use, as the findings of this study clearly indicate.

Likewise, El Masri's (2021) examination of Raseef22, the Pan-Arab website launched in 2013 as a strong voice for the Arab Spring revolutions, reveals how the internet became an important space for deliberative democracy, and how it enabled the emergence of deliberative, digital public spheres, while acting as a vibrant platform for several counter-publics to emerge, representing different ideological orientations, emanating from, and contributing to, the Arab Spring uprisings. This cacophony of differing – and sometimes conflicting and clashing – voices, identities and subjectivities, exemplifying different political positionalities, and representing different narratives and counter-narratives, is also in line with the results of this study.

Finally, as Menshawy (2021) rightly states in his chapter in this volume, which analyses why and how former MB members disengaged from the group, there has been an increase in this phenomenon after the Arab Spring, as the post-2011 sociopolitical shifts, with all their entanglements, challenges and complexities, facilitated their disengagement and departure from the ranks of this group, for a variety of reasons. Interestingly, Menshawy (2021) sheds light on how the shifts in pronouns, juxtaposing the individual 'I' with the collective 'we', reflect parallel shifts in the power dynamics, resistance mechanisms and identity markers among members of the MB. These findings are consistent with this study's results, which point to an increasing disillusionment among the new generation of the MB, especially after the derailment of the Egyptian revolution of 2011, and its aftermath. This explains the emergence of identity frames and discourses, related to 'defeat', 'despair' and 'helplessness' among some of them during this period.

This is also consistent with Bayat's (2013) argument that Islamists, among others, were not suddenly changed by the revolution itself but rather, by the specific context of the transformations and transitions that accompanied and followed it, and their aftermath, which allowed them to expose and revisit the post-Islamist transformations they were experiencing, even before the eruption of the revolution.

Here again, these findings are perfectly in line with the results of this study, which clearly indicate a shift in the formation and articulation of the post-Arab Spring and post-Egyptian revolution 2011 identities of the members of this group, as well as why and how the processes of formulating and expressing these shifting identities have taken different forms, degrees and directions during the post-revolutionary phase, in particular, with all the obstacles, failures and reversals encountered in it.

Research limitations

Some of the obstacles confronted while conducting this research study were the shortage in archived information and documents pertaining to this important phase in Egypt's modern history, as well as the fact that the online versions of the newspapers being examined did not always mention their news editing policy on their websites.

The study did not yield widely generalizable results, due to its exploratory nature, limited sample size and limited scope. The purposive nature of the research sample also limited the applicability and generalizability of the research findings. Moreover, the study focused on print and digital media content, and did not include other forms of mediated communication such as televised content, which may have yielded different results.

Directions for future research

One area of research worthy of further investigation is how the dynamic and ongoing processes of framing and reframing (Kaufman et al. 2003) could contribute to conflict management and conflict resolution, in the long run, rather than to conflict escalation and proliferation, as the results of this study seem to suggest. This is especially important in the context of such a highly volatile and transitional part of the world as the Arab region, which has been witnessing tumultuous waves of political change, characterized by conflict, tension and even violence, in recent years.

Also, more in-depth discourse analysis research needs to be conducted, moving forward, to better analyse the content and tone of the mediated messages that are being exchanged by the various political actors, through different platforms and modes of communication. This could allow for a better and deeper understanding not only of the mediated messages but also of the underlying identity frames that are embedded and perpetuated through them, as well as the overall context through which these acts of communication are being grounded, exchanged and proliferated. This deeper investigation could, in turn, draw our attention to new cultural practices, modes of communication, political actors and identity frames, which are worthy of further exploration.

Concluding remarks

An important factor to reconsider, in light of the findings of this study, is the importance of revisiting the notion of 'techno-euphoria' (Khamis 2019), or the tendency to privilege the powers and potentials of social media, and the myriad roles they can play to aid the process of sociopolitical transformation. The complexity, hybridity and intersectionality of the set of factors that revealed themselves before, during and after the Arab Spring uprisings and their tumultuous waves (Mohamed and Douai 2021), compel us to question the notion of 'technological determinism', revisiting the capacities and potentials, as well as the limitations and shortcomings, of the phenomenon of cyberactivism, bearing in mind the constant interplay between online and offline activism(s), realities and discourses (Mohamed and Mohamed 2021; Zayani 2015). The findings of this study also compel us to question the limitations of the phenomenon of framing (Druchman 2001), including identity framing, and the many constraints impacting its effectiveness, outreach and outcome.

After all, we cannot begin to fully grasp the scope and magnitude of the unfolding transformations in this region and their myriad impacts on the formation and transformation of the identities of different political actors and players, without taking into account the ecologies of the anti-authoritarian uprisings (Rinke and Röder 2011), a term which compels us to consider how and why different forms of communication are deployed by different revolutionary actors during different phases and across varying spatial and temporal settings.

It is safe to conclude that the Arab Spring waves triggered a 'tumultuous period of cultural, political and social realignments in the region' (Mohamed and Douai 2021, p. 1), with long-term ripple effects and far-reaching implications, not just on the political and mediated landscapes in various Arab countries but also on the shifting discourses of resistance and opposition, which shape and are shaped by the complex identities of various political actors in this equally shifting region.

The fact that many of the conditions which initially gave birth to the eruption of the Arab Spring uprisings (Lynch 2011), in the first place, still exist until this moment politically, economically and socially, and the fact that a second wave of Arab Spring uprisings, or 'Arab Spring 2.0', as Momani (2019) refers to them, erupted in countries such as Algeria and Sudan, are clear indications that these waves of public anger and popular revolt are most likely to continue well into the future, albeit with different paces, forms and outcomes. With the continuation of these waves, new political players and actors will also continue to emerge, assuming new roles of leadership, expressing new discourses and formulating new identities.

It is wise to predict that these contestations in the Arab public sphere will continue to take place both offline and online, utilizing social media as vital tools for resistance, opposition, mobilization or even manipulation, with varying degrees of effectiveness – or lack thereof – since, as Mohamed and Douai (2021) rightly put it, 'The Arab uprisings have captured a unique moment in history where media and culture are shaping Arab publics' defiance of autocratic regimes and the quest for inclusive and democratic forms of governance' (Mohamed and Douai 2021, p. 8).

These ongoing, complex phenomena compel scholars of Arab politics and Arab media to take a closer and deeper look at the forces behind the formulation and expression of these oftentimes ambivalent, paradoxical, obscure or conflicting identities, and why and how they are (re)inventing and (re)framing themselves, through myriad discourses, messages and platforms.

References

Abbas, W. (2016). ['Camp 30 Sonia wins Great Britain']. Available at: https://hunasotak.com/article/23011 [accessed 16 June 2017].

Abdalla, N. (2013). 'Egypt's revolutionary youth: From street politics to party politics', *SWP [Stiftung Wissenschaft und Politik / German Institute for International and Security Affairs]*, 11, pp. 1–8. Available at: https://www.swp-berlin.org/fileadmin/contents/products/comments/2013C11_abn.pdf [accessed 11 April 2017].

Akhavan-Majid, R. and Ramaprasad, J. (2000). 'Framing Beijing: Dominant ideological influences on the American press coverage of the Fourth UN Conference on Women and NGO Forum', *International Communication Gazette*, 62, pp. 45–59.

Al-Anani, K. (2016). *Inside the Muslim Brotherhood: Religion, identity, and politics*. Oxford: Oxford University Press.

Al-Awadi, H. (2013). 'Islamists in power: The case of the Muslim Brotherhood in Egypt', *Contemporary Arab Affairs*, 6(4), pp. 539–51.

AlMasry Al Youm. (2016). ['Alaa Abdel El-Fattah from inside his prison: "I lost hope. I regret staying in Egypt"'], 24 January. Available at: http://www.almasryalyoum.com/news/details/880193 [accessed 7 August 2017].

AlSharq Al Awsat. (2005). ['Mahdi Akef: "We are not revolutionary people… and we have no interest in the fall of the regime"'], 12 May. Available at: http://archive.aawsat.com/details.asp?article=298875&issueno=9662#.WCXdJy0rLIU [accessed 30 July 2017].

Bayat, A. (2013). 'The Arab Spring and its surprises', *Development and Change*, 44(3), pp. 587–601.

BBC Arabic. (2015). ['Egyptian activist Alaa Abdel-Fattah sentenced to five years in prison'], 23 February. Available at: http://www.bbc.com/arabic/middleeast/2015/02/150223_egypt_court_alaa_abdelfattah_verdict [accessed 5 April 2017].

BBC. (2019). 'Egypt protests: Activist Alaa Abdel-Fattah arrested amid rare unrest', 29 September. Available at: https://www.bbc.com/news/world-middle-east-49873463 [accessed 19 April 2021].

Bostick, J.N. (2005). *Second-level agenda-setting and political advertising: A content analysis of the framing dimensions used by the 2004 presidential candidates.* M.A. Thesis. Texas Tech University. Available at: http://dspace.lib.ttu.edu/bitstream/2346/1104/1/thesis_merged.pdf [accessed 30 December 2017].

Brassinga, I. (2013). 'Meet Wael', *The Activist Hive*, 7 July. Available at: https://www.activisthive.org/tag/wael-abbas/ [accessed 30 June 2017].

Busher, A. (2006). *Framing Hillary Clinton: A content analysis of the New York Times news coverage of the 2000 New York senate election.* M.A. Thesis. Georgia State University. Available at: http://etd.gsu.edu/theses/available/etd-04282006-110950/unrestricted/busher_amy_200606_mast.pdf [accessed 3 June 2017].

De Vreese, C.H. (2005). 'News framing: Theory and typology', *Information Design Journal*, 13(1), pp. 51–62.

Drake, L.E. and Donohue, W.A. (1996). 'Communicative framing theory in conflict resolution', *Journal of Communication Research*, 23, pp. 297–322.

Drezner, D.W. and Farrell, H. (2008). 'The language of blogging', *Hand Book for Bloggers and Cyber-Dissidents*. Reporters without Borders. Available at: https://ifap.ru/library/book414.pdf [accessed 30 May 2021].

Druchman, J.N. (2001). 'On the limits of framing effects: Who can frame?', *The Journal of Politics*, 63(4), pp. 1041–66.

Dulcan, E. (2006). *A content analysis of news frames in English and Spanish language newspapers.* M.A. Thesis. University of Missouri-Columbia. Available at: http://edt.missouri.edu/Summer2006/Thesis/DulcanE-090106-T5666/short.pdf [accessed 20 December 2018].

Duncan, J.F. (2007). *Framing African genocide: Location, time and gender in the coverage of genocide in Rwanda and Sudan.* M.A. Thesis. University of Missouri-Columbia. Available at: http://edt.missouri.edu/Winter2007/Thesis/DuncanF-050407-T6891/research.pdf [accessed 30 August 2017].

Dunne, M. and Hamzawy, A. (2017). 'Egypt's secular political parties: A struggle for identity and independence', Carnegie Endowment for International Peace, 31 March. Available at: http://carnegieendowment.org/2017/03/31/egypt-s-secular-political-parties-struggle-for-identity-and-independence-pub-68482 [accessed 12 August 2018].

El Masri, A. (2021). 'Hybridity and online public spheres after the Arab Spring: The case of Raseef22', in A. Douai and E. Mohamed (eds.) *New media discourses in Egypt and the Middle East: Culture and politics after the Arab Spring uprisings*, pp. 129–146. London: I.B. Tauris.

El Nahass, N. (2015). *Framing of political forces in liberal, Islamist and government newspapers in Egypt: A content analysis*. M.A. Thesis. The American University in Cairo. Available at: http://dar.aucegypt.edu/handle/10526/4801 [accessed 10 April 2017].

Elnaili, S. (2021). 'Promoting Libyan nationalism concepts via Facebook: A critical discourse analysis', in A. Douai and E. Mohamed (eds.) *New media discourses in Egypt and the Middle East: Culture and politics after the Arab Spring uprisings*, pp. 147–158. London: I.B. Tauris.

El-Nawawy, M. and Elmasry, M.H. (2018). *Revolutionary Egypt in the eyes of the Muslim Brotherhood: A framing analysis of Ikhwanweb*. Lanham, MD: Rowman & Littlefield.

El-Nawawy, M. and Khamis, S. (2013). *Egyptian Revolution 2.0: Political blogging, civic engagement, and citizen journalism*. New York: Palgrave Macmillan.

Entman, R.M. (1993). 'Framing: Toward clarification of a fractured paradigm', *Journal of Communication*, 43(4), pp. 51–8.

France 24 Arabic. (2011). ['The Muslim Brotherhood announces the establishment of the Freedom and Justice Party to participate in the elections'], 30 April. Available at: http://www.france24.com/ar/20110430-egypt-after-mubarak-era-muslims-brotherhood-to-create-political-parti [accessed 7 May 2017].

Front Line Defenders. (2018). 'Detention of Wael Abbas', 24 May. Available at: https://www.frontlinedefenders.org/en/case/detention-wael-abbass [accessed 19 April 2021].

Gamson, W.A., Croteau, D., Hoynes, W. and Sasson, T. (1992). 'Media images and the social construction of reality', *Annual Review of Sociology*, 18(1), pp. 373–93.

Gardner, R. (2003). 'Identity frames', in G. Burgess and H. Burgess (eds.) *Beyond intractability*. Conflict Information Consortium: University of Colorado, Boulder. Available at: https://www.beyondintractability.org/essay/identity-frames [June 2003 original publication; updated June 2017].

Gitlin, T. (1980). *The whole world is watching: Mass media in the making and unmaking of the new left*. Berkeley: University of California Press.

Goffman, E. (1974). *Frame analysis: An essay on the organization of experience*. Cambridge: Cambridge University Press.

Hallahan, K. (1999). 'Seven models of framing: Implications for public relations', *Journal of Public Relations Research*, 11(3), pp. 205–42.

Hallahan, K. and Baysha, O. (2003). 'Media framing of the Ukrainian political crisis, 2000–2001', *Journalism Studies*, 5(2), pp. 233–46.

Hashem, M. (2016). 'The great Brotherhood divide', Carnegie Endowment for International Peace, 2 March. Available at: http://carnegieendowment.org/sada/62942 [accessed 11 August 2017].

Howard, P.N. (2011). *The digital origins of dictatorship and democracy: Information technology and political Islam*. London: Oxford University Press.

Hunt, S.A., Benford, R.D. and Snow, D.A. (1994). 'Identity fields: Framing processes and the social construction of movement identities', in E. Laraña, J.R. Gusfield and H. Johnston (eds.) *New social movements: From ideology to identity*, pp.185–208. Philadelphia, PA: Temple University.

Iyengar, S. (1991). *Is anyone responsible? How television frames political issues*. Chicago, IL: University of Chicago Press.

Kandil, H. (2014). *Inside the Brotherhood*. Cambridge: Polity Press.

Kaufman, S., Elliott, M. and Shmueli, D. (2003). 'Frames, framing and reframing', in G. Burgess and H. Burgess (eds.) *Beyond intractability*. Conflict Information Consortium: University of Colorado, Boulder. Available at: https://www.beyondintractability.org/essay/framing [originally published September 2003; updated June 2013, June 2017].

Kerlinger, F. N. (2000). *Foundations of Behavioral Research*. San Diego, CA: Harcourt College Publishers.

Khamis, S. (2019). 'The online public sphere in the Gulf: Contestation, creativity, and change', *Review of Middle East Studies* (RoMES), 53(2),pp. 190–9. Available at: https://www.cambridge.org/core/journals/review-of-middle-east-studies/article/online-public-sphere-in-the-gulf-contestation-creativity-and-change/98494CA7E0AD7F0BE9EEBB8BEAB9512D [accessed 30 December 2020].

Khamis, S. (2020). 'Dueling discourses of power and resistance: The cultural contexts of the shifting revolutionary rhetoric of three Egyptian political actors', in K. Krippendorff and N. Halabi (eds.) *Discourses in action: What language enables us to do*, pp. 143–57. London: Routledge/Taylor & Francis.

Khamis, S. and Vaughn, K. (2011a). 'Cyberactivism in the Egyptian revolution: How civic engagement and citizen journalism tilted the balance', *Arab Media & Society*, 29 May. Available at: https://www.arabmediasociety.com/cyberactivism-in-the-egyptian-revolution-how-civic-engagement-and-citizen-journalism-tilted-the-balance/ [accessed 20 January 2021].

Khamis, S. and Vaughn, K. (2011b). '"We are all Khaled Said": The potentials and limitations of cyberactivism in triggering public mobilization and promoting political change', *Journal of Arab & Muslim Media Research*, 4(2&3), pp. 139–57.

Kingsley, P. (2013). 'Protesters across Egypt call for Mohamed Morsi to go', *The Guardian*, 30 June. Available at: https://www.theguardian.com/world/2013/jun/30/mohamed-morsi-egypt-protests [accessed 26 June 2017].

Lia, B. and Al Banna, J. (1998). *The Society of the Muslim Brothers in Egypt: The rise of an Islamic mass movement, 1928–1942*. Reading, UK: Ithaca Press.

Lynch, M. (2011). 'Media, old and new', in M. Lynch (ed.) *The Arab uprisings explained: New contentious politics in the Middle East*, pp. 93–110. New York: Columbia University Press.

Menshawy, M. (2020). *Leaving the Muslim Brotherhood: Self, society and the state*. Cham, Switzerland: Palgrave.

Menshawy, M. (2021). 'The revolution of "pronouns": Shifts of power and resistance in Egypt's Muslim Brotherhood', in A. Douai and E. Mohamed (eds.) *New media discourses in Egypt and the Middle East: Culture and politics after the Arab Spring uprisings*, pp. 103–128. London: I.B. Tauris.

Mitchell, R.P. (1969). *The Society of the Muslim Brothers*. London: Oxford University Press.

Mohamed, E and Douai, A. (2021). 'The "Arab Spring" waves: Media, culture and social protest', in A. Douai and E. Mohamed (eds.) *New media discourses in Egypt and the Middle East: Culture and politics after the Arab Spring uprisings*, pp. 1–18. London: I.B. Tauris.

Mohamed, E. and Mohamed, E. (2021). 'Do Egyptians still care about the Arab Spring?: Computational cultural assessment of online and offline activism', in A. Douai and E. Mohamed (eds.) *New media discourses in Egypt and the Middle East: Culture and politics after the Arab Spring uprisings*, pp. 37–54. London: I.B. Tauris.

Momani, B. (2019). 'Arab Spring 2.0: New protests, same failures that plague the Middle East', *The Globe and Mail*, 10 April [updated 11 April]. Available at: https://www.theglobeandmail.com/opinion/article-arab-spring-20-new-protests-same-failures-that-plague-the-middle [accessed 20 January 2021].

Negm, N. (2014). ['The sound of silence of half a bird bleeding'], *Tahyyes*, 15 January [Blog]. Available at: http://tahyyes.blogspot.com.eg/2014/01/blog-post.html [accessed 30 July 2017].

Page, B.I., Shapiro, R.Y. and Dempsey, G.R. (1987). 'What moves public opinion?', *The American Political Science Review*, 81(1), pp. 23–44.

Pan, Z. and Kosicki, G. (1993). 'Framing analysis: An approach to news discourse', *Political Communication*, 10(1), pp. 55–75.

Park, J. (2003). 'Contrasts in the coverage of Korea and Japan by US television networks: A frame analysis', *International Communication Gazette*, 56(2), pp. 145–64.

Rinke, E.M. and Röder, M. (2011). 'The Arab Spring media ecologies, communication culture, and temporal-spatial unfolding: Three components in a communication model of the Egyptian regime change', *International Journal of Communication*, 5, pp. 1273–85.

Saleem, N. (2007). 'U.S. media framing of foreign countries' image: An analytical perspective', *Canadian Journal of Media Studies*, 2(1), pp. 130–62.

Saleh, Y. and Kalin, S. (2014). 'Sisi won 96.91 percent in Egypt's presidential vote – Commission', *Reuters*, 3 June. Available at: http://www.reuters.com/article/us-egypt-election-results/sisi-won-96-91-percent-in-egypts-presidential-vote-commission-idUSKBN0EE1UO20140603 [accessed 30 July 2017].

Weaver, M., Owen, P. and McCarthy, T. (2013). 'Egypt protests: Army issues 48-hour ultimatum-as it happened', *The Guardian*, 1 July. Available at: https://www.theguardian.com/world/middle-east-live/2013/jul/01/egypt-stanoff-millions-protest [accessed 25 June 2017].

Williams, P.A. (2007). 'Framing the youth in Campaign 2004: Twenty million strong – or weak', *American Behavioral Scientist*, 50(9): 1273–9.

Wimmer, R.D. and Dominick, J.R. (2006). *Mass media research: An introduction* (8th ed.). Belmont, CA: Thomson Wadsworth.

Zayani, M. (2015). *Networked publics and digital contention: The politics of everyday life in Tunisia*. Oxford: Oxford University Press.

Chapter 5

E-SHEIKHS: HOW ONLINE ISLAMIC DISCOURSE CAN REPRODUCE AUTHORITARIAN POWER STRUCTURES

Dina Abdel-Mageed and Grant Bollmer

Introduction

The media landscape in the Arab world today has been largely shaped by the dynamics of the post-Arab Spring political struggle between Islamists and Arab regimes. Discourses on both sides seem equally manipulative of religion as both attempt to project the competition for power in Islamic terms, defending contradictory stances. The challenge Islamists posed in the wake of the Arab Spring made it necessary for the state to contain their influence by both cracking down on them and discrediting their discourse, which has largely been done through the media. The media war between the two sides is described by Anas (2016, p. 57) as a 'war of disinformation', where both sides have been attempting to use the influence of social media, among other media outlets, for their advantage. In this article, the role of social media as a platform for free, rational deliberation – as it has largely been framed throughout the Arab uprisings – will be revisited in favour of a more realistic understanding of its complex function invoked by the new political situation in the Arab world. By highlighting the political undertones of an influential type of online Islamic discourse, this chapter will demonstrate the negative influence of political polarization and hegemonic political and religious discourses on the potential role of the internet as an Islamic public sphere.

The context of the debate

Political failure, a fierce media war and an unrelenting government crackdown have all led to Islamism losing a big part of its appeal among large social segments in the Arab world (*The Economist* 2014) as well as a sense of apathy towards the Arab uprisings, as reflected in Eid Mohamed and Emad Mohamed's work (2021). This has by no means resulted in a less significant role for Islam in the political game. Religion has always been part of the political formula in the Arab world because it is 'too important as a source of political legitimacy to be ignored by autocrats' (Fattah 2013, p. 292). Rulers in Muslim-majority countries have tried over the centuries to use Islam as a source of legitimacy. Islam's role in politics came to the forefront during the Arab uprisings because of the rise of Islamists to power in a number of Arab countries.

Today, Islam still occupies an important place in political discussions in the Middle East (Fattah 2013, p. 287). This is particularly true if we keep in mind Foucault's broad definition of politics, which 'is not confined only to the realm of state and governance but has also to do with the creation of an organizing discourse: values, symbols and meanings undergoing within the social and cultural spheres' (cited in El-Sherif 2006, p. 8). Some scholars argued that political Islam had died. For example, Bayat (2007, p. 145) claimed that Islamism stopped being a mainly political project and had turned into merely an 'Islamic phenomenon': 'a struggle against secular values in order to elevate personal piety, morality, Islamic identity, and ethos … ' But according to other views, the Arab Spring has revitalized the role of political Islam. Fattah (2013, p. 287), for instance, argues that 'Islamists appear to be the main winners of the so-called Arab Spring'. Ten years on, Fattah's argument can easily be challenged. What was true before and during the Arab Spring is different from what has emerged since its retreat. The initial success of political Islam resulted in a strong backlash from Arab regimes, whose reaction to its perceived threat has been 'clumsy and horribly damaging' in Brown's (2016, para. 3) words. For most of their history, Arab regimes have been at war with Islamists – one of a few political alternatives capable of mobilizing the masses. And in the several years following the uprisings, the Arab world has witnessed a new phase of the struggle between what Wise (2003, p. 8) describes as 'the state's construction of "official" Islam versus "unofficial" Islamism'.

An Islamic public sphere online?

According to Habermas et al. (1974, p. 49), the public sphere is 'a realm of our social life in which something approaching public opinion can be formed'. In other words, the public sphere is a social space where individuals can assemble and express their opinions freely about 'matters of general interest' (ibid.), which should ideally lead to forming a unified opinion that serves the common good. The public sphere, according to this line of reasoning, acts as a mediator between society and state. Critiques of the theory revolve around its idealism, classism, sexism, narrowness and Eurocentricity (Anderson 2003, p. 892); however, the theory is still 'a compelling situational approach for the study of divergent views online' (El-Nawawy and Khamis 2009, p. 6).

A wide range of studies on the role of media technologies as a new Muslim public sphere point in different directions. Although some scholars, such as Castells (1996, p. 19), argue that the rise of Islamic fundamentalism is a reaction to globalization and modernization, others attribute the emergence of a new Muslim public sphere to the advances in digital communication (Mandaville 2001, p. 179). According to the latter view, the Arab state's monopoly over mediated religious discourse has been gradually broken by the advent of modern education and media technologies (Echchaibi 2014, p. 82). Proponents of this line of reasoning say that 'translocality' has enabled Muslims to challenge 'the dominant powers within Islam' by offering them a platform to come up with 'counter-hegemonic discourses' (Mandaville 2001, p. 179), and developments in information technology have resulted in a 'globalization from below' (Eickelman and Anderson 1999, p. 10).

This chapter adopts the view that the public sphere is not necessarily a secular space, and that the internet in general and social media in particular can play conflicting roles, depending on the larger context. Where religious discourse is concerned, social media does not seem in all cases to be a space for rational deliberation. Political polarization and post-Arab Spring power relations have undermined the potential role of social media as a public sphere for freely debating Islam in the Arab world.

Why critical discourse analysis?

This study applies critical discourse analysis (CDA) to the online discourse of a number of prominent Muslim preachers. Therefore, in this section, I will provide a brief background of the multidisciplinary approach to the study of texts. First developed by Fairclough, CDA merges Foucault's theories of discourse and power with what is known as functional linguistics (Hjelm 2014, p. 858). In this context, discourse is defined as 'language in use' and linguistic analysis is closely connected to social analysis (Richardson 2007, p. 26). Hjelm (2014, p. 857) argues that 'we live in an age of discourse', where a large number of the details of our lives depend on our ability 'to construct, control, and manipulate texts and symbols' (ibid.). Therefore, theoretical implications of CDA can enrich our understanding of discourse in multiple contexts, including online Islamic spaces.

It is important to note that CDA is the subject of much academic debate (Breeze 2011; Reed 1998; Stubbs 1997). Some scholars raise concerns about the representativeness of the text analysed, especially when qualitative discourse analysis is undertaken. However, other scholars argue that techniques of corpus linguistics give limited attention to context, which does not allow for careful reading and informs us only about the 'verbal domain' (Tenorio 2011, p. 198). This article adopts a qualitative approach to CDA, a choice made for a number of reasons.

First, such a qualitative approach allows for looking at the wider social, historical and political contexts at a critical moment in the history of the region. In line with CDA's 'holistic approach to text' (Hardt-Mautner 1995, p. 3), the discourse analysis in this research project is done from a Foucauldian perspective, which takes into consideration what is beyond the communicative act, such as history, power and authority structures (Wall 2015, p. 262). The choice by some preachers to post about certain historical events, for example, at specific points and its relevance to contemporary political developments cannot be captured by corpus-informed techniques. Also, visual language or what is left unsaid about certain major events in the discourse of preachers cannot be accounted for by narrow approaches that focus only on the verbal domain. Second, it enables a close reading of text that looks at a variety of textual features and linguistic structures. The range of discursive techniques explored in this study cannot be easily captured by quantification.

Because textual analysis is 'inevitably selective' (Fairclough 2003, p. 14), this research project does not attempt to present a detailed account of all Muslim preachers' religious discourse on Facebook. Rather, the focus of this study will be some representative posts from well-known preachers, which will allow readers to have an overview of an influential type of Islamic discourse on the social network and how it can reproduce political and religious dominance. In choosing texts, the search was confined to a period of three years, from 2013 to 2016. A wide range of posts commenting on the events of the Arab Spring and its aftermath were examined. A number of posts that demonstrate the discursive strategies which will receive special attention in this study – reference, sentence construction and presupposition – were chosen for analysis. I believe the limited size of the sample does not affect the representativeness of the posts because the ideological positions of the preachers covered in this study are publicly expressed, so the significance is in the interdiscursivity between religious and political discourses, the diversity of ways the language is used to express their biases and how the influence of social media comes into play. Thus, I am looking here at how certain Islamic discourses manifest themselves online.

As I will show in my analysis, preachers loyal to either their country's regimes or Islamic groups manipulate language in their Facebook posts to reproduce hegemonic religious and political narratives. I will draw on the three levels of analysis explained by Fairclough (1992, p. 73): (1) textual analysis, (2) analysis of discourse practice and (3) analysis of social practice. In my analysis, I will depend largely on the approach by Richardson (2007), whose work on the media coverage of Islam is quite relevant to this study. For Fairclough (2003), analysing texts involves looking at the processes of meaning-making – 'the production of the text, the text itself, and the reception of the text' (p. 10). One of the limitations of this study is that it focuses mostly on the first two elements, which has been imposed by constraints of time and space; therefore, my suggestion for further research is to study the readers' comments and the negotiation processes through which meanings are made.

Muslim preachers and social media

One factor that largely influences Islam's role as an ideological tool in the political game is the position of Muslim preachers. There is no lack of examples of sheikhs taking sides in political disputes and mobilizing their religious authority as so-called spokespersons for Islam to support one faction against another. The advent of Facebook has clearly encouraged the tendency among sheikhs for self-presentation and for participation in political debates by giving their opinions a wider outreach and allowing them to assume a greater role in the ongoing discussions. Since the onset of the Arab Spring in 2011, social media usage in the Arab world has been largely focused on politics. 'Facebook sheikhs' – as some people like to call them – have been an integral part of that phenomenon. Muslim preachers have become keen to engage in political discussions in cyberspace to express their views which, as we will see later in this study, are frequently positioned as religious injunctions. As a result, in many instances, online Islamic discourse performs ideological functions. This results in not only polarization across religious and political lines but also a greater tendency for manipulating religion by other players. As a result, those who criticize political Islam manipulate religious discourse too for their own advantage when necessary.

This study analyses some Facebook posts published by well-known Sunni Muslim preachers. The common characteristic among those posts is that despite, their religious phrasing, they have political undertones relevant to the political situation in the region. The main themes I came across while looking at the postings analysed below are (1) condemning political competition, (2) projecting religious/historical narratives on contemporary politics and (3) manipulating sectarian grievances.

Online vs offline preaching

One of the differences between online and offline preaching is manifested in what van Dijk (1988, p. 26) describes as the 'overall organizational pattern'. Religious sermons in real life are relatively long talks delivered in a mosque. Some of the elements of a traditional sermon are a standard introduction, where God and the prophets are praised, and a standard conclusion, which usually includes *du'aa* ('supplication'). Thanks to the influence of the social network, most of the posts on sheikhs' Facebook pages, including the ones discussed below, are rather brief, straightforward messages, with few rhetorical linguistic ornaments.

Nevertheless, the linguistic style of the social media preaching examined in this study seems to be similar to its offline counterpart. According to van Dijk (1988, p. 27), 'stylistic variation is not simply free or arbitrary'; rather 'style is a major indication of the role of the context. It may signal personal or social factors of the communicative context' (ibid.). Although Facebook discussions are largely characterized by informality, the stylistic choices in the posts discussed below reveal how authors assume more of a pedagogic role while addressing their audience, which has ideological importance. Also, despite the fact that social media is expected to bring about more intimacy and immediacy between users, the use of classical Arabic in most of the posts analysed below reflects a more formal style, which can imply authority and positions the speaker and the audience in a defined relationship. Facebook preaching conforms to the offline 'rules of the genre' (Fairclough 2003, p. 81) in some aspects. For instance, Islamic content on Facebook pages is more of a monologue. Sender–receiver interaction on sheikhs' pages, which are supposed to be spaces for dialogue, is considerably weak as sheikhs hardly respond to comments and interaction happens mainly between page visitors. Despite the assumed egalitarian nature of social media, we still can see on those pages what Fairclough (2003, p. 78) describes as 'inequalities … [that] can be attributed to social relations between participants'. The audience's comments and questions are ignored more often than not, topics are largely chosen by sheikhs and readers' 'right' to comment can be easily restricted using some of Facebook features. This can be seen as a reflection of a 'decline in substantive public debate', as perceived by Fairclough, which in turn affects the possibility of the existence of a real public sphere (2003, p. 79).

The CDA in the upcoming sections attempts to shed light on the characteristics of some Muslim preachers' discourse online, revealing how it reproduces authoritarian power structures. It highlights how the political stances of some Muslim preachers are presented in religious language in their Facebook posts, which allows religion to function ideologically. The preachers included in this study belong to different traditions and theological understandings. Some of them have classical/official religious training, which is either acquired through prestigious Islamic institutions or respected senior scholars. There might be different interpretations of their importance. While some of them appeal to certain social segments, others acquire their influence from their affiliation with powerful Islamic groups, such as the Muslim Brotherhood (MB). And there are also those sheikhs who have the power of official positions. Some cases and countries will receive more attention. Egypt, for example, will occupy an important part in the forthcoming analysis because of its central role as a cultural hub in the region.

Condemning political competition

The two posts discussed below were published by the Yemeni scholar Habib Ali Al-Jifri. The fifty-year-old sheikh, who gained most of his fame – along with the New Preachers[1] – in the early 2000s, has an online presence that ranges from his personal website to a verified Facebook page that is followed by more than six million people. Al-Jifri's case renders categorization difficult because, despite his traditional background and appearance, he first emerged as a part of the new religious discourse era. Like other fellow preachers, Al-Jifri's ability to approach new segments of society – both in real life and through media – brought him into direct confrontation with the state. In the mid-2000s, the Sufi scholar was declared persona non grata by the Egyptian government (*Al Arabiya* 2006). However, Al-Jifri's anti-Islamism stance has made him welcome again by the region's old guard in the post-Arab Spring era. As we will see again later in this chapter, the official stance towards certain preachers varies depending on how beneficial their discourse can be to the state at a specific point.

The first post was shared by Al-Jifri on 25 July 2013, (Figure 4.1) and it quotes Sheikh Mohamed Metwally el-Shaarawi. The quote goes:

الحبيب علي الجفري
July 25, 2013 · Cairo · ✎

"لا أحبُّ أن أحكمْ أنا بالإسلام ولكن أحب أن أحكم بالإسلام .. لأن طالب الولاية لا
يُولّى .. نقول له ابعد عنها "

"استنفقوا هذه الشمعة .. استنفقوها لتأخذوا منها النور للمحب والنار للمبغض"

"واعلموا أنا لا نستطيع أن نكون كلمتُنا من رأسنا إلا إذا كانت قوتُنا من فأسنا"

" يا قوم لا تستمعوا إلى أحد لأن ديكم واضح .. دينكم فطري .. واعلموا أن خصوم
الإسلام لم يقدروا على الإسلام من ذواتهم، فدخلوا عليه من أبنائه .. وجعلوا لكل
واحد أملا في أن يكون أميرا أو حاكما ..

ولذلك أعلنت دائماً: أنا لا أريد أن أحكم بالإسلام ولكني أريد أن أحكم بالإسلام "
نصيحة ونوجهه من شيخنا الإمام الشعراوي رحمه الله وكأنه يعيش اليوم بيننا!
ما أحوجنا إلى الاستماع إليها حيدا فقها ما يحتاج الناس إليه للتبصّر.
اللهم لطفك نطلب ورحمتك نرجو وعمووك وعافينك نسأل وعليك نتوكل ..
يا رؤوفا بالعباد

الحبيب علي الجفري Alhabib Ali Al Jifri

حقائق عن مصر لم يقتلها الزمن بصوت
الشيخ الشعراوي
حقائق عن مصر لم يقتلها الزمن بصوت الشيخ الشعراوي

YOUTUBE.COM

Like · Comment · Share · 👍 1,135 💬 54 ➦ 1,150

Figure 4.1 Al-Jifri quoting Shaarawi.

I do not want to *rule* by myself according to Islam, but I would like to *be ruled* according to Islam because those who seek political leadership should not be leaders; we tell them stay away from [leadership] … And be aware that the enemies of Islam could not defeat Islam, so they decided to focus on the children of Islam by making everyone want to become an emir or a ruler.

The quote is followed by an approving sentence and a supplication from Al-Jifri, who urges people to listen to Shaarawi's 'advice', which gives a feeling 'as if he is living with us today'.[2]

Both explicit and implicit intertextuality is manifested here. The first intertextual element is the quote from Shaarawi, which invites association. By creating an interrelationship between the two texts, the author uses the quote to support the argument behind the post. The second intertextual element is in the quote itself, where a reference is made to the prophetic tradition: 'We do not assign the authority of ruling to those who ask for it, nor to those who are keen to have it' (Bukhari, hadith 263, volume 9, book 89). Intertextuality here draws on readers' prior knowledge of religious texts, and again the antecedent source is used for persuasive goals. According to Hiramoto and Park (2010, p. 179), 'mediatization is inherently intertextual' because it restructures the speech behaviour of the speaker and introduces it in another 'stream of representation' (ibid.). In this case, a religious sermon essentially given in a mosque no less than a decade ago and probably recorded for television is reframed in a Facebook post to pass judgement on a current political situation. Interdiscursivity also comes into play here. Despite endeavouring to discredit political Islam, the post clearly intertwines Islamic and political discourses, backing political views with religious arguments.

Along similar lines, on 6 May 2014 (Figure 4.2), Al-Jifri published a quote superimposed on a picture of him preaching as a background, where he said: 'We need the type of religiosity that occupies us with perfecting building our countries, not the type of religiosity that occupies us with the struggle to rule our countries.'[3] In both posts ideographic puns are used, with the words '*ahkom* ('rule') and '*ohkam* ('be ruled') in the first post, and the words *nohkem* ('perfect') and *nahkem* ('rule') in the second post. Another interesting aspect about the pun in the first post here is that the change of the sound of one of the letters alters the sentence construction from active '*ahkom* to passive '*ohkam*. In this linguistic form, the actor is deleted, leaving the passivized verb without agent, which adds vagueness to the sentence. This kind of alteration removes 'a sense of specificity and precision from the clause' (Richardson 2007, p. 55). Such transformations affect agency and change the way we see the roles of the participants involved in the process (p. 13). So, although political Islam is criticized here, there is no emphasis on who should rule or what kind of political system should be adopted as long as people are 'ruled according to Islam', no matter how vague this might sound. Who, in this case, would rule, according to Islam? According to Richardson (p. 70), this kind of word play is considered by some as 'a merely entertaining aspect', but it often highlights a 'political agenda', which is arguably true in this case. A referential strategy is applied using the skilful manipulation of possessive pronouns, such as 'we' and 'our', which, according to van Dijk (1997, p. 34), 'has many implications for the political position, alliances, solidarity, and other socio-political position of the speaker'. The use of pronouns here also 'implies an authority to speak for others' (Pennycook 1994, p. 176). So, in these posts, an 'ingroup' (van Dijk 1997, p. 34) is being constructed, and the most important characteristic of its members is that they are religious people who are not occupied with the 'struggle' to rule their countries.

Figure 4.2 Al-Jifri criticizing political competition.

Turning to the contextual level, the two posts attempt to discredit Islamists by implying that seeking political leadership reflects greed and hunger for power. Rather than a normal dynamic of political life, competition for power is portrayed here negatively, and it is even associated with disunity and conspiracies against Islam. The two posts in their current construction play to the benefit of the post-Arab Spring political order because this type of discourse discourages political opposition, and implicitly supports what Bayat (2007, p. 173) describes as the 'secularreligious' autocrats of the region. Fattah (2013, p. 293) notes that the 'secularreligious agenda' of the ruling elites embraces 'positions, discourses, and laws with roots in both religious and secular values'. In this context, religious representations and pretexts are used to maintain political legitimacy. Therefore, despite their fierce war against Islamism, Arab states strive to portray themselves in public as the protectors of religion (pp. 292–3). Arguably, the legitimacy conferred by Muslim preachers plays a major role in giving power to the ruling elites against other political discourses rooted in Islam.

The timing of the two posts is significant because they were published after the military's ousting of the MB president in Egypt in 2013. Brookings researchers describe the event as one of the twin shocks (the other being the rise of ISIS) that have forced re-examining the main ideas about Islamism (Hamid and McCants 2016). Removal of the Islamist president Mohamed Morsi was followed by a security crackdown on Islamic groups and their supporters and orchestrated government efforts to demonize political Islam. On a regional level, the wealthy Gulf monarchies, with the exception of Qatar, moved against Islamists, particularly the MB, supporting the attempts to curb their influence using tools such as the media and their financial leverage (*The Economist* 2014). Such Facebook posts, especially by popular Muslim preachers, can help legitimize efforts to suppress political Islam. The focus of many sheikhs' social media posts on Egyptian current affairs, despite their different nationalities, reflects Egypt's status as a major player in the region. Brown (2014) makes a compelling argument when he says that what has happened in Egypt 'has already affected thinking throughout Islamist circles everywhere' (para. 17), encouraging governments across the region to crackdown on Islamists and urging Islamists to reassess their environments.

Historical narrative and contemporary politics

One of the themes that emerged during analysis is the use of historical narrative as a source of moral authority (Chilton 2004, pp. 189–93). Drawing on the Muslim tradition of revering Prophet Mohamed's family and his companions, preachers use the shared familiarity with certain historical events of religious significance to connect with their audience. By presenting references that they presume to be recognizable to the reader, they attempt to validate their current stances on religion and politics. Two examples of this are posts made by Al-Jifri and the popular Kuwaiti preacher Tariq Al-Swaidan. The latter is well known for his motivational talks and his approach, which connects Islam to self-development and material

Figure 4.3 Al-Swaidan supports his political stance using a historical narrative.

success. A MB enthusiast, Al-Swaidan expressed a clear-cut support for Islamists in the post-Arab Spring power struggle in the region, which cost him his job at Al-Risalah – one of the most prestigious Islamic satellite channels in the Arab world – as well as some of his popularity (*USA Today* 2013).

In his post (Figure 4.3), which he published on 7 November 2013, Al-Swaidan says:

> Those who fought the Commander of the Faithful Ali were sure that they were on the side of truth. But according to the scholars' consensus, our master Ali (may Allah be pleased with him) was on the right side. [This is a reminder] from me to the coup's supporters before [it is too late to] regret [their stance].[4]

Here Al-Swaidan is referring to the first Muslim civil war, where the fourth Muslim caliph, Ali Ibn Abi Talib, fought a number of Muslim factions to quell rebellion. The Kuwaiti preacher uses emotional, ambiguous terms such as 'truth' and 'consensus' to influence his audience. Who decides who was on 'the side of truth' in a civil war? What does he mean by 'consensus' – a slippery term that Muslims have struggled with over the centuries? The hidden association in the first part of the text between the historical event and contemporary politics is then revealed explicitly at the end of the text through Al-Swaidan's pedagogic reminder for the 'coup supporters'. In this context, the preacher draws on history to support a contemporary political stance. The use of the term 'coup supporters'[5] is significant from a CDA perspective because it marks his position and that of his opponents in the debate.

On the other hand, on 29 June 2013, Al-Jifri wrote:

> Our master al-Hassan bin Ali accepted the fall of the caliphate to prevent further bloodshed. So how can we accept bloodshed in order to restore the caliphate? And what is even more important than that is that the Prophet – peace be upon him – had [prospectively] supported the choice of his grandson al-Hassan more than thirty years before the occurrence when he had said: 'My son here is a master. May Allah make him reconcile between two big factions of Muslims'. Narrated by Bukhari.[6]

Al-Jifri uses emotionally charged words, such as 'bloodshed' (*safk al-dima*') and 'caliphate' (*al-khilafah*), as well as intertextuality by including a prophetic tradition

الحبيب علي الجفري
June 29, 2013

قيلَ سيدنا الحسن بن علي أن تُهدَم الخلافة في سبيل حقن الدماء .. فكيف نستبيح سفك الدماء في سبيل إستعادة الخلافة ؟

والأهم من ذلك أن النبي صلى الله عليه وآله وسلم قد أثنَ اختيار سبطه الحسن قبل الحادثه بما يريد على النلائس سنه فقال: (إن ابني هذا سيد، ولعل الله يصلح به بين فئتين من المسلمين عظيمتين) .
رواه البخاري

علي الجفري
Follow

قيل سيدنا الحسن بن علي أن تُهدم الخلافة في سبيل حقَن الدماء .. فكيف نستبيح سفك الدماء في سبيل إستعادة الخلافة ؟

Reply   Retweet   Favorite   More

Figure 4.4 Al-Jifri projects historical narratives on contemporary politics.

to solidify his argument. There is also presupposition that embodies the author's opinions. According to Richardson (2007, p. 63), a presupposition is 'a taken-for-granted, implicit claim embedded within the explicit meaning of a text or utterance'. The question in the quote presupposes not only that Islamists want to re-establish the caliphate but also presupposes that the only way to power is through violence. These presuppositions fit with the ideological stance of Al-Jifri, who condemned political competition in a previous post.

The posts discussed above reveal the complications involved in using political discourse on Islamic grounds. The two posts show the blatant contradictions in Islamic discourses that attempt to use narratives from Islamic history – products of human reasoning and their historical moments – as references upon which Muslims can base their views on contemporary politics. We have two sheikhs on two sides of the political division paradoxically calling up parallels in the first Muslim civil war to support two opposite stances. Since each side presents a one-sided account, ignoring other interpretations of reality, it can be argued that both discourses function ideologically by suppressing 'alternative constructions of the world' (Hjelm 2014, p. 860). This point connects with Ferjani's (2010, p. 93) argument about the contradiction between Islam and the concept of the public sphere. By making the argument that their opinions are based on prophetic traditions or actions of some of the Prophet's most revered companions, the two authors aim to 'disarm dissenters' (ibid.). And when political stances are derived from what Ferjani calls 'absolute knowledge' (ibid.), there is little space for rational arguments, a prerequisite for the existence of a functioning public sphere.

The discourse of Islamists, who adopt anti-regime political rhetoric on religious grounds, does not seem to be less hegemonic than that of regime supporters. Their religious justifications make it difficult for opponents to present counter-arguments, and when they do, they are obliged to frame it in religious terms too. This is reminiscent of Eickelman and Piscatori's (2004, p. 89) discussion of the role of Islamist discourses in drawing boundaries within their own societies and creating the 'internal Other'. But it can be argued that 'othering' opponents is a trait of both Islamist discourse and Arab regimes. Both discourses are equally hegemonic; they encourage conceiving politics in absolutist terms of good and evil, highlight a selective approach to Islam and attempt to construct discursive hegemony around how events of the Arab Spring are to be perceived. So, on the one hand, we see the representations of Islam as an 'official religion', which produce a religious discourse that manipulates the sacred to serve state interests. On the other hand, we have Islamism, which attempts to mobilize truth and raises vague slogans like 'Islam is *the* solution', ignoring the fact that different players offer different interpretation of Islam. And arguably in both cases Islam is used as an ideology. To explain what 'ideology' is, I borrow Soroush's definition, which – echoing the Marxist view – describes it as 'an exclusionary truth claim' (cited in Ghamari-Tabrizi 2013, p. 251). According to him, this 'not only distorts the reality of religion but also facilitates the establishment of totalitarianism' (ibid.). This definition is in harmony with CDA's critical perception of ideology, which describes it as 'meaning in the service of power' (Hjelm 2014, p. 860).

Sectarian grievances

Regional power relations play a major role in shaping preachers' media discourse. The war zones stretching from Libya to Syria to Iraq to Yemen are not the only battlefields. There are also wars of discourses, symbols and identities taking place via the media, especially social networking websites. Arab-Iranian and Sunni-Shiite relations are recurrent themes in many Facebook posts, which deal with issues ranging from regional wars to the volatile situation of Shiite minorities in the Arab world and the Sunni minority in Iran. As we will see in this section, sheikhs' discourses on such topics are heavily charged with religious terminology and sectarian references. Muslim preachers, particularly those from the Gulf countries, tend to portray the thorny situation as a Sunni-Shiite conflict rather than a geopolitical struggle for domination between regional and international powers.

I will discuss below two examples of posts published by the Saudi sheikhs Aaidh Al-Qarni and Saud Al-Shuraim. Al-Qarni, who has more than 16 million followers on Facebook and around 18 million followers on Twitter, is an independent Saudi traditional scholar, poet and published author. The sixty-two-year-old sheikh has been mediating his preaching through different modes of media, from cassette tapes to satellite TV and the internet. He was jailed, banned from travelling and his preaching activities were restricted for ten years by the Saudi authorities as a result of his opposition to the government and his objection to the Western military deployment in his country during the Second Gulf War (Lacroix 2011, pp. 203–4). The prominent Saudi scholar, who has been described recently by the Islamic State group (ISIS) as one of the imams of *kufr* ('apostasy'), was the target of an assassination attempt in the Philippines in March 2016 (*The Guardian* 2016). On the other hand, Al-Shuraim is an official Saudi religious figure, a former student of some of the most well-known Saudi orthodox scholars, such as Abdulaziz bin Baz and Abdullah bin Jibreen. Al-Shuraim's social media following is relatively modest compared to other sheikhs: 1.7 million Twitter followers.[7] But arguably his most important status marker is that he is one of the imams of the holy mosque in Mecca, which means that he leads some of the prayers in the most sacred mosque for Muslims. This gives the Saudi sheikh a special spiritual standing that goes beyond the borders of his country. Both scholars hold doctorate degrees in Islamic studies from Saudi universities.

In the tweet reposted on Facebook on 18 January 2016 (Figure 4.5), Al-Shuraim wrote: 'There is nothing strange about the coalition between the Safavids, Jews, and Christians against Muslims. History has been a witness to similar occurrences. However, what actually causes bewilderment is the minds of people who do not understand this fact until this moment.'[8] Van Dijk's (1988, p. 62) argument about actual discourses being 'much like the proverbial icebergs' is relevant here because the amount of information required to understand the short Facebook post is immense. What van Dijk calls 'the top of the information' is visible (ibid.). Yet, interpreting the text largely depends on information and beliefs shared by the audience. A referential strategy is applied here when Al-Shuraim uses the word *Safawiyyeen* ('Safavids' in English) to refer to Iranians, which has both historical and religious significance. By using the rhetorical device of allusion, Al-Shuraim reveals his bias against Shi'ism, expecting his audience to understand the derogatory intention behind using the name of a dynasty that ruled Persia in the sixteenth century to refer to Iranians today. The Safavid dynasty established a theocracy, where the official religion of the state was Shi'i Islam. According to historical accounts, Shi'ism, which was 'totally foreign to Iranian culture' at that time, was imposed on the then mostly Sunni population (BBC 2009). So, by using the word *Safawiyyeen* here, the Saudi scholars purposefully invokes sectarian grievances to comment on current events. From a CDA perspective, the referential strategies used here aim for the demonization of the 'Other'. In his post, Al-Shuraim refers to an alliance between 'the Safavids, Jews, and Christians against Muslims', assuming that to be the normal state of affairs but failing to specify what he means by the generalized terms of 'Jews' and 'Christians'. Reflecting on Fairclough's (2003, p. 88) discussion of the issue of 'equivalence and difference', it can be argued that there is a tendency here towards 'creating and proliferating differences' and that the process of categorization presents a world where Muslims are under attack from an ambiguous alliance that includes the Kingdom's geopolitical foe, Iran. Arguably, this again helps to solidify the authority of the state by using the technique of fear mongering that puts Muslims in a position of animosity with elusive, foreign enemies.

On the other hand, Aaidh al-Qarni's post (Figure 4.6), which was published on 5 January 2016, goes:

#Salman of the Haram
Oh, Son of Saud hit with your sword
The heads of the Zoroastrians and let us stamp on them[9]

Figure 4.5 Al-Shuraim capitalizes on sectarian grievances.

Figure 4.6 Al-Qarni describes Iranians as Zoroastrians.

The religious and sectarian references in the post are significant, from a CDA perspective. At the beginning of his post, Al-Qarni uses the hashtag 'Salman of the Haram' (the holy mosque in Mecca), referring to the Saudi king, who officially calls himself 'Custodian of the Two Holy Mosques'. The phrase has important implications, given the audience's shared belief in the holiness and importance of the mosque in Mecca. Thus, readers can suppose that the Saudi king is a significant figure in Islam, not just a political leader in his country. Al-Qarni also quotes a few lines from one of his colloquial poems, where he uses a referential strategy again when he calls Iranians *majoos* ('Zoroastrians' in English). Arguably, the referential strategy here suggests that Iranians are not Muslims, an opinion that is entertained by some conservative Muslims. Factually speaking, the reference is wrong. But it is important for establishing a coherence relation with the first part of the sentence, which urges the Saudi king to kill them. The use of force is normalized in both the brief quote and the video.

Using their rhetorical ability, the sheikhs here are manipulating religious language to construct consensus around political goals, empowering the ruling elite by giving religious legitimacy to political domination. The referential strategy of 'us versus them' and verbal derogation are manipulatively utilized here, turning politics into a battlefield for religious and sectarian identities. The 'Other' is demonized in both posts and derogatory terms are used to describe those portrayed as enemies in the official political discourse. 'Boundary maintenance', as described by Hjelm (2014, p. 861), is achieved here by 'reframing competing belief systems as evil'. This also connects to van Dijk's (1998, p. 42) concept of the ideological square: 'say a lot about Our good things and Their bad things, and say little about Our bad things and Their good things'. Such polar perceptions of political stances are also reflected in Elnaili's work (2021).

Such posts reflect the successful formula that Fattah (2013, p. 301) explains: 'Practically, if the 'umara (princes) and 'ulama agree, then there is little room for generalized dissent.' It can be argued that the Sunni-Shiite conflict in the region is a power struggle in disguise. The conflict in the region, which is characterized by thorny power relations between the Sunni kingdom of Saudi Arabia on one side and the Shiite theocracy of Iran on the other, is projected in sectarian terms that make mobilizing the masses easier. And the media plays a significant role in that struggle. The media discourse, particularly that propagated by prominent sheikhs, increases polarization by dividing the world into separate camps and renders dissent more difficult. Besides securing internal support for the Kingdom's foreign policy, this discourse also validates what Wehrey (2013, para. 8) describes as 'the entrenched sectarianism in Saudi society and government policy'. Discrimination against the country's Shiite minority – who continuously faces accusations of being loyal to Iran – and the resulting backlash has been a constant source of tension for the Kingdom. And framing the relationship with Iran and the wars in places like Syria and Yemen in sectarian terms has exacerbated suspicion between Saudi's two sects (ibid.). Also, such a discourse made it easier for other Gulf countries to intervene militarily in Bahrain to end a potential revolution in 2011 by the predominantly Shiite population against their Sunni rulers. The official discourse of the Gulf states at that time portrayed the uprising as a Shiite/Iranian conspiracy (Al-Rasheed 2011). On reading this, it can be argued that – as a part of the sectarian discourse in general – the posts analysed above can help in the furthering of sectarian inequality. By using stereotyping and generalization as central rhetorical tropes, such a discourse helps maintain power relations domestically between the ruling Sunni majority and the Shiite minority and regionally between the Sunni kingdom of Saudi Arabia and its Shiite rival, Iran.

Conclusion

In the above sections, this article has examined how online Islamic discourse can help reproduce the offline hegemonic power relations in the Arab world. Abdul-Latif (2011) looks at religious references in political speeches, and the interdiscursivity formula he describes is quite relevant to the subject of this article. By manipulating the elements of religious discourse to achieve political goals, he argues, speakers make use of not only 'the persuasive and emotional effects of religious discourse' (p. 51), but also they take advantage of 'the restrictions that govern how "believers" respond to "divine" discourse' (ibid.). So, by presenting political opinions in a religious context, such as the Facebook posts discussed above, some Muslim sheikhs reframe politics and allow it to take over some meanings and features associated with religion. And this is how political references achieve their function. A close look at those preachers' textual practices as they appear in their posts and their social practices represented in where they position themselves in the ongoing power struggle in the Arab world reveals how their media discourse helps consolidate the hegemonic narratives of both the state and its Islamist rivals. My main reference here is Fairclough's (2003, p. 8) argument about the social effects of texts. According to him, texts have both immediate and long-term causal effects, which range from 'changes in our knowledge ..., our beliefs, our attitudes, values and so forth' (p. 13) to shaping our identities, social relations, and the material world. Yet, those causal effects can be attributed to linguistic form 'only through a careful account of meaning and context' (ibid.), which I have been trying to do here.

It can be argued that 'power [is] ... increasingly exercised through the use of persuasive language instead of coercion' (Hjelm 2014, p. 860). This is particularly true in the case of online discourse of preachers. Although some Muslim preachers' social media discourse in the post-Arab Spring world is frequently couched in the language of truth, good, piety and public interest, it acts ideologically to legitimize power and domination. Using both syntactic and discursive elements, those sheikhs' discourse creates ambiguity, discredits political opponents on religious grounds, defines the world in dichotomous terms and manipulates sectarian tension for political reasons – all of which help preserve the existing power structure. By sociopolitically situating their discourse, it is possible to uncover power relations that are often concealed and demonstrate how they are exercised and negotiated through discourse, as explained by Fairclough and Wodak (1997). By using the German sociologist Habermas's theory of the public sphere as a theoretical framework to think through these issues (Habermas et al. 1974), this study has revealed how the wider sociopolitical context has put limitations on the role of new media as an Islamic public sphere, considerably reducing the space for critical-rational deliberation on religion in the post-Arab Spring Arab world.

Notes

1   A group of young lay preachers collectively known as *al-du'aah al-judud* ('The New Preachers'), who turned into satellite television celebrities in the late 1990s and early 2000s.
2   The Arabic text was translated by one of the authors (Dina Abdel-Mageed).
3   The Arabic text was translated by one of the authors (Dina Abdel-Mageed).
4   The Arabic text was translated by one of the authors (Dina Abdel-Mageed).
5   Labelling what happened in Egypt on 3 July 2013 has not been less controversial than describing the wave of protests that swept the country in January 2011. The military

intervention to oust Mohamed Morsi, the first democratically elected president after the 25 January 2011 revolution, has been described by its supporters as a 'revolution', given the alleged popular opposition to the rule of the Muslim Brotherhood president. However, many observers and mainstream media outlets describe the event as a 'coup'.

6   The Arabic text was translated by one of the authors (Dina Abdel-Mageed).
7   It seems that the Twitter account for Al-Shuraim has been deactivated since this article was written. But several media outlets, including Reuters, at that time reported on the controversial tweet.
8   The Arabic text was translated by one of the authors (Dina Abdel-Mageed).
9   The Arabic text was translated by one of the authors (Dina Abdel-Mageed). It would seem the Al-Qarni post has been deleted since this article was written.

References

Abdul-Latif, E. (2011). 'Interdiscursivity between political and religious discourses in a speech by Sadat', *Journal of Language and Politics*, 10(1), pp. 50–67.

Al Arabiya. (2006). 'Al-Jifri reveals the secrets behind his wealth, videos of the private sermons, and imprisonment' 19 October. Available at: http://www.alarabiya.net/articles/2006/10/19/28400.html[accessed 2 May 2015].

Al-Jifri, H.A. (2013a). 'no title', 27 June. Available at: https://www.facebook.com/permalink.php?story_fbid=588980661141918&id=196704400369548 [accessed 2 May 2015].

Al-Jifri, H.A. (2013b). 'no title', 25 July. Available at: https://www.facebook.com/permalink.php?story_fbid=602827183090599&id=196704400369548 [accessed 2 May 2015].

Al-Jifri, H.A. (2014). 'no title', 4 May. Available at: https://www.facebook.com/permalink.php?story_fbid=759049750801674&id=196704400369548 [accessed 20 June 2015].

Al-Rasheed, M. (2011). 'Sectarianism as counter-revolution: Saudi responses to the Arab Spring', *Studies in Ethnicities and Nationalism*, 11(3), pp. 513–26.

Al-Swaidan, T. (2013). 'no title', 7 November. Available at: https://www.facebook.com/Dr.TareqAlSuwaidan/posts/10152532305351677 [accessed 1 March 2015].

Anas, O. (2016). 'Arab social media: From revolutionary euphoria to cyber realism', in B. Gunter, M. Elareshi and K. Al-Jaber (eds.) *Social media in the Arab world: Communication and public opinion in the Gulf states*, pp. 45–67. London: I.B. Tauris.

Anderson, J.W. (2003). 'New media, new publics: Reconfiguring the public sphere of Islam', *Social Research*, 70(3), 887–906.

Bayat, A. (2007). *Making Islam democratic: Social movements and the post-Islamist turn*. Stanford: Stanford University Press.

BBC. (2009). 'Safavid Empire (1501–722)', *Religions*, 7 September. Available at: http://www.bbc.co.uk/religion/religions/islam/history/safavidempire_1.shtml [accessed 2 May 2015].

Breeze, R. (2011). 'Critical discourse analysis and its critics', *Pragmatics*, 214 (4), pp. 493–525. Available at: https://www.researchgate.net/publication/259484653_Critical_Discourse_Analysis_and_Its_Critics [accessed 2 May 2015].

Brown, N.J. (2014). 'The future of Egyptian democracy: Political Islam becomes less political', *The Immanent Frame*, 11 March. Social Science Research Council (SSRC).

Available at: https://tif.ssrc.org/2014/03/11/political-islam-becomes-less-political/ [accessed 2 April 2015].

Brown, N.J. (2016). 'Rethinking language: "Islamism" as a dirty word', *Rethinking Political Islam Series*, April. Project on US Relations with the Islamic World at Brookings. Available at: https://www.brookings.edu/wp-content/uploads/2016/07/Jonathan-Brown_FINAL.pdf [accessed 20 December 2016].

Bukhārī, M.I. (1966). *Sahih Bukhari*. Karachi: Muhammad Sarid.

Castells, M. (1996). *The Rise of the Network Society*. Oxford: Blackwell Publishers.

Chilton, P.A. (2004). *Analysing political discourse: Theory and practice*. London: Routledge.

Echchaibi, N. (2014). 'Altmuslim: Media spaces for a modern Muslim voice', in J.H. Mahan (ed.) *Media, religion and culture: An Introduction*, pp. 82–3. New York: Routledge.

Eickelman, D.F. and Anderson, J.W. (1999). 'Redefining Muslim publics', in D.F. Eickelman and J.W. Anderson (eds.) *New media in the Muslim world: The emerging public sphere*, pp. 1–18. Bloomington: Indiana University Press.

Eickelman, D.F. and Piscatori, J.P. (2004). *Muslim politics*. New Jersey: Princeton University Press.

Elnaili, S. (2021). 'Promoting Libyan nationalism concepts via Facebook: A critical discourse analysis', in A. Douai and E. Mohamed (eds.) *New media discourses in Egypt and the Middle East: Culture and politics after the Arab Spring uprisings*, pp. 147–158. London: I.B. Tauris.

El-Nawawy, M. and Khamis, S. (2009). *Islam dot com: Contemporary Islamic discourses in cyberspace*. New York: Palgrave Macmillan.

El-Sherif, A. (2006). 'Democratic Islamic yuppies: Post-Islamism or another Islamism?', Association of Muslim Social Scientists (AMSS) 35th annual conference: *Muslim identities: Shifting boundaries and dialogues*. Hartford Seminary, 27–29 October. Hartford, Connecticut.

Fairclough, N. (1992). *Discourse and social change*. Cambridge: Polity Press.

Fairclough, N. (2003). *Analysing discourse: Textual analysis for social research*. London: Routledge.

Fairclough, N. and Wodak, R. (1997). 'Critical discourse analysis', in T.A. Van Dijk (ed.) *Discourse as social interaction*, pp. 258–84. London: Sage.

Fattah, M.A. (2013). 'Islam and politics in the Middle East', in J.L. Esposito and E. Shahin (eds.) *The Oxford Handbook of Islam and Politics*, pp. 289–306. New York: Oxford University Press.

Ferjani, Riadh (2010). 'Religion and television in the Arab world: Towards a communication studies approach', *Middle East Journal of Culture and Communication*, 3, pp. 82–100.

Ghamari-Tabrizi, B. (2013). 'Abdulkarim Soroush', in J.L. Esposito and E. Shahin (eds.) *The Oxford Handbook of Islam and Politics*, pp. 246–59. New York: Oxford University Press.

Habermas, J., Lennox, S. and Lennox, F. (1974). 'The public sphere: An encyclopedia article', *New German Critique* 3, pp. 495–5.

Hamid, S. and McCants, W. (2016). 'Rethinking political Islam', *Brookings Report*, 6 May. Available at: http://www.brookings.edu/research/reports2/2015/08/rethinking-political-islam [accessed 4 October 2016].

Hardt-Mautner, G. (1995). '"Only connect": Critical discourse analysis and corpus linguistics'. Available at: https://www.researchgate.net/

publication/238287338_%27Only_Connect%27_Critical_Discourse_Analysis_and_
Corpus_Linguistics [accessed 18 May 2021].

Hiramoto, M. and Park, J.S.-Y. (2010). 'Media intertextualities: Semiotic mediation across time and space', *Pragmatics and Society*, 1(2), pp. 179–88.

Hjelm, T. (2014). 'Religion, discourse and power: A contribution towards a critical sociology of religion', *Critical Sociology*, 40(6), pp. 855–72.

Lacroix, S. (2011). *Awakening Islam: The politics of religious dissent in contemporary Saudi Arabia*. Cambridge, MA: Harvard University Press.

Mandaville, P. (2001). *Transnational Muslim politics: Reimagining the umma*. New York: Routledge.

Mohamed, E. and Mohamed E. (2021). 'Do Egyptians still care about the Arab Spring? Computational cultural assessment of online and offline activism', in A. Douai and E. Mohamed (eds.) *New media discourses in Egypt and the Middle East: Culture and politics after the Arab Spring uprisings*, pp. 37–54. London: I.B. Tauris.

Pennycook, A. (1994). 'The politics of pronouns', *ELT Journal*, 48(2), pp. 173–8.

Reed, M. (1998). 'Organizational analysis as discourse analysis: A critique', in D. Grant, T. Keenoy and C. Oswick (eds.) *Discourse and organization*, pp. 193–213. London: Sage.

Richardson, J.E. (2007). *Analysing newspapers: An approach from critical discourse analysis*. New York: Palgrave Macmillan.

Stubbs, M. (1997). 'Whorf's children: Critical comments on critical discourse analysis', in A. Ryan and A. Wray (eds.) *Evolving models of language*, pp.100–16. Clevedon: Multilingual Matters.

Tenorio, E.H. (2011). 'Critical discourse analysis: An overview. *Nordic Journal of English Studies*, 10(1), pp. 183–210.

The Economist. (2014). 'Islamism is no longer the answer', 20 December. Available at: http://www.economist.com/news/middle-east-and-africa/21636776-political-islam-under-pressure-generals-monarchs-jihadistsand [accessed 8 June 2016].

The Guardian. (2016) 'Sheikh Aaidh al-Qarni, Saudi preacher, shot in Philippines', 2 March. Available at: http://www.theguardian.com/world/2016/mar/02/sheikh-aaidh-al-qarni-saudi-preacher-shot-philippines [accessed 6 April 2016].

USA Today. (2013). 'TV director fired for ties to Muslim Brotherhood', *News*, 18 August. Available at: http://www.usatoday.com/story/news/world/2013/08/18/saudi-prince-muslim-brotherhood/2668443/ [accessed 11 June 2015].

Van Dijk, T.A. (1988). *News as discourse*. Hillsdale, NJ: Lawrence Erlbaum.

Van Dijk, T.A. (1997). 'What is political discourse analysis?', *Belgian Journal of Linguistics*, 11(1), pp. 11–52.

Van Dijk, T.A. (1998). 'Opinions and ideologies in the press', in P. Garrett and A. Bell (eds.) *Approaches to media discourse*, pp. 21–62. Oxford: Blackwell.

Wall, J.D., Stahl, B.C. and Salam, A.F. (2015). 'Critical Discourse Analysis as a review methodology: An empirical example', *Communications of the Association for Information Systems*, 37(11). Available at: http://aisel.aisnet.org/cais/vol37/iss1/11 [accessed 18 November 2015].

Wehrey, F. (2013). 'Will change come for Saudi Arabia's Shia minority?', *Sada*, 12 February. Available at: http://carnegieendowment.org/sada/?fa=50920 [accessed 18 November 2015].

Wise, L. (2003). '*Words from the heart*': *New forms of Islamic preaching in Egypt*. M. Phil. Thesis. St. Antony's College, Oxford University. Available at: http://users.ox.ac.uk/~metheses/Wise.pdf [accessed [accessed 4 April 2015].

Chapter 6

THE REVOLUTION OF PRONOUNS: SHIFTS OF POWER AND RESISTANCE IN EGYPT'S MUSLIM BROTHERHOOD

Mustafa Menshawy

Introduction

If you seek to understand Egypt's Muslim Brotherhood, a mass corpus of literature will direct you to who and what is inside it (e.g. Al-Anani 2016; Kandil 2014; Skovgaard-Petersen and Gräf 2009; Zollner 2009). Scholars adopting this line of analysis justify this focus on the inside for what seem like legitimate logical reasons: unravelling significant structural dimensions, modes of operation and dynamics of evolution pertaining to what is Egypt's largest opposition movement (e.g. Gerges 2018; Lia 1998; Mitchell 1969). The fact that the Brotherhood is an underground movement and that it also cultivates a tradition of secrecy and unanimity adds to the validity of the biased focus on all these internal elements. Still, this limitation has a number of drawbacks. First, it attributes too much homogeneity or coherence to the group as a *catch-all* unit of analysis. Second, it serves or at least accords with the attempts by the Brotherhood itself to control scholars' access to its 'inside' or to direct their attention to specific concepts or practices of interest related to it (e.g. Abed-Kotb 1995). Third, aspects that lie on the opposite side, i.e., those related to what or who is *outside* the Brotherhood, have always been underexplored or un-explored in the literature (e.g. Al-Awadi 2013). Members who have left the group gain their value not as cases of individual disengagements but as sources informing and educating us on new perspectives of what is inside the group (Wickham 2013). The events that happened from 2011 onwards, including the protests which the Brotherhood took part of it after an initial hesitation, the resignation of President Hosni Mubarak and the rise of Brotherhood's Mohamed Morsi to power, ended this symbolic annihilation (Skalli 2011) which had been inadvertently shared by the movement and the scholars studying it.

The outside has become as significant as the inside at more than one level (Menshawy 2020). First, the cases of departures from the Brotherhood are now higher in number and level, especially as of 2011. The group can no longer succeed at condemning, trivializing 'dissidents' or denying them membership in the first place (Interview, Sha'ban 2020).[1] Scholars could not avoid investigating the phenomenon of increasing numbers of members leaving the Brotherhood, including a plethora of big names such as Leader's Deputy Mohamed Habib and a member of its influential Guidance Bureau, 'Abdel-Mon'im Aboul-Futouh. They are of a high-level status that the group cannot disown or downsize, and they have long played influential roles that scholars can also not ignore. Ex-members come from all over Egypt and they belong to different age and sex groups. We know about this variety of former members due to the second level justifying the re-direction of focus towards the outside – that is, docoumented publicity. As of 2011, many individuals have announced their departure live on TV, sending their resignation letters to newspapers, even before notifying the group's leaders of their decisions, as well as writing dozens of autobiographies (e.g. *Altaghieer* 2012). This publicity has created the unique spectacle of disclosure as members no longer maintain secrecy and silence in their disassociation, or opt to be 'ordinary leave-takers' (Bromley 1998, p. 15) in order to avoid the wrath of an oppressive state suspicious of their intentions. They have been emboldened into these media-led disclosures as the 2011 revolutionary transformations led to the demise of the state itself. Many former members have become of the 'apostate' type (ibid.), i.e., those who dramatically and publicly 'reverse' their loyalties and even at sometimes become a 'professional enemy' of the movement they have left' (Introvigne 1999, p. 84). A simple search on Facebook or YouTube can lead to hundreds of self-proclaimed ex-Brotherhood members and who have put their narrations into audiovisual or online formats. Supported by contextual shifts as global as increasing forms of 'mass self-communication' (Castells 2015, p. 6) and as local as a high level of contentious politics based on claims and counter-claims (see Tarrow and Tilly 2015), exiters found more reasons to maintain their visibility amidst state-led security crackdowns and media campaigns to expose their former group especially after losing power in 2013 (Interview, Aboul-Sa'd 2017).

This chapter is an attempt to understand how members have disengaged, despite all social, psychological and even political pressures not to, and how the post-2011 socio-politics have created opportunities – or not – to facilitate the disassociation. The chapter also covers the aforementioned lacunae in the literature by giving exiting members the power of narration. It is the language used by these members that can represent and also create disengagement itself. What is analysed is texts varying from content of former members' appearances in traditional media and social media. Analysis mainly includes a genre of autobiographies with which dozens of exiting members have chosen to tell stories or describe events that happened to them either separately or along with other means of communication.

The discourse analysis of these narrational outlets moves at both levels of what is *linguistic* and *extra-linguistic*. The two specific pronouns 'I' and 'we' are traced, grouped and analysed. They are studied as they are textured in the variable means of narration/communication through consistency and coherence drawn on repeating or reinforcing the same 'frames' in different texts and means of narrating experiences on disengagement. The extra-linguistic level is based on an understanding of these two pronouns (selected for specific reasons detailed below) as tools of dominance and resistance marking the relationship between exiting members and their former group. They are also understood as parts of geo-political and sociopolitical shifts in Egypt and beyond. These shifts, providing sources for the *articulation* and *operationalization* of a 'discourse of exhood', are also drawn on other factors such as the phenomenon of re-spatialization which has led many former members to relocate in countries such as Turkey and the UK, and to seek the support of the Egyptian state's resources.

Methodology and sources of data

Critical discourse analysis is the main approach for this study. As there are many perspectives on this approach, I take disengagement as a discourse moving across Fairclough's (1992) three-level conceptualization. Still, this does not exclude other perspectives, including van Dijk's (1980) conceptualization of discourse through the prism of 'semantic macrostructures', where we can trace and group 'thematized meanings' of the disengagement in texts.

At the first level of Fairclough's conceptualization; 'discourse as a text' (Fairclough 1992, pp. 74–8), the paper addresses both questions of form and questions of content or meanings pertaining to the semantics of the two specific pronouns 'I' and 'we'. The textuality of the two pronouns is traced in two ways. The first way is through 'textual surface structures, including words, sentences, paragraphs or presentation formats' (van Dijk 1988, p. 170). The 'local-level meanings' of these elements are made in the pronouns' frequency as well as relations such as those of synonymy between sentences or propositions carrying them when exiting members assign meanings to their disengagement (ibid.). The second way is an exploration of the 'global meanings', i.e., how fragmented elements of texts and their meanings coalesce into 'topics, themes, perspectives, as well as overall schematic forms' (ibid.). These global meanings create 'topical' or 'thematic' structures of the texts but they are still drawn on smaller 'atomized' local units of these texts such as 'titles' and 'keywords' or 'metaphors' and which can 'abstract' and 'summarize' the whole 'discourse of exhood' (ibid., p. 10). I group the two levels of meanings and identify them as frames. The 'I' pronoun is a frame not only by its repetition in texts but also by its association with other linguistic formulations that support its articulation at local and global levels of meaning-making.

At the second level of Fairclough's conceptualization, 'discursive practices', interest expands into the production and interpretation of texts, i.e., how certain topics or themes of texts as well as their meanings (now grouped for the sake of organization as frames) gain salience and emphasis through features as 'force', 'coherence' or 'intertextuality' (Fairclough 1992, pp. 78–86). This level of analysis allows moving beyond exhood-related texts. For example, via intertextuality, exiting members resorted to texts of *existing* members as resources from which they have drawn, in order to construct their 'cues', in Fairclough's words (ibid., p. 80), building their own texts. In this process of transforming prior texts and restructuring existing discourses related to the Brotherhood, exiting members can generate a new discourse, the discourse of exhood, through which they can resist, challenge and counter the hegemony of the Brotherhood and its pre-emptive/ punitive measures against disengagements. For example, exiters produce their rising 'I' as a frame by re-interpreting and reconstructing the meanings of the group's dominant frame of the pronoun 'we' and discursive strategies related to it.

This leads to Fairclough's third level of analysis, 'discourse as social practice' (1992, pp. 86–91). From a less abstract and more contextualized semantic analysis which I also fruitfully adopted in other works of mine (Menshawy 2017, 2019), this chapter investigates the two pronouns/frames in relation to ideology and to power. In other words, it is about how the evolution of the two pronouns in texts has drawn on an evolution of power relations and hegemonic struggle and resistance related to the Brotherhood and broader social and political structures in which they dis/function. By ideology, I mean the 'thematized meanings' (van Dijk 1998, p. 113) projected onto individual members by their leaders and which they must adhere to. Focusing on cases of disengagement announced or made after 2011 is thus justified as the production, consumption and interpretation of the two pronouns can be explored against specific workings of the sociopolitical in 2011 and afterwards. During this time, including a short span of three years in which the Brotherhood challenged, gained and lost power, the 'I' and 'we' are fully re-positioned in opposite seats and also have become full-fledged politicized pronouns of power and resistance, respectively.

This chapter combines different data sources in the study of the disengagement phenomenon. The data includes autobiographies written by former members and published between 2011 and 2017, and transcribed interviews conducted with thirty-two other ex-members who had announced their departure from the group within the same period (Table 5.1).

Table 5.1 Interviewees who are ex-members of the Muslim Brotherhood (MB)

Name	Joined MB	Left MB	Age	Profession	Interview Date	Interview Place
Ghandi Antar	2000	2012	35	Journalist and researcher	3-3-2017	Turkey
Abdallah El-Qaddoum	2000	2006	20	Documentary maker	5-3-2017	Turkey
Tareq El-Labban	2000	2009	35	Journalist	3-3-2017	Turkey
Mohamed Ali Zaqzouq	2002	2012	32	Journalist	4-3-2017	Turkey
Ibrahim Mohamed Ibrahim	1987	2011	30	Lawyer	12-5-2017	Egypt
Ahmed Salah Rashwan	1998	2012	31	Arabic teacher	2-5-2017	Egypt
Amina Zayed	1993	2012	51	Housewife	17-5-2017	Egypt

Rafi Shaker	2003	2014	31	Cameraman	10-5-2017	Egypt
Salman El-Shaf'y	1990	2011	28	Journalist	11-5-2017	Egypt
Sayyed Milad	2006	2014	31	Merchant	11-5-2017	Egypt
Tareq Aboul-Sa'd	1985	2011	50	School Vice-Principal	12-5-2017	Egypt
Tareq El-Beshbeshy	1984	2013	53	Government employee	16-5-2017	Egypt
'Ala El-Shaf'y	1984	2011	52	Engineer	9-5-2017	Egypt
Mohamed Ibrahim 'Anan	2010	2013	26	Engineering student	8-5-2017	Egypt
'Emad Ahmed 'Ali	2002	2017	33	Student	12-5-2017	On Skype
'Abdel-Rahman Jom'a	1986	2014	32	Pharmacist	3-3-2017	Turkey
Islam 'Outewy	2012	2015	24	Political science student	4-3-2017	Turkey
Haitham Aboul-Khalil	1989	2011	49	Media practitioner	4-3-2017	Turkey
Mohamed Aboul-Gheit	1989	2011	28	Journalist	13-1-2017	Britain
Mohamed El-Qassas	1987	2011	42	Deputy Chairman of Strong Egypt Party	20-8-2017	Egypt (on phone)
Islam Lufty	1984	2011	40	Lawyer	25-1-2017	Britain
'Ibrahim Rabi'	1979	2013	53	Government employee	24-2-2017	Egypt (on phone)
Ibrahim El-Za'frany	1965	2011	66	Physician	24-2-2017	Egypt (on phone)
Kamal El-Helbawy	1951	2012	79	Writer	20-1-2017	London
Ahmed 'Abdel-Gawwad	1977	May 2011	41	Secretary General of Strong Egypt Party	11-2-2017	Egypt (on phone)
Khaled Fouad	1999	2015	39	Writer and researcher	5-3-2017	Turkey
Mohamed Saber	2007	2013	33	Building contractor	12-3-2017	Turkey
Ahmed Yehia	2001	2013	34	Journalist	13-3-2017	Turkey
Ahmed Nazily	1983	2011	40	Businessman	2-9-2017	Qatar
Mohamed Affan	1998	2011	38	Researcher and writer	5-3-2017	Turkey
Mohamed Hegazy	2005	2013	29	PhD student	5-3-2017	Turkey
Mus'ab El-Sawah	2010	2014	23	Student	4-3-2017	Turkey

Other acts of texturing by ex-members including posts on social media or TV appearances are also included as part of the analysis. I adopt this 'triangulation', i.e., the combination of data sources in the study of the same phenomenon (see Denzin 1978; Denzin and Lincoln 2005), for a number of reasons. Firstly, it secures a richer and thicker data set, grounded in a more well-rounded investigation of a topic considerably under-explored in the literature. Secondly, we deal with different frames encompassing thematic meanings of a subjective nature and which are mainly constructed in the minds of exiting members. Combining sources of narration by different ex-members who had belonged to the same movement can, at the same time, help the convergence towards truthfulness and full meaningfulness about the whole phenomenon of disengagement itself. The truthfulness is created by the confirmation and corroboration among frames that cover all domains of the disengagement phenomenon and that could be contradictory or conflictual. The frames, based on human experience and understanding, refer to subjective accounts and events brought into a textual shape from the opinions and memory of exiting members. Therefore, the best option is to compare and contrast the frames as multiple outcomes of different departure narratives. The bias inherent in any one particular data source can be cancelled out (or perhaps confirmed) when used in conjunction with the other source. Analysis also adds another layer of verification, this time beyond the level of texts of narrativization. I go to the original sources as a necessary step of gaining knowledge.

Admittedly, the sampling in interviews are subject to biases as the thirty-two individuals were selected on a 'snowballing' basis. For example, in Turkey, ex-members whom I interviewed on the first day of my arrival in Istanbul introduced me to their friends and acquaintances who also departed from the same group and who could share the same characteristics. As the sample builds up in this 'non-probability' technique, also adopted in Egypt, the UK and Qatar, the data was gathered. However, the technique can be justified as I was looking for a variety of exiting members including those who were hidden and difficult to locate, especially in Egypt's conflict environment, full of suspicion and mistrust drawn from the official anti-Brotherhood hostility and public outrage. The snowballing technique is justified to avoid more problems in this kind of research, problems that also have to do with the characteristics of exiting members who are ready to talk to researchers and the public in general. The interviewees who are ready to talk are mostly those of the apostate type, i.e., those who have 'louder' voices as they can dramatically and publicly narrate their experiences, 'reverse' their loyalties and even become 'professional enemies' of the movement they have left (Bromley 1998; Introvigne 1999). I was not the first one to talk to the apostate type of those exiting members as they enjoy a wider access to other researchers and media outlets in and out of Egypt. Benefitting from contextual shifts such as the Egyptian state's attempts to use every tool to crack down on the Brotherhood and its existing members, some of those apostate ex-members found additional reasons to enhance their visibility. They not only narrated their experiences, but they also shared the regime's goals of exposing their former group. One could even suspect this visibility and ubiquity in the 'quit literature' that abounds in the literature on the Brotherhood within a short space of time could not have been possible without the tacit approval, if not outright encouragement, of the regime of Abdel-Fatah El-Sissi, Egypt's president. The list of interviewees thus includes ordinary leavers, such as Mohamed Ibrahim 'Anan and Amina Zayed, who had never narrated their disengagement publicly, and those who have drifted away quietly without fanfare or revealing themselves to the media or researchers, or writing autobiographies. It was important to enroll in this study those voices that are 'most common and least often discussed' and which have long been 'marginalized' at the expense of the louder voices of the apostate type (Introvigne 1999, p. 84). Again, this helped boost the reliability of my findings as the frames of the quiet individual interviewees s always stand as a tool corroborating the frames of the louder apostate type of ex-members, who could hold stronger feelings, radical views and revengeful attitudes when they narrated their past. This desire for corroboration, coupled with that of seeking a higher degree of comprehensiveness and truthfulness, also manifested in variations inside the interview samples. As thousands of Brotherhood members are now relocated in Turkey, the latter became a key location for interviews. The sample also reflects variations in interviewee jobs, with a bigger focus on the middle class and professionals (which accords with the Brotherhood's policies of taking them as the main 'source of recruitment').[2]

As the Brotherhood's recruitment also 'targets children' especially 'kids of its members' (Mensshawy 2020, p. 15), The sample reflects this targeting by showing how most of the interviewees joined the group at a younger age. The duration of staying in the Brotherhood as well as the age groups is also fairly evenly represented and distributed in the sample on basis of the data available on Brotherhood recruitment and membership.

Once the interviews were conducted, they were transcribed and the data from them, along with the autobiographies, was qualitatively analysed for identifying and reporting patterns within it. I read over the texts repeatedly to become as familiar with them as possible. During each reading of the transcripts, I would note my preliminary impressions and interpretations in the left margin, in codes referencing the participants' style of meaning-making, forms of language, apparent contradictions and patterns within the data. The right margin was subsequently used to place these initial codes into frames that were meant to capture the 'salience' and 'selection' qualities of these accounts (Entman 1993, p. 52).

Units of analysis: The 'I' and 'we'

I selected the pronouns 'I' and 'we' as my main units of analysis because of their significance in the relationship between individual members and the group. The semantics of the two pronouns are symbolically important, as uttering them can signify who and who is not a Brotherhood member. They are such makers/markers of identity that 'we can recognize a Brotherhood member who use either one of the two pronouns once she or he opens her/his mouth before and after the exit' (Interview, Brown 2018[3]; see also Interviews, El-Tahawy 2016 and Sha'ban 2020). In addition, the two pronouns are a reflection of some of the well-established policies inside the Brotherhood which are based on 'renunciation' and 'communion'. Renunciation is the way the Brotherhood reduces the interaction of individuals with people outside the Brotherhood in order to enhance their attachment to the group-related 'we'. This not only denies 'I' its individuality and originality as it must always be part of the 'we'. It also separates the 'we', and the submerged 'I', from the 'they' now implicitly identified as the non-Brothers in the taxonomy of deliberately naming the group as *Ikhwan Muslimoon* ('Muslim Brothers'). This clear-cut separation between the 'I/we' merger on the one hand and the 'they' on the other has led to the development of what Gamson (1995, p. 102) calls 'adversarial framing' and other scholars (Hunt, Benford and Snow 1994, p. 194) call 'boundary framing' with it. Separated from the outside world (symbolized by the 'they'), the 'I' gets an assumed unanimity and a will to exclusion by 'communion'. The latter ensures full conformity of individual members to the group (symbolized by the 'we') and to avoid any 'free-riding' (Fillieule 2015, p. 47), which was thought implicit in any significant assertion of individual autonomy (which can be also symbolized by the rise of the 'I' as a lead to disengagement from the group). Therefore, the movability of the two pronouns in the texts of exiting members (including whatever verbal and written) can reveal the process of disengagement from these policies themselves.

There is one more reason to analyse engagement/disengagement via the semantic movability of the two pronouns. The latter are constituent parts of the literature of the Brotherhood itself. For example, in the autobiography of the founder of the Brotherhood, Hassan El-Banna, and which is still studied as a key element of the curricula inside the group, the 'I' is dismissed, downsized and subjugated as a static invariant of the discursive life of the 'we'. El-Banna applied this fixity and stability by 'intertextual chaining' (Fairclough 1992, p. 130) as is obvious in these citations from his autobiography: 'I am only one of [we] Muslims serving their religion', and 'I dedicate myself to the *Da'wa* [which we are carrying] to God' (El-Banna 2012, p. 227). As will be detailed below, El-Banna posits the two pronouns less as mere vocabulary and more as lexical items of *sanctification* or *canonization*. It is therefore interesting and revealing to understand how exiting members shifted and re-aligned the semantics of the pronouns that have long operated within a complex yet coherent 'macrostructures', to borrow the term from van Dijk's 1980 book title, of Islam as a religion.

The personal 'I'

The pronoun 'I' predominates as all former members adopt a first-person narration style in their texturing of their interviews and autobiographies. This clears the texts of any 'ambivalence of voice' (Fairclough 1992, p. 108) and adds to the narration an 'authoritative assertion' (p. 173) since we are all the time reminded of who talks or writes. The other functional benefit of this first person style is relational, as exiters make it clear that they have a full agentive control over their group or its leaders who are referred in texts under analysis in the third-person format (e.g. 'it', 'he', 'they'). The lexical choice of the 'I' also serves meanings of what van Dijk (1988, p. 184) calls the 'amplification process' judged by occurrence, frequency and size of the pronoun itself as the leading 'discourse referent'. One manifestation of this amplification is 'density' or 'overwording'. The 'I' appears as part of every answer and almost in every page of texts by exiting members. Some of the latter use several different wordings that are synonyms or near synonyms to convey the same meanings (Fairclough 1992, p. 193), and the pronoun takes a rhetorically iterative manner in the same clause or sentence. These are examples mentioned in answers to my main question on reasons behind exiting the group: 'I wanted to be an I' (Fayez 2011, pp. 17-18), 'I wanted to restore the I' (Interview, Aboul-Gheit 2017), 'I wanted to be an I' (Interview, Nazily 2018), 'It is a search for the I' (Interview, El-Shaf'y 2018) and 'I won myself by exiting the group' (Interview, Rashwan 2018).

The rhetorically emphasized meanings are sustained by complementarity granted by other linguistic constructions such as metaphors. The latter serve significant ideational functions as they can 'structure the way we think and the way we act, and our systems of knowledge and belief, in a pervasive and fundamental way' (Fairclough 1992, p. 194). Two main metaphors prevail in the texts, constituting engagement as 'slavery' or 'imprisonment' and disengagement as 'emancipation'. El-Khirbawy, sixty-one years old, metaphorized his twenty-year membership as a 'human chain of slavery' since it 'chained my body and soul' (2012, pp. 16–17). Across his text, El-Khirbawy provides further clauses and sentences adding functionality to his metaphorical construction by such linguistic features as 'enhancement', 'extension' and 'elaboration' (Halliday 1985, pp. 202–27). On enhancement, he refers to specific times, places, manners and incidents in which the group's leaders imposed a house arrest as a punitive measure against his disobedience of their orders. On extension, he cohered the metaphor as part of other global meanings related to other genres such as novels. He describes his crude experience as similar to those ready-made experiences in Shawshank State Prison, from the movie *The Shawshank Redemption* (1994) adapted from Stephen King's novel, and Kunta Kinte, the fictional African who became an American slave in Alex Haley's book *Roots* (1976) and the 1977 American television mini-series based upon it. On elaboration, he emphasized the metaphorization of reality by repeated occurrences and frequencies as these examples indicate: 'I have felt for a long time that this group is a prison for me'; 'I am a prisoner who cannot move towards his freedom'; 'Heavy are my chains [set by] by the officers of the prison' (El-Khirbawy 2012, pp. 16–17). The metaphoric construction became naturalized as it was described, reworded and clarified to convey the same meanings in these quotes.

Building further coherence, exiting members link the metaphor with another, to the effect of emancipation, a conditional sequentially ordered linkage based on explicit adversative collocation. In other words, individuals are emancipated as this state or action is conditioned as a consequence of the other state or action of imprisonment or slavery, and both constitute the course of disengagement. The texts are full of descriptions which use the word literally as 'emancipation' or metonymically by referring to indicative features such as breathing. These are quotes from two separate texts by exiting members: 'Outside the Brotherhood, I can breathe air. The air can be polluted, but I have the freedom to breathe it or not' (Interview, Rashwan 2018); and it is about 'feeling that I breathe a fresh air' (Interview, El-Shaf'y 2018). The comparison is necessitated by *animating* it, i.e., every living being has no option but to breathe. As such, breathing, a metaphor for life, can disguise the constructive effect that individuals draw on the reality of their sociocultural dis-affiliation from the group. The two metaphors also stabilize the subjective emotional meanings pertaining to disengagement by borrowing from the style register of various types of objectified bodily processes such as breath deprivation and physical imprisonment/slavery. In this dual sense, the very act of disengagement allows individuals to regain both the mental functioning and the bodily functioning of their selves (Fesmire 1994). Noticeably, the clauses and sentences carrying the metaphors centralize the mention of the 'I' as a keyword representing individuals who undergo acts such as breathing. Mostly mentioned at the initial clause of sentences, the 'I' keeps its position as a 'focus of struggle' (Fairclough 1992, p. 236) in all the syntactic formulation of the metaphors against the attempts to stop former members from breathing, as implied in their descriptions of 'enslavement' and 'imprisonment'.

The 'I' and all linguistic configurations serving its rise in texts of ex-members, including rhetorical wordings with the same meanings and metaphorization, are not moving in isolation. They are connected to and shaped by prior texts of the Brotherhood, as if they are responding to them, a feature of discourse-making in the name of 'intertextuality' if the connection is manifest or 'interdiscursivity' if they are implicit or indirect (Fairclough 1992, p. 10). The Brotherhood has long acted as a 'centripetal' force of language, i.e., imposing 'unity', 'centralization' and 'correctness' on texts used by its members (Bakhtin 1981, p. 269). This ideologically saturated imposition made it feasible, or indeed easier, to recognize a common language inside the Brotherhood as members share the conventions of its use (Kandil 2014; Interview, Brown 2017). As a result, the group's reigning language stood against any language plurality that might reflect differences among individuals or sub-groups divided along lines related to generation or gender (Biagini 2017). By treating language as a socio-ideological unifier, the 'I' representing each individual member and her/his personal self was supplanted and subsumed within the 'we' representing the group and its reigning proto-language. The latter practices what Bakhtin (1981, p. 270) described as an act of 'enslavement', a striking similarity with the metaphoric constitution of engagement with the group, as alluded to above. Therefore, intertextuality is a necessary step as it can show us that the dynamics and moments of the evolution of the 'I' and the 'we' in texts of *exiting* members are in fact a reaction to prior texts inculcated by exiting members' former leaders and still shared by the group's *existing* members.

For example, as mentioned above, in the autobiography of El-Banna (2012), the founder of the group, the 'I' submerges as an un-identifiable part of the 'we'. Due to the sanctification and canonization of the two pronouns, El-Banna's instructions and the principles of Islam and its holy book, the Quraan, were 'reduced', 'stored' and 'retrieved' (van Dijk 1980, p. 14) in the minds of members of the group as two juxtaposed pronouns. For example, the founder's autobiography defined the 'we' as representing those who are 'Muslims applying what is mentioned by Quran and adopted by Prophet Muhammad' and who sacrifice their personal selves for the sake of this purpose (El-Banna 2012, pp. 54, 90). This microstructurally formulated sanctification projected on the 'we' adds factualness and presupposition, and thus makes it harder – or anti-Islamic – for potential exiters to raise their 'I', evidenced by their desire to criticize, question, judge or reject the orders of their superiors in the group. In order to do so, these individuals have the formidable task of re-modifying or de-constructing Islam itself in which the 'we' is lexicalized and sanctified as well as chained. From this same perspective, the Brotherhood reacted to individuals raising the 'I', including simple acts of raising questions or debating hierarchically based decision-making process, by labelling them 'apostates', 'less Islamic', and 'Satan followers' or 'heretics' (Interviews with Aboul-Sa'd 2017; Nazily 2018; Lutfy 2017; El-Sawah 2017; and El-Qaddoum 2018). This brings to mind all the Quranic anecdotes of the past in which Satan had disobeyed God by attempting to raise the 'I'. Satan sets himself apart from other angels, who kneeled down in front of God stylistically referring to Himself in some spaces of Quran with the majestic plural 'we'. Therefore, most exiting members remember how their leaders reacted to their objections to their instructions by requests to 'perform more prayers' and 'read more Quraan' to dismiss 'Satanic ideas growing in our minds' (Interview, Nazily 2018).

As part of intertextual or interdiscursive connectivity with this past and that background information, slavery/imprisonment and emancipation can be thus considered counter-metaphors through which exiting members can stand up to the Brotherhood's hegemonic discourse. In its literature, the group has used the slavery metaphor as a positive commendable act in which the 'I' must submit to the orders of God and the Brotherhood. On the other side, the emancipation metaphor means each individual's ability to contain or get rid of her or his personal 'psychological needs' and 'biological luxuries' and avoid falling into 'lust' and corrupt souls all for the sake of giving primacy to the 'renaissance of the *Umma* ('Islamic nation') (El-Banna 2012, pp. 172–73). In other words, the emancipation of the personal self is realized by enslaving it to part of a holy or sanctified collective self. What exiting members have done is flip these metaphors around by rewording them to convey opposite meanings without losing what van Dijk (1980, p. 32) calls the discursive 'satisfaction'. The latter is ensured by 'mutual connectedness', 'compatibility' and 'coherence' of such metaphorical combinations in the past and in the present (ibid., pp. 32–33). To oversimplify, what exiting members carry out is an intertextuality by reverse. Evidently, El-Banna and his writings are heavily mentioned in texts as 'retrieval cues' (ibid., p. 14) for exiting members to criticize, refute or falsify Brotherhood claims (e.g., El-'Agouz 2011). The texts are full of exegetical attempts to re-interpret the Quraan and its imaginable facts (as long established in the minds of the Brotherhood members) in order to validate and construct their own disengagement as adherent to Islam not against it as El-Banna and other leaders have long claimed (e.g. 'Eid 2014a).

The social 'I'

The accentuation of the 'I' ness meanings at the lexical, grammatical or semantic levels building a discourse as texts is associated with discourse as a social practice, another level of Fairclough's (1992) conceptualized analysis. These practices include the way exiting members *talk* in order to frame their experience of disengagement, as a regaining of their 'I'. For example, some individuals whom I met, as well as writers of the autobiographies, used expletives to describe the Brotherhood and its leaders, always sanctified as 'godly people' under the intertextual chaining between the group and Islam, as '*welaad weskha*' (Interview, Anan 2017). The curse used by Shaker, a thirty-one-year-old press cameraman who left in 2014 after an eleven-year-membership, is a common Arabic slang expression or curse that literally means 'sons of a dirty woman,' akin to the English 'son of a b***h' or the Spanish *hijo de puta* ('son of a whore'). The cursing and the use of expletives is a symbolic announcement of regaining one's 'I' by challenging the rules accentuating the 'we', where all members are asked to abide by 'linguistic politeness' as part of their collective identification. Article 7 of the Brotherhood's General Law states, 'Bluntness, crudeness, and abuses in words or by hints must be avoided at all cost' (Lia 1998, p. 110). Therefore, clean or correct language has become institutionalized in what Watts (2003, p. 10) calls 'expectable behaviour' on what and how to speak. As part of their disengagement, exiters now build their own linguistic reservoir, to shape their own meanings without commitment to the Brotherhood's rules of propriety.

The social practices associated with the rise of the 'I' and the way of texturing it as a main part of the disengagement experience are also evidenced in discarding other symbolic activities related to appearance or dress codes. Mus'ab El-Sawah, a twenty-three-year-old man who left the Brotherhood in 2014 after four years, came to meet me in a café in Istanbul with pony-tailed hair, a forbidden Westernized behaviour inside the Brotherhood. He consciously reasoned it as an attempt to carve a space for himself or as he put it: 'I want to be myself' (Interview, El-Sawah 2017). Mohamed El-Qassas, a forty-two-year-old who stayed in the group for twenty-four years until leaving in 2011, said he now wore sunglasses in public 'after always being banned by the group' (Interview, El-Qassas 2017). Another interviewee (Interview, Saber 2018) met me while combing his long hair to the back. Thirty-three years old and a member for sixteen years, until his exit in 2013, Saber did not deny the change is 'revolutionary' as it relates to his desire of regaining his 'I' by getting rid of the group's rules and dress codes, including 'that I have to comb my hair to the right side'.

The social practices supporting the texturing of disengagement also include shifts in friendship practices in which the discourse of disengagement can be borne or circulated by interaction and interpretation. For example, 'Abdel-Mon'im (2011) replaced her Brotherhood friends with new ones as evidenced in her Facebook list of 'friends'. In February 2018, she posted a picture of herself on Facebook with a 'friend' from China who had written her master's thesis on 'Abdel-Mon'im's writings, after the latter had changed careers upon leaving the Brotherhood. 'Abdel-Monim continued posting images of new friendships made as she travelled to new countries, including Spain, and as she engaged in more activities related to her career shift. Her list of friends also included novelists, writers and columnists, further removing her from the Brotherhood's social milieu. Almost all departing members narrated similar experiences of building up new networks of friendships during or after their exit. Tracing changes in the Facebook lists of friends and posts of other exiters, one can identify similar patterns (e.g. Interviews with Aboul-Gheit 2017; and Nazily 2018). Other exiters re-accommodated the 'we' by modifying rather than severing ties with the past. They have built friendships with others who had left the Brotherhood before or after 2011. Photos posted on Facebook pages for Aboul-Sa'd and other exiting members show that they were meeting on a regular basis. Captioned with a new 'we', the pictures show how this regularity of contact created solidarity based on sharing the pronoun and all the like-mindedness and similar behaviour disposition associated with it. The solidarity expanded to career activities, making up for the loss of the Brotherhood's membership as a safe economic haven. For example, in a workplace such as the London-based *Al-Araby* TV station, I was able to identify several ex-Brotherhood members, most of whom identified their connectivity also as 'we are friends'. It was a brotherhood based on the ex-Brotherhood.

All these practices support the texturing of the disengagement discourse as represented in the shifts by re-prioritization in the 'I' and 'we' pronouns at different levels. For example, by consolidating friendships with other ex-members, individuals shift the *semanticness* of the 'we' and power relations drawn on it; that is, the 'we' becomes more of a 'solidarity semantic' drawn on a 'symmetrical' relationship based equal reciprocity of power (Brown and Gilman 1960, p. 257). It thus replaces the 'we' of the Brotherhood, denoting a power semantic drawn on hierarchism, whereby some members/friends are endowed with superior power. Obligations of a member in the 'we' of solidarity require cooperation and mutual support, whereas the other 'we' requires subordination to the group's leaders, who are 'people above' (Interview, Nazily 2018; Interview, Aboul-Gheit 2017), a common code used in the group as part of asymmetrical power semantics ritualized and regularized inside the Brotherhood. This is evidenced by images of exiters seated equally in a circle at a local café, a practice banned during their membership in the Brotherhood (Interviews with Nazily 2018 and El-Qassas 2017). Furthermore, the new 'we' of solidarity supported the rise of the 'I' during and after disengagement from the group as it had a therapeutic purpose, drawing on a sense of unembarrassability by repeatability in action. They would share experiences and advice in this interaction, which attributes another level of unity, counterbalancing that of the Brotherhood. Many exiters partly traced their disengagement to a point of contact with exiters (Interview, Aboul-Sa'd 2017). Indeed, many friends, couples or family members entangled in an onerous and restrictive socialization under the Brotherhood also ended up disengaging together or followed one another in departing from the group (e.g. Interviews, Zayed 2017 and El-Shaf'y 2018). By this collectivization of departure, those individuals create a socialization in the very act of de-socialization from the Brotherhood and its circles.

The significance of these new practices such as socialization and re-socialization practices also lies in their power to neutralize or de-actualize the Brotherhood's hegemonic practices including social tools long used to restrict the movability of the 'I' and 'we' to serve its own interests. For example, the group has long asked members to adopt *depersonalization,* defined as 'a shift towards the perception of self as an interchangeable exemplar of some social category and away from the perception of self as a unique person' (Turner et al. 1987, p. 50; see also Goffman 1974). This is made possible as the group controls all means of communication with the 'real kinship' referring to biological family members and 'imagined kinships' referring to friends and all social circles of the outside world ('Eid 2013), and also as the group can punish potential exiters or disgruntled members through 'ostracism', 'boycott' (Interview, Milad 2018) and 'smear campaigns' (Interview, Zaqzouq 2018) or more acutely by 'forced divorce' (Interviews with El-Helbawy 2018 and 'Affan 2018). The group has also long enhanced the exclusive nature of its 'we' by renunciation and communion, described above as two key concepts of its discourse.

Ideological/organizational 'I'

As mentioned above, the 'I' is an expression referring to a presentist texturing phenomenon, supported by current social practices such as social re-assimilation. However, the 'I' is also shaped as individuals were attempting to resist the hegemony of ideological and organizational forces inside the Brotherhood. One major practice symbolizing this evolution of the 'I' is reading. Under the Brotherhood's rules, reading was a controlled collective practice in which the 'we' was both articulated in texts and materialized in the act of reading them. Members, representing the collective 'we', had to read the group's censored and excerpted texts, themselves calling for full commitment to the 'we'. Collectively, they had to do this practice together in supervised weekly sessions of each Brotherhood family. Potential exiters have always attributed their disassociation to occasions where they repeatedly challenged this practice and texts enforced in it as a necessary reading in the past. Mohamed Aboul-Gheit (Interview 2017) began out of curiosity by examining some books by Brotherhood leaders that had been excluded from the group's curricula. His reaction was more of a dialogue with a rising 'I'. The 28-year-old, who announced an end to 21 years of membership in the group in 2011, said: 'I began to ask myself: "Why do they [the leaders of the Brotherhood] not allow us to study even those critical thinkers who are still part of the group?" I found no answers convincing to myself' (Interview, Aboul-Gheit 2017).

Aboul-Gheit's reading habits expanded, taking him to the writings of non-Brotherhood members including, significantly, the Egyptian Nobel laureate,

Naguib Mahfouz, and 'I realized that this magnificent novelist is not against Islam or the group as my leaders has been used to telling me' (Interview, Aboul-Gheit 2017). He took his passion to online forums on unrestricted and uncensored reading. He said, 'Members of the forum gradually encouraged me to read books of different viewpoints. I began to think independently and critically and this led me to disengagement'. Aboul-Gheit provided particular incidents such as him being awarded the 'best participation' prize because of 'my passionate involvement in the activities of the forum' (Interview, Aboul-Gheit 2017). This helped him socially assimilate into a different, non-Brotherhood milieu as he began to attend other activities, such as reading clubs, without the approval of his leader; he also changed his career from being a medical doctor to a journalist/writer, an activity more conducive to the cumulative transformations drawn from his reading habits (ibid.).

Socially, the reading-related practice outside the remit of the Brotherhood triggered or boosted disengagement by creating with it a desire for 'anticipatory socialization', involving the 'adoption of values of a group to which one aspires but does not yet belong' (Merton and Merton 1968, p. 265). More significantly, reading is a cognitive act as it ends the dissonance based on following a line of ideas in the Brotherhood while believing in another line of convergent ideas. For example, Aboul-Sa'd (Interview, 2017) said he began his journey by reading the autobiographies of other exiting members months before effecting his disengagement in 2011. Having said that, disengagement through reading becomes a 'mental process' where individuals could 'stop and think', and this 'mental process' empowered him to disengage from the group and to frame this disengagement itself as an option to be considered (Dewey 1938, p. 62). Reading in these loose, uncontrolled and globalized mediums such as online forums boosts the 'I' by being an individualistic act where each member can 'frame purposes, to judge wisely, to evaluate desires by the consequences which will result from acting upon them' (pp. 63–4).

Again, one can find in the language of texts evidence of the *ideologized* evolution of the 'I' as part of thematized meanings first drawn in the mind of each reading member. There is much space dedicated to showing the relationship with the Brotherhood as a battle of minds; i.e., the 'I' mind against the 'we' mind. Take this repeated and frequent mention of the word itself across autobiographies: The book is an attempt to 'take my mind out of any attempts to freeze it' (El-'Agouz 2012, p. 8); the book is a 'search for my critical mind' ('Abdel-Mon'im 2011, p. 210); the book is 'the by-product of half my mind, as the group destroyed the other half' (Ban 2013, p. 7). Ban included in his autobiography his full resignation letter, from February 2012, which mentions how 'the group fixated in my mind some unreasonable and unjustified facts which we have to abide by for the sake of promotion into its ranks' (p. 256).

Intertextually, part of the resonance of this mind-based juxtaposition is in its relationship with the Brotherhood's hegemonic discourse, where the 'we' is always described as a 'mind-liberating' force or, to go with the metaphor, the 'group has a mind'. By being a full member, the first pillar of the 'Oath of Allegiance' which every member has to take is called 'Comprehension', a faculty which draws on the use of mind, as the group's founder also stressed on several occasions, to show how the group's ideology 'liberates the mind' (El-Banna 1990, p. 393). Therefore, exiting members engaged in full force to show in their narrativization the dissonance between claims and practises in the Brotherhood's framing process of the mind. They mentioned occasions where claims of comprehension were overrun by the *Al-Sam' wal T'a* ('hearing and obedience') principle, which is included in 'obedience' as the 6th pillar of the Oath of Allegiance. They showed how they had clashes with rules warning them not to get involved in debating 'meanings of the Quran' or to discuss subjects that were controversial in Islam, such as the historical disagreements between disciples of Prophet Muhammad. They criticized aspects of the cultivation curriculum, stressing 'the necessity of bringing Muslims together around a single interpretation of Islam' and 'turn[ing] away from debate and arguments' (cited in Kandil 2014, p. 30). Expectedly, many exiting members dedicated large parts of their texts to re-interpreting the Quran or sanctified events long stabilized inside the group as part of its hegemonic discourse (e.g. 'Eid 2014a, b). This practice of re-interpretation supports the 'I' and challenges the 'we' as it ends the group's rules of 'same-saying', where everyone has to accept its version of truth to avoid *fitna* ('division') (Amghar and Khadiyatoulah 2017, p. 62) and get involved in a 'systematic search for consensus (*ijma*)' (ibid.).

The significance of the frame based on the mind reference also serves the rise of the 'I' through one other way: metonymy. In texts, many former members used the mind and brain not as separate entities but indistinctively and interchangeably (e.g. one recurring description in autobiographies is 'the group is a body without the brain part of it'). This signals that the mind is only a 'part' of the whole of the Brotherhood's 'body', or what Lakoff and Johnsen (1980, pp. 37–8) refer to as 'the part for the whole'. The metonymy serves the framing process by adding 'salience' based on 'selection' of characteristics of the group (Entman 1993, p. 52) as highlighted by exiting members. In other words, 'which part we pick out determines which aspect of the whole we are focusing on' (Lakoff and Johnsen 1980, p. 36).

As examples mentioned above indicate, ex-members highlight certain aspects of what was being referred to in the ideological disengagement. When they thought of the Brotherhood's 'mind', ex-members were not thinking of it, in and of itself. They thought of it in terms of its relation with the group's lacking power of imagination, recognition, appreciation, the ability to process different views or new ideas in which the 'I' ness of individual members could develop. In addition, the metonymical use of the mind as one key part of the body coheres well with other forms of physicality conveyed in the framing processes, through such metaphors as slavery, imprisonment, emancipation and breathing which were alluded to earlier. It is this coherence which conveys the meaning that the Brotherhood fully controls the different parts of the 'body' of its members to ensure the full submission of the 'I'.

This metonymical use of the mind and body to refer to the Brotherhood as an ideology supports the articulation of the 'I' as a key frame in the disengagement process through personification. Viewing something as abstract and theoretical as ideology in human terms thus has an explanatory power of the sort that makes sense to most people. This not only gives a 'specific way of thinking' about ideology, now being a person with a body and a brain/mind, but also a way of 'acting toward it' (Lakoff and Johnsen 1980, pp. 33–4). In individual disengagements from the Brotherhood, exiting members could see the whole group or its ideology as another 'person' who could be attacked, hurt or even destroyed as an adversary, at least at the discursive level.

The political 'I'

The sections above have demonstrated the movability of the 'I' either as a moment of articulation in texts, and a moment of materialization in concrete real social practices such as the way exiting members talk, get dressed or re-socialize as well as the way they *re-ideologize* by adopting new frames of constituent thematized meanings in acts such as reading. Still, all these processes of textual articulation and social materialization are mainly internal, i.e., they relate to the workings and dynamics of interaction between individuals and the group or interpretation of meanings agreed or contested between them. This section will seek to prove that the 'I' was enabled at both levels *externally* by political practices that Egypt has witnessed since 2011. These practices included mass protests leading to the resignation of Mubarak on February 2011; the rise of the Brotherhood to power, culminating in the election of Morsi in June 2012 after long decades of only challenging it; and the dramatic loss of power, as military leader Abdel-Fatah El-Sissi led a coup against them in 2013. It was within these events, including changes pertaining to the Brotherhood by challenging, gaining and losing power, that the 'I' found an opportunity to be better articulated and resources to be fully materialized or operationalized within the workings of the surrounding environment. If I have been oversimplifying the process of disengagement through the prism of the personal, social and ideological/organizational facets of its emergence, this section could be seen as a pronouncement of the rise of the political 'I'.

During the time period that began with protests that erupted in 25 January 2011 and ended with the resignation of Mubarak three weeks later, the 'I' and discourse related to it gained salience due to a number of reasons. First, the nature of the revolution itself was conducive to the rise of this pronoun/frame. Unlike the revolutionary movements that had emerged around the world in the 1960s and 1970s, which espoused a powerful 'socialist, anti-imperialist and anticapitalist, and social justice impulse' (Bayat 2017, p. 11) the Egyptian revolution was preoccupied with issues that relate to what is 'personal' (Idle et al. 2011, p. 10). Protestors raised slogans on the 'I'-related issues such as human rights and personal identity (especially as many of these slogans were individually and spontaneously constructed during the protests). Second, the revolution was leaderless, which means that the 'I' became emancipated from restraints imposed by the state and the Brotherhood as they both are hierarchical entities always seeking to collectivize or suppress the 'I' for the sake of the 'we'. In this atmosphere, marked with a 'lack of ideology, lax coordination, [and the] absence of any galvanizing leadership and intellectual precepts' (Interview, Lutfy 2017), many individual members of the Brotherhood challenged their leaders' orders not take part in protests or to go home. Responding to internal pressures without losing fears of revenge in case the regime did not fall down, the group's leaders asked members to participate in protests 'on individual basis' (Hadeyah 2011a), which unprecedentedly boosted the pronoun by decoupling it from the collective 'we'. Indeed, it was a moment of the efficacy of 'I' inside the Brotherhood, as the 'we' was too cumbersome as the 'body of the movement is too big, to be mobilized in such a short time' (Beshara 2016, p. 397). The discourse of the Brotherhood became cracked and less unified as many members now saw it as 'hesitant', 'confused' and 'contradictory' (Interviews with Nazily 2018 and Lutfy 2017). On the other hand, many of the group's members, especially younger ones, joined another 'we' of a more nationalist and less Islamist identity that was more organized and well coordinated by secular forces. However, this alternative 'we' did not intend to overcome the 'I'. If anything, it might have been the opposite. With the occupation of Tahrir Square, the 'I' gained another boost due to the dominant sense of ownership of both place and 'self', drawing an unprecedented feeling of entitlement. Exiters narrated occasions where, by getting 'fully and somehow independently' (Interview, Nazily 2018) involved in organizing the Tahrir sit-in, they gained power over their Brotherhood leaders as they, to borrow from Volpi and Jasper (2018, pp. 15–16), now became key players with their own arena, to share goals and identities with others. 'Had I not intervened to talk with fellow organizers to let them in, those Brotherhood leaders would not be there,' said Nazily (Interview, 2018). The forty-year-old, who exited the group in 2011 after thirty-five years of membership, showed me a picture of himself, leading two senior Brotherhood figures at the square. All such forms of horizontality, marked with an aversion to representation and decentralized forms of power, allowed members to de-emphasize the Brotherhood's 'we'. For example, leading young members of the Brotherhood ensured that the group raised none of its slogans during the protests and that their senior leaders had no hegemonic or 'too much presence' in the discourse delivered on the main podium in the middle of Tahrir Square (Beshara 2016, p. 503). This was another manifestation not only of the battle of discourses between the group and its disgruntled members (and soon-to-be exes). It was a battle of pronouns since the square showed no collective identity other than the sum of all 'I'-symbolized individuated identities of its occupants (i.e. ordinary protestors).

The fall of Mubarak witnessed the return of the Brotherhood as a strong political force making its way into power. Still, this did not dissipate the rise of the 'I'. Many of its members who played leading roles during the early days of the protests demanded to take the revolution inside the group. In March 2011, around 300 Brotherhood members took the individual initiative and publicly met in one of Cairo's big hotels to hold a conference despite the objection of the group's leaders. Demands were mostly all related to internal reform based on 'meritocracy not loyalty', an end to 'hearing and obedience' and democratization in the sense put by one participant as such: 'I have a voice and I want to be heard' (*Alahram2009* 2011). As the Brotherhood ignored these demands, as part of its 'apathy towards freedom of expression' and 'authoritarian repression of Egyptian plurality and diversity through the state censorship of almost all platforms of expression' (Mohamed and Momani 2014, p. 206), subsequent individual disengagements of many of those who had participated in the conference took place.

More political events benefitted attempts to regain the 'I'. In March 2011, the same month as the conference, the Supreme Council of the Armed Forces, which had taken over after the resignation of Mubarak, introduced the Political Party Law, which eased restrictions on the legal establishment of new political parties in Egypt. This led Mohamed Habib to apply for the foundation of his political party in July of the same year, and his application came only two days after announcing his resignation from the Brotherhood, ending a thirty-five-year membership in it (Hadeyah 2011b). Other leaders also exited the group, directly joined newly founded political forces such as *Al-Tayyar Al-Masry* and *El-Nahda*, and then ran in the presidential elections, against the desire of the group's leaders.

Another opportunity, and a source for the rise of the 'I', arose when the Brotherhood took power after the election of Morsi. Many members felt disillusioned as the group had become institutionalized and its authentic or uncompromising face, based on an original contentious position was diluted by negotiating with or co-opting Mubarak's old state. Its leaders also faced accusations of losing the utopian impetus drawn from serving the 'Islamic project', and politically unskilled as they failed to translate their social and religious successes into political influence. By dominating the same political system they had long sought to challenge, those leaders served their own self-interests, according to one of the main arguments made in the texts under study. The description considering Morsi as another face of Mubarak permeates the texts of exiting members and is also substantiated by examples of corruption and nepotism based on forming a kind of nomenclatura or a Muslim 'aristocratic elite' (Amghar and Khadiyatoulah 2017, p. 63). The allegation is based on claims that the leaders exclusively shared among themselves state positions and privileges after coming to power (see Mohamed and Momani's references on 'Brotherhoodization' 2014, pp. 20507). Disillusionment with leaders continued after the coup against Morsi, where the group involved in internal division among leaders representing 'two Brotherhoods'. If anything, the 'we', long boasted inside the Brotherhood as the basis of unity and consensus and according to which each leader could be a plural 'we' in the sense of being a 'summation of his people and can speak as their representative', was fragmented into more than one 'we'. The sanctified 'we' lost its reverential position and those 'earthly self-serving leaders' (Interview, El-Sawah 2017) were denied the exclusivity of religion, which was their strongest source of legitimacy, appeal, mobilization and, indeed, existence. El-Sawah regretted that his one-year imprisonment along with the group's leaders increased his disillusionment as the latter 'sounded to me selfish, hesitant and ignorant' (ibid.). Gone was the sense of comaraderie, resulting from a common fate or a common task involved in belonging to the 'we'. Exiting members othered the Brotherhood leaders as impersonal, collective subjects, pronominally categorized as 'they'. These are random quotes from different interviews: 'They told us,' (ibid.), 'they nominated a weak stupid candidate' (Interview, Lutfy 2017), 'they frantically changed their views' (Interview, Saber 2017) and 'they asked us to adopt their wrong decisions' (Interview, Nazily 2018).

This switch into the opposite pronoun distances the speaker furthermore from the referents that are their former leaders, and it also makes expressions of anger and disapproval stronger than expressions of sympathy. Demands to 'hold those leaders into account' as they were responsible for mistakes of the past including the 'blood of Brotherhood victims spilt' in clashes with police forces during the Brotherhood-staged Rabi'a Al-'Adawiyya sit-in after the coup (Interview, Saber 2017).

Remarkably, the state, consciously or not, partially has supported the rise of the pronoun 'I' and the related texturing of it. It is less suspicious and more tolerant of exiting individuals as evident in the fact that some of these interviews were conducted in Egypt and at a time the state was escalating its crackdown of detention, torture and assassinations against the Brotherhood's existing members. The state's biggest and main publishing house unprecedentedly published the autobiography of 'Abdel-Mon'im (2011). This support has taken a more systematic shape as the state has appropriated its control of tools of cultural capital to serve the publicizing and circulation of exiters' perspectives, ideas and products. For example, the state's heavily censored mouthpiece, the newspaper *Al-Ahram*, has opened space to 'Abdel-Mon'im to express some of her views through a genre other than the autobiography. The state also granted her the prestigious State Encouragement Award. To build on Bourdieu's classifications (2011), these state resources have allowed 'Abdel-Mon'im and her texturing on disengagement to possess the three aspects of 'states' of 'cultural capital': (1) the 'objectified' state, e.g., widely publicized novels in her name; (2) the 'institutionalized' state, e.g., by being recognized and accredited as a novelist (a title which, in her autobiography, she blamed the Brotherhood for depriving her of and (3) the 'embodied' state, which can now control her means of communication and self-presentation. What these 'states' share is providing the individual disengagements with 'publicness', which make them 'effective' and 'legitimized' (van Dijk 1988, p. 183). The texturing of 'Abdel-Mon'im was supported by what Bourdieu conceptualized as economic and social capital. For example, 'Abdel-Mon'im boastfully acknowledged on her Facebook page a recent trip to Spain where she had networked and promoted her writings by giving talks and making media appearances. She continued to post news about new awards added to her name or new editions of her novels being printed. In contrast, the state drained the Brotherhood's 'existing' members of all these forms of capital by such actions as confiscating their properties or banning the group's media outlets.

The state also boosted the 'I' by expanding its wave of arrests to thousands of ordinary members of the Brotherhood. This has deprived the leaders, who had been the ones targeted by regimes such as Mubarak's, of claiming legitimacy on the basis of representing and safeguarding the 'we' through their own self-sacrifice (El-Nawawy and Elmasry 2018). For example, the wide-spread detention campaigns unprecedently included many female members of the group. This has led to demands for a bigger say in running the affairs of the male-dominated group. These demands are all about an attempt to regain the 'I' exactly like the ones identified in the texts of exiting members. Biagini, who closely and insightfully investigated the internal dynamics of engagement inside the Brotherhood after 2013, quoted a female member challenging the orders of her male leaders as such: 'It is my role to be there! I am part of society and I am part of this group' (Biagini 2017, p. 9). In these sentences, as well as others cited by Biagini, the 'I' pronoun enjoys the same levels of salience by such textural features as intensity or overwording as well as sociopolitical practices such as sharing decision-making.

Nevertheless, the state's rewards came at the price of limited access to politics. El-Qassas, a deputy leader of the *Misr Al-Qawia* ('Strong Egypt') whom I interviewed in 2016, was arrested two years later, in February 2018, on charges of 'serving the goals of a banned movement' [in reference to the Brotherhood] (*Al Jazeera* 2020). Aboul-Futouh, who founded the party and magnetically attracted many exiting members of the Brotherhood, was also detained at the same time after publicly criticizing President El-Sisi in a TV interview. The opportunity which the party offered to exiters, especially given its inclusion of reference to Islam in its platform and which made it a more convincing alternative for Brotherhood members not seeking a full 'discursive rupture' with their past, was lost. Furthermore, the state's coupling of members and ex-members in its campaign against the Brotherhood could sound like throwing the baby out with the bath water. Many exiters narrated how the disengagement of Aboul-Futouh (still in prison at the time of writing this chapter in January 2020), a charismatic influential character taken as a mentor especially among young Islamists including those I interviewed, was a key factor facilitating their own disassociation. Even more, many exiters took part in his presidential campaign in 2012, where he ran against the Brotherhood's candidate, Morsi, and also joined his party, *Misr Al Qawia*, whose platform calls for 'respect for individuals freedoms', 'the right of self-expression' and 'participatory democracy' (*Misr Al Qawia Party* n.d.). His detention therefore could send mixed messages affecting the pace of disengagement from the Brotherhood.

Conclusion

This chapter has sought to cover a lacuna in Brotherhood-related literature by exploring the group from the outside in and by taking individuals, i.e., exiting members, as the main points of reference. The benefit of this change of direction is well worth it as it leads to new and significant findings, one of which is that disengagement is about the rise of the 'I' – not merely based on changes in structural tactics of recruitment or dynamics of association. The findings could not have been possible without the adoption of critical discourse analysis, as the 'I' pronoun is not merely a deictic construction. It is a discursive event attached to texts, practices, rules and relations within, across and beyond texts of exiting members. The 'I' has been analysed semantically in its interaction and interpretation against its plural, the 'we' symbolizing engagement in and belonging to the Brotherhood. By bringing an interest in the centrality of both discourses such as the one carried in this functional language of pronouns and the individuals shaping or being shaped by it, I hope to raise to the attention of other researchers the notion that disengagement can be less of a process of well-defined stages or easily demarcated turning points. Fragmented, random or arbitrary experiences of individual disengagements which are always discarded in other scholars' search for systematisity in analysis, were found to be useful in the analysis done here. Even more, disengagement itself can occur in and by texts which carry these experiences.

However, the rise of the 'I' as detailed above is not a matter of texts or semantics. It is a matter of social practices, where objectivized relations, interests and rules pertaining to the group, its structure or ideology, as well as pertaining to the state, have actualized and materialized any shifts or transformations in the *pronoun-ing*. The actualizing or materializing context, for example, provides structural opportunities such as the geographic re-spatialization of power from the Brotherhood's head office in Muqatam, at the outskirts of Cairo, to Tahrir Square in the capital's centre and where members feel freer to act. Tahrir Square also provides discursive opportunities where the 'I' integrates into a new 'we' drawn from unique sentiments of community or togetherness, counterbalancing those of the Brotherhood. For example, the slogans and chants in Tahrir Square stood as both an interpretive tool and a subjective opening where members of the Brotherhood repeat wordings no longer hierarchically made or approved by their group. Despite the fact that the 'we' of the square was also building another collectivity that can chain the individual to a collective structure or mentality, it was uniquely personalized. The rise of the 'I' pronoun therefore has a cognitive correlation as it was grounded in what Castells calls the 'fundamental psychological mechanism to overcome fear' (2015, p. 10) of challenging both Mubarak's regime and the Brotherhood's regime at the same time. By treating the revolution as spaces of autonomy that provide 'sufficient resources' (Melucci 2001, p. 71) for individuals, the 'I' has found the opportunity to rise and thrive. The fact that the 'I' has gained this centrality of position by positive evaluation as a tool of 'emancipation' associated with practical steps of re-assimilation and re-accommodation could justify my interest in extending this research into identity-making processes associated with the discursive processes of disengagement.

Notes

1   All interviewees identified by a name and date can be found in Table 5.1. I am grateful to the insights provided by Mahmoud Sha'ban, an Istanbul-based journalist and researcher on political Islam, during my fieldwork.

2   On the Brotherhood's official English-language website, it explains its structure as follows: 'The MB group does exist in all the classes, from the upper one to the lower, but it's mostly dominant in the middle one, which is the main source for recruitment' (Muslim Brotherhood 2007).

3   Thanks to Professor Nathan Brown for the illuminating comments provided during our informal chat in Doha as part of discussing the findings of my fieldwork.

References

'Abdel-Mon'im, I. (2011). *Hekayati ma' Al-Ikhwan* ['My story with the Muslim Brotherhood']. Cairo: Al-Hayaa Al-Misriyya Al-'ama leil Kitab.

Abed-Kotob, S. (1995). 'The accommodationists speak: Goals and strategies of the Muslim Brotherhood of Egypt', *International Journal of Middle East Studies*, 27 (3),pp. 321–39. Available at: http://www.jstor.org/stable/176254 [accessed 29 October 2018].

Alahram2009. (2011). 'Mu'atamar Shabab Al-Ikhwan' ['Conference of Muslim Brotherhoods youth'], 28 March. Available at: https://www.youtube.com/watch?v=nKD9vrrKseU [accessed 29 October 2018].

Al-Anani, K. (2016). *Inside the Muslim Brotherhood: Religion, identity, and politics*. Oxford: Oxford University Press.

Al-Awadi, H. (2013). 'Islamists in power: The case of the Muslim Brotherhood in Egypt', *Contemporary Arab Affairs*, 6(4), pp. 539–51.

Al Jazeera. (2020). 'Tajdid habs al-Qassas naeb hezb 'Misr al-Qawiyya' ['Renewing the arrest of El-Qassas, the deputy leader of the Strong Egypt Party'], 22 January. Available at: http://bitly.ws/cUMz [accessed 21 April 2021].

Altaghieer. (2012). 'El-Helbawy Yualen Istiqalatahu 'ala Al-Hawaa' ['El-Helbawy announces his resignation live'], 31 March. Available at: https://www.youtube.com/watch?v=PyAX7tVBAzs [accessed 10 September 2018].

Amghar, S. and Khadiyatoulah, F. (2017). 'Disillusioned militancy: The crisis of militancy and variables of disengagement of the European Muslim Brotherhood', *Mediterranean Politics*, 22(1), pp. 54–70.

Bakhtin, M.M. (1981). *The dialogic imagination: Four essays*. Edited by M. Holquist and C. Emerson, translated by M. Holquist. Austin: University of Texas Press.

Ban, A. (2013). *Al-Ikhwan al-muslimoon wa mehnat al-watan wal deen* ['The Muslim Brotherhood and the predicament of nation and religion']. Cairo: Al-Neel Centre for Strategic Studies.

Bayat, A. (2017). *Revolution without revolutionaries: Making sense of the Arab Spring*. Stanford, CA: Stanford University Press.

Beshara, A. (2016). *Thawret Masr: Men Jumhuryet Yulyu ella Thawret Yanayir* ['The Egyptian Revolution: From Egypt's July revolution to January 25 revolution'], vol. I. Beirut: Arab Center for Research and Policy Studies.

Biagini, E. (2017). 'The Egyptian Muslim Sisterhood between violence, activism and leadership', *Mediterranean Politics*, 22 (1), pp. 35–53. Available at: http://doi.org/10.1080/13629395.2016.1230943.

Bourdieu, P. (2011). 'The forms of capital (1986)', in I. Szeman. and and T. Kaposy (eds.) *Cultural theory: An anthology*, pp. 81–93. West Sussex, UK: John Wiley and Sons.

Bromley, D.G. (1998). 'The social construction of contested exit roles: Defectors, whistle-blowers, and apostates, in Bromley', in D.G. Bromley (ed.) *The politics of religious apostasy: The role of apostates in the transformation of religious movements*, pp. 19–48. London: Praeger.

Brown, R. and Gilman, A. (1960). 'The pronouns of power and solidarity', in T.A. Sebeok (ed.) *Style in language*, pp. 253–76. Cambridge, MA: MIT Press.

Castells, M. (2013). *Communication power*. Oxford: Oxford University Press.

Castells, M. (2015). *Networks of outrage and hope: Social movements in the Internet age*. Cambridge, UK: Polity Press.

Denzin, N.K. (1978). *The research act: A theoretical introduction to sociological methods.* New York: Praeger.

Denzin, N.K. and Lincoln, Y.S. (2005). 'Introduction: The discipline and practice of qualitative research', in K. Denzin and Y. S. Lincoln (eds.) *The Sage handbook of qualitative research* (3rd ed.), pp. 1–28. Thousand Oaks, CA: Sage.

Dewey, J. (1938). *Experience and education.* New York: Touchstone.

'Eid, S. (2013). *Tajribati fi Saradeeb Al-Ikhwan* ['My experience in the basements of the Muslim Brotherhood']. Cairo: Jazeerat Al-Ward.

'Eid, S. (2014a). *Al-ikhwan Al-muslimoon: Al-hader wal Mustaqbal, Awraq fil Naqd Al-zati* ['The Muslim Brotherhood: The present and the future: Papers from self-criticism']. Cairo: Al-Mahrousa.

'Eid, S. (2014b). *Qissati ma' Al-Ikhwan* ['My story with the Muslim Brotherhood']. Cairo: Mahrousa.

El-'Agouz, A. (2012). *Ikhwani Out of The Box* ['A Muslim brother out of the box']. Cairo: Dewan.

El-Banna, H. (1990). *Majmu't Rasael Al-Imam El-Shahid Hassan El-Banna* ['A collection of epistles of the Martyr Imam Hassan El-Banna']. Alexandria, Egypt: Da'wa.

El-Banna, H. (2012). *Muzakerat Al-d'awa wal Da'ia* ['The memoirs of the preaching and the preacher']. Kuwait: Afaq.

El-Khirbawy, T. (2012). *Ser Al-M'abad: Al-Asrar al-khafiya li gama't Al-Ikhwan Al-Muslemeen* ['The temple's secret: The hidden secrets of the Muslim Brotherhood']. Cairo: Nahdet Masr.

El-Nawawy, M. and Elmasry, M.H. (2018). *Revolutionary Egypt in the eyes of the Muslim Brotherhood: A framing analysis of Ikhwanweb.* Lanham, MD: Rowman and Littlefield.

Entman, R.M. (1993). 'Framing: Toward clarification of a fractured paradigm', *Journal of Communication*, 43(4), pp. 51–58.

Fairclough, N. (1992). *Discourse and social change.* Cambridge: Polity Press.

Fayez, S. (2011). *Janat Al-Ikhwan: Rehlat al-khuroug min al-gam'a* ['The Muslim Brotherhood paradise: The journey of getting out of the group']. Cairo: Al-Tanweer.

Fesmire, S.A. (1994). 'Aerating the mind: The metaphor of mental functioning as bodily functioning', *Metaphor and Symbolic Activity*, 9 (1), pp. 31–44. Available at: http://doi.org/10.1207/s15327868ms0901_2.

Fillieule, O. (2015). 'Disengagement from radical organizations: A process and multilevel model of analysis', in B. Klandermans and C. Van Stralen (eds.) *Movements in times of democratic transition*, pp. 34–63. Philadelphia, PA: Temple University Press.

Gamson, W.A. (1995). 'Constructing social protests', in H. Johnston and B. Klandermans (eds.) *Social Movements and Culture*, vol. 4, pp. 85–106. Minneapolis: University of Minnesota Press.

Gerges, F. (2018). *Making the Arab World: Nasser, Qutb, and the clash that shaped the Middle East.* Princeton, NJ: Princeton University Press.

Goffman, E. (1974). *Frame analysis: An essay on the organization of experience.* Cambridge: Cambridge University Press.

Hadeyah, S. (2011a). 'Al-Ikhwan tuhadid 3 dawabet leil musharaka fi muzaharat 25 Yanayir' ['The Muslim Brotherhood sets three rules for taking part in the January 25 protests'], *Youm7*, 23 January. Available at: http://bitly.ws/cULL [accessed 23 April 2021].

Hadeyah, S. (2011b). 'Istiqalat Mohammed Habeeb min al-Ikhwan wa endhimamih ella hizb al-nahdhah' ['Mohammed Habeeb resigns from the Muslim Brotherhood and joins al-Nahdhah Party'], *Youm7*, 13 July. Available at: https://bit.ly/2EpSQBO [accessed 29 October 2018].

Haley, A. (1978). *Roots*. New York: Doubleday.

Halliday, M.A.K. (1985). *An Introduction to functional grammar* (1st ed.). London: Edward Arnold.

Hunt, S.A. Benford, R.D. and Snow, D.A. (1994). 'Identity fields: Framing processes and the social construction of movement identities', in E. Laraña, J.R. Gusfield and H. Johnston (eds.) *New social movements: From ideology to identity*, pp. 185–208. Philadelphia, PA: Temple University Press.

Idle, N., Nunns, A. and Soueif, A. (2011). *Tweets from Tahrir*. New York: OR Books.

Introvigne, M. (1999). 'Defectors, ordinary leave-takers, and apostates: A quantitative study of former members of New Acropolis in France', *Nova Religio: The Journal of Alternative and Emergent Religions*, 3(1), pp. 83–99.

Kandil, H. (2014). *Inside the Brotherhood*. Cambridge, UK: Polity Press.

Lakoff, G. and Johnson, M. (1980). *Metaphors we live by*. London: University of Chicago Press.

Lia, B. (1998). *The Society of the Muslim Brothers in Egypt: The rise of an Islamic mass movement, 1928-1942*. Reading, UK: Ithaca Press.

Melucci, A. (2001). 'Becoming a person: New frontiers for identity and citizenship in a planetary society', in M. Kohli and A. Woodward (eds.) *Inclusions and exclusions in European societies*, pp. 71–86. London: Routledge.

Menshawy, M. (2017). *State, memory, and Egypt's Victory in the 1973 War: Ruling by discourse*. Cham, Switzerland: Palgrave.

Menshawy, M. (2019). 'Constructing state, territory, and sovereignty in the Syrian conflict', *Politics*, 39(3), pp. 332–46.

Menshawy, M. (2020). *Leaving the Muslim Brotherhood: Self, society and the state*. Cham, Switzerland: Palgrave.

Merton, R.K. and Merton, R.C. (1968). *Social theory and social structure*. New York: Simon and Schuster.

Misr Al Qawia Party. (n.d.) [Facebook]. [The official party page]. Available at: https://www.facebook.com/MisrAlQawia [accessed 12 December 2020].

Mitchell, R.P. (1969). *The Society of the Muslim Brothers*. London: Oxford University Press.

Mohamed, E. and Momani, B. (2014). 'The Muslim Brotherhood: Between democracy, ideology and distrust', *Sociology of Islam*, 2(3-4), pp. 196–212.

Muslim Brotherhood. (2007). 'Structure & Spread', Ikhwanweb: The Muslim Brotherhood's Official English Website, 13 June. Available at: http://www.ikhwanweb.com/article.php?id=817 [accessed 23 April 2021].

Skalli, L.H. (2011). 'Constructing Arab female leadership: Lessons from the Moroccan media', *Gender and Society*, 25 (4), pp. 473–95. Available at: http://doi.org/10.1177/0891243211411051

Skovgaard-Petersen, J. and Gräf, B. (eds.). (2009). *Global mufti: The phenomenon of Yusuf al-Qaradawi*. New York: Hurst/Cambridge University Press.

Tarrow, S. and Tilly, C. (2015). *Contentious politics*. Oxford: Oxford University Press.

Turner, J.C., Hogg, M.A., Oakes, P.J., Reicher, S.D. and Wetherell, M.S. (1987). *Rediscovering the social group: A self-categorization theory*. Oxford: Blackwell.

Van Dijk, T.A. (1980). *Macrostructures: An interdisciplinary study of global structures in discourse, interaction, and cognition*. New Jersey: Lawrence Erlbaum Associates.

Van Dijk, T.A. (1988). 'Semantics of a press panic: The Tamil invasion', *European Journal of Communication*, 3(2), pp. 167–87.

Van Dijk, T.A. (1998). *Ideology: A multidisciplinary approach*. London: Sage.

Volpi, F. and Jasper, J.M. (eds.) (2018). *Microfoundations of the Arab uprisings: Mapping interactions between regimes and protesters*. Amsterdam: Amsterdam University Press.
Watts, R. J. (2003). *Politeness*. Cambridge: Cambridge University Press.
Wickham, C.R. (2013). *The Muslim Brotherhood: Evolution of an Islamist movement*. Princeton, NJ: Princeton University Press.
Zollner, B. (2009). *The Muslim Brotherhood: Hasan al-Hudaybi and ideology*. London: Routledge.

Chapter 7

HYBRIDITY AND ONLINE PUBLIC SPHERES AFTER THE ARAB SPRING: THE CASE OF RASEEF22

Azza El Masri

The so-called 'Arab Spring' uprisings, which saw Arabs demanding social justice, democracy and basic human rights in 2011 across Tunisia, Egypt, Bahrain, Yemen, Libya and Syria, and their consequent failure (Achcar 2016), propelled liberal Arab millennials to find new spaces where they could deliberate and reconcile their hybrid identities. Indeed, with the advent of globalization and the internationalization of communication, Arab millennials grew up embracing liberal Western principles, which they fused with their Arab perceptions and realities. However, the failure of the upheavals, which were by and large sparked by youths, has left Arab millennials with an inability to reconcile their values with their realities.

In 2013, a new independent digital website called Raseef22 (Arabic for 'sidewalk 22'), provided a platform where Arab identity could be negotiated at the intersection of politics, culture, economy and lifestyle across the twenty-two Arab countries. In turn, Raseef22 promised to create an online public sphere where millennial concerns about and perspectives on Arab realities could be shared without fear of persecution in their respective countries.

Indeed, this would not be possible if it was not based in Beirut, Lebanon. One of the smallest countries in the Middle East, Lebanon enjoys the freest media, the highest literacy rate and the largest ethnic diversity in the region. Whereas traditional media is scrutinized by outdated laws that date as far back as 1962, digital journalism remains an area outside of government jurisdiction, allowing considerable freedom to publish online. Local and pan-Arab traditional media, with the exception of a few countries, is government-owned and strictly censored. Thus, the Internet provides an opportunity for urban Arab youths to exchange opinions, perspectives and ideas.

This chapter will examine the hybridity of Raseef22's journalists and audiences, through a qualitative content analysis of twelve articles published between 13 March and 4 April 2017. More importantly, the chapter will provide tentative answers to the following research questions: Can independent media platforms break the trend of traditional media dependency for young Arab publics? Did the uprisings of 2011 help create a new pan-Arab public sphere where controversial issues such as sex, censorship and religion can be laid bare?

Habermas and the public sphere(s)

In his seminal work, Habermas argued that the rise of early modern capitalism led to the creation of 'the bourgeois public sphere' (1989, p. xvi). Indeed, the conditions that facilitated this phenomenon were the rise of private poverty, literary influences, coffee houses and salons and an independent, market-based press (ibid.). In that sense, Habermas characterized the public sphere as separate from the state, the formal economy and the family, where private individuals come together to deliberate over the current state of political, economic and social affairs within a rational-critical framework.

This definition, which has been largely adopted since its first translation, has given rise to numerous questions on the scope of the public sphere and its representativeness. Indeed, the main critique of this definition is that it is too narrow due to its inability to recognize the existence of multiple publics (Breese 2011; Fraser 1990). This is partly due to a paradigm shift in cultural and global communication research towards a more postmodern understanding of the world that recognizes the multiplicity of realities, depending on which viewpoint is adopted. Indeed, Fraser reimagines a model of the public sphere that goes beyond the bourgeois and recognizes the existence of multiple publics in modern society. However, Fraser (1990, p. 68) contends, publics take on different forms depending on the type of society, of which there are two. The first is a stratified society, where inequality is rampant and structured, leading to the creation of *counterpublics*. Counterpublics exist in 'a subordinate position to the dominant class' (Breese 2011, p. 131). In that sense, counterpublics arise from a position of dissent to the dominant bourgeois class and function as spaces where one's marginalization produces counter-discourses of revolt, dissent and emancipation. On the other hand, Fraser (1990, p. 72) notes the abstract existence of a more egalitarian modern state that is classless, where political dissent is replaced by a more civic understanding of the public sphere.

However, a more definitive framework and typography has been proposed by Breese (2011, p. 134), who places public spheres on two continua: scale and content. Indeed, the author posits that the public sphere appears on a spectrum with face-to-face interaction on one end and symbolic or mediated interaction on another, with varying degrees of civic or political orientation. Breese's framework comes as an answer to a general inconsistency in research, offering academics the opportunity to detach themselves from Habermas' narrow definition. Following in Fraser's footsteps, Breese recognizes the postmodern conceptualization of the public sphere into multiple public spheres, articulated on different scales and included in different spaces (e.g., institutions, media, groups.) where 'discourse, action, representation, and criticism' are presented and negotiated. The author places Habermas' conception in the *political* public sphere. In that realm exist social movements, groups that take political action and media that act as watchdogs of the state. *Civic* public spheres, on the other hand, are most notably exemplified by civic associations, voluntary organizations, as well as social clubs. In that sense, civic publics' goal is to promote unity and 'camaraderie' in society, while affiliation to political publics is an act of 'solidarity' (p. 136). The conceptualization of the public sphere has endured changes since its first introduction in the late twentieth century, but the role of the press – both traditional and new – in the creation, reproduction or dismantling of publics deserves a more scrutinizing examination.

Mass media and the reinvention of the public sphere

Habermas' (1989) conception of the role of mass media in the public sphere comes from a position of scepticism that recognizes the barriers to access set up by media organizations that prop up certain interest groups' agendas that usually do not match the interests or will of the people. An exception, however, is when mass media serve as platforms for civil society groups during times of mass mobilization and crises. Habermas' understanding, while not comprehensive, echoes critical communication scholars' examination of mass media under a neoliberal system and its ramifications on public opinion (Downing 2014; Harvey 2005; McChesney 2004). Indeed, in a neoliberal context, mass media enter the free market. The ultimate objective, then, is to turn media outlets such as television channels and newspapers into economies of scale. In other words, the bottom line weighs more than the media's role of disseminating accurate and fair information. This is brought on by a wave of media concentration wherein horizontal and vertical integrations effectively have eroded competition, in favour of what McChesney (2004) calls an oligarchic media system. What, then, can be the consequences of such developments on the public sphere?

As corporate interests continue to play an active role in influencing the news media (Beers 2004), the voices that receive coverage and whose representation is legitimized are further filtered, away from the public's will. In turn, these representations and biases exert their own pressures on public opinion, which is then moulded to fit the corporate interests. Schulz (1997) refers to mass media as the gatekeepers of the public sphere. Editorial boards pressured by executives in a concentrated media environment decide which public actors gain access and whose voice merits projection. As has been demonstrated repeatedly, mass media privileges the elite as well as the state due to their perceived credibility, which is imbued by their position of authority. This, coupled with increased media dependency by the public, propels us to rethink the previous conceptions of the public sphere. Schulz, in turn, advances a new conceptualization of the public sphere in the era of booming mass media, which he calls 'media constructed public sphere' (p. 60).

This conceptualization arises from the public's increased dependency on mass media for information, with the expectation of it being factual, objective and fair. This information is then deliberated in interpersonal and, more recently, computer-mediated settings. Likewise, media's spotlighting of some viewpoints over others, usually in favour of the dominant discourse, makes them spaces where counterpublics compete for coverage and acknowledgement. Furthermore, the professionalization of journalism – which has standardized coverage methods and newsworthiness criteria – plays an active role in constructing the public sphere (McChesney 2004). Moreover, the overspecialization of media content and the proliferation of television channels, magazines and radio stations that cater to different interests have helped fragment the public. In that sense, it may seem impossible in this mediated context to refer back to the Habermasian definition of the public sphere. Instead, Fraser's (1990) conceptualization of multiple publics seems more in tune with the changing media landscape, which further legitimizes Breese's typography (2011). Schulz (1997), who examined Germans' television viewing, is cautious about generalizing his findings to non-European media systems), although similar trends have been found in the Arab world (Kraidy 2012), the United States (McChesney 2004) and Canada (Beers 2004).

Public sphere 3.0: The Internet as space for deliberative democracy

With the advent of the Internet, scholars were optimistic of its impact on democracy, especially as geographical constraints became obsolete (Sunstein 2001). However, this optimism – which transpires with every innovation in media technology – was soon replaced with scepticism of the Internet's democratizing ability. As Bohman (2004) argues, this scepticism is underlined by scholars' general ignorance as to how computer-mediated communication and the Internet truly function.

The Internet has, undeniably, revolutionized the way we think about the public sphere, as online news sites with comment sections and discussion forums have eroded the traditional boundaries between news and deliberation (Brundidge 2010). More importantly, the Internet has also helped audiences seek out information from news sources that may not be part of massive conglomerates, with the added benefit of not having to worry about cost. In that sense, the Internet has become a marketplace of ideas in its truest sense.

However, as audiences take further control of their communication, a threat may be posed on deliberative democracy. Sunstein (2001) argued that the Internet would, in fact, increase users' propensity to seek out content that matches their worldviews and belief systems. This increased selectivity will lead to further fragmentation (Galston 2003). The increased political polarization that has swept the world with the proliferation of misinformation, disinformation online and its offline consequences certainly offer credence to this theory.

Yet, another general argument in mass media research posits that the weakening of social boundaries, previously imposed by face-to-face communication, motivates Internet users to seek out others and information that may not subscribe to their beliefs. Benkler (2006) goes further, by implying that a new public sphere has emerged due to Internet users' transformation from passive receivers to active participants in political deliberation. In that sense, there is a general trend in acknowledging the existence of a networked public sphere whose protocols of communication do not correspond with traditional understanding of the public sphere. In fact, the rise of social media networks, independent online news media and blogs as spaces of political deliberation and dissent (Papacharissi 2009) signals a new era of democratization. Independent media, which have burgeoned with the commercialization of the Internet, provide citizens with the opportunity to hold traditional media and their parent companies accountable (Beers 2004). Independent media, then, become spaces of counterpublics (Fraser 1990), especially as the Internet becomes more accessible and widespread. A principal difference between traditional and independent media is that the latter is 'owned, operated, and structured to allow reporting and commentary that compensates for and counters corporate media consensus' (Beers 2004, p. 116). With his experience in founding an independent online newspaper in Canada, Beers provides an example of a sustainable online news source that maintains thousands of free subscribers in British Columbia (p. 114).

With more people on the Internet than ever before, the potential to extend the public sphere becomes undeniable. This is particularly relevant for younger generations, who are becoming more and more plugged in. Moreover, the cheap costs of news production and dissemination on the Internet limit the conventional barriers of access that once privileged corporate media due to their horizontal and vertical integration. Likewise, the Internet has returned agency back to the citizen who, no longer a passive consumer, is able to comment, contract, acquiesce or debate the merits of credibility of a news item. Instead of a vertical one-to-many relationship, the Internet has led to 'many-to-many' communication that places the citizen at either ends.

The rise of pan-Arab media

Although Hallin and Mancini (2004) developed a model of media systems that takes the nation-state as a unit of analysis, Kraidy (2012) argues that this conception largely discounts the importance of transnational systems, as is the case of pan-Arab media. Indeed, the introduction of Arab satellite television in the 1990s has led to an increased rise in pan-Arab channels that supersede national broadcasting systems due to 'agendas [that] converge and compete with nation-state policies' (ibid., p. 177). The author further explains: 'Contemporary Arab media consist of an unevenly integrated (pan-Arab) market, superimposed onto national systems and increasingly integrated into the global media market, although in many respects distinct from both: It is a transnational media system' (ibid.).

Cleavages exist in this system. Gulf countries, consisting of wealthy but conservative oil monarchies such as Saudi Arabia, Qatar and Bahrain, are a sharp contrast to the Levant countries (Jordan, Lebanon, Syria and Palestine) as well as to the North African countries of the Maghreb (Algeria, Morocco and Tunisia). These differences are explained by the varying political and media systems whereby the twenty-two Arab countries can be placed on a spectrum that places

Saudi Arabia's Islamic authoritarian regime and 'quiescent media' on one end and Lebanon's fractured consociational democracy and pluralist media on the other (Kraidy 2012, p. 178).

However, it was Saudi funding that helped expand Arab media to a transnational system as it is understood today (Kraidy 2012). Indeed, Saudi princes and businessmen launched channels in London and Dubai and collaborated with Lebanese media professionals and institutions such as the Lebanese Broadcasting Corporation (LBC), giving rise to a new Arab media landscape made of multi-platform conglomerates that include Rotana, MBC Group and LBC Group (Kraidy 2012). LBC, launched at the height of the Lebanese Civil War in 1985 by the Christian-nationalist party Lebanese Forces, is the longest running privately owned Arab television channel (Salloukh et al. 2015). After the end of the Civil War in 1989, Pierre Daher, LBC's founder and chief executive, reformed the television channel to cater to an encompassing Lebanese audience. With an emphasis on entertainment programs, LBC began broadcasting Ramadan programs, expanding its viewership among Muslim audiences. The channel's popularity in the Lebanese media scene helped it gain momentum, especially in Saudi Arabia, when it launched its satellite channel in 1996 (Kraidy 2012). Moreover, Saudi investments came pouring in, with tycoon Prince al-Waleed bin Talal buying 49 per cent of the channel's total shares. Al-Waleed's Rotana, a satellite channel broadcasting music videos not unlike MTV, later merged in 2007 with Pierre el-Daher's LBC satellite channel, to expand into the pan-Arab media market.

Another immensely popular satellite broadcast channel that launched in 1996 was the Doha-based Al-Jazeera Channel (AJC). Unlike LBC's private funding, AJC was funded by the Qatari state. The channel dedicated itself to news and current affairs, and stationed foreign correspondents in every Arab country (Sakr 2001), as opposed to the entertainment-heavy LBC. Although established by the Emir of Qatar, AJC's editorial content was largely independent from government meddling (ibid.). Its staff, made of seasoned journalists trained by the BBC, reflected the diversity of the Arab world. In turn, AJC covered stories that other Arab media would not, which increased its appeal to pan-Arab audiences. In other words, satellite channels such as LBC and AJC were compelled to do away with national intricacies in order to integrate into the pan-Arab media market (Kraidy 2012). As AJC began breaking taboos on air and LBC developed reality shows with audience participation, tensions between nations ran high as unique national values clashed with the pan-Arab market's interests. The audience, however, was riveted. Only recently, a seven-nation media habits survey conducted by the Northwestern University in Qatar has shown the Internet and television vying for first place as primary sources for news and information (Dennis, Martin and Hassan 2019).

Arab Spring: Burgeoning ideas

In December 2010, Mohamad Bouazizi, a Tunisian street vendor, set himself on fire to protest police corruption and humiliation (Fahim 2011). Bouazizi's self-immolation, against the backdrop of growing frustration with dire socio-economic conditions and crony authoritarian governance, sparked widespread protests in Tunisia, which in turn influenced waves of unrest in Egypt, Yemen, Libya, Bahrain, Syria and other Arab countries in 2011. Dubbed 'Arab Spring', the uprisings, led by Arab youths, highlighted a shared dissatisfaction of corruption and rampant youth unemployment. According to Dhillon, 65 per cent of the pan-Arab population is under thirty years old (Dhillion 2008). Armed with values of democracy and social justice, youths across the Arab world marched to protest their disenfranchisement from the political process and the lack of economic equity. In 2016, 30 per cent of Arab youths were unable to find a job, stoking fears of another revolt (*The Economist* 2016). But the Arab Spring revolutions, broadcast to the world on satellite television channels such as AJC, brought about new questions pertaining to communication technology, especially with the advent of new media technologies.

Were social media websites such as Facebook and Twitter instrumental in mobilizing populations and bringing down despotic rulers? The mainstream media seemed to think so at first (Vargas 2012), because several academics stipulated it (Khamis and Vaughn 2011). In June 2010, Internet penetration in the Arab world was at an estimated 19.6 per cent, compared to 29.2 per cent for the rest of the world (Rinnawi 2011). On the eve of the Arab Spring revolutions, Internet access in the Arab world seemed scarce, partly due to high IT costs, a crumbling, old infrastructure and a negligible if absent access in rural areas (ibid.). In that sense, that the Arab Spring revolutions were brought on by the use of the new media technologies, namely the Internet, takes away from the power of interpersonal communication and takes for granted the role of these technologies in causing attitudinal change (Dajani 2012). More importantly, those who had access to the Internet at the time were able to afford it, bringing us back to the Habermasian notion of the bourgeois public sphere. Indeed, in 2010, the Arab Internet was largely dominated by English-language content, which effectively alienated the majority of the pan-Arab population. In fact, the Internet was best used by highly skilled Arab professionals from the middle to upper middle classes (Rinawai 2011). But this has been rapidly changing. In 2013, Internet penetration among Arabic speakers was at 32.4 per cent, 41.6 per cent in 2016 and 54.6 per cent in 2019 (ITU 2020). With this rapid expansion, Arab users have been able to utilize these new communication technologies to create spaces, no longer confined to those able to speak English, where the issues that pushed protesters in 2011 to take to the streets were still being debated online.

Raseef22, the voice of the Arab Spring

Raseef22, or 'sidewalk 22', launched in 2013 as an online platform meant to carry the problems of youths to cyberspace after the failure of the Arab Spring uprisings. It was a pan-Arab venture; the first of its kind. Founded by Syrian millionaire Kareem Sakka, Raseef22 provided an independent outlet for news and viewpoints that fill a cultural gap in Arab-language online media landscape. According to Sakka (2019), Raseef22 is headquartered in Beirut, Lebanon, and receives contributions from more than 150 journalists and activists. First launched exclusively in Arabic, Raseef22 quickly added an English portal to appeal to an Arab diaspora and an Arab upper class whose command of their native language is decreasing. This duality between the usage of English and Arabic is reflective of the impact of colonization and, later, globalization and their discursive powers in education, culture, media and other institutions. This hybridity will be explained further below, using examples from the online platform.

Raseef22 targets Arab millennials whose interests are as diverse as the countries the platform aims to report on. From devout 'digital age muslims' who want to understand their faith beyond its clerical interpretations, to alternative journalists and activists looking for Arabic content that comes from their peers and Arab readers around the world whose demands for social justice and a reformed political discourse have not been subdued, Raseef22's target is to speak to the disenfranchised, fragmented and lost youth of the Arab world. For example, murdered Saudi activist Jamal Khashoggi was a regular contributor to the website. According to Raseef22's publisher and co-founder Karim Sakka (2019), in 2019, the website boasted 12 million yearly readers.

Methodology

A qualitative content analysis of eleven Raseef22 articles was conducted to examine the nature of the public sphere emerging through the website. Articles were selected from the emailed newsletters sent by Raseef22's editorial team. Every newsletter included eight articles. The author chose the last three newsletters sent on 18 March, 25 March and 1 April 2017, respectively, and randomly sampled four articles from each newsletter. In total, eleven articles – five in Arabic and six in English – were examined (Table 6.1).

Table 6.1 The 11 Raseef22 articles examined in this analysis

Author(s)	Target Country/Audience
Aya AbdelRahman (English)	Arab world
Tareq Ali (English)	Syria
Emad Bazzi (English)	Lebanon
Bobker Belkassem (Arabic)	Algeria
Dia Bousselmi (Arabic)	Tunisia
Mostafa Fathi (English)	Egypt
Fadi Hosni (Arabic)	Palestine
Hiba Ahmad Hilal and Rania Hilal (Arabic)	Arab world
Ali Khalil (Arabic)	Egypt
[Anonymous author] Raseef22 (English)	Saudi Arabia
Sherif Zeitouni (English)	Tunisia

The information collected included the following:

- *Headline*: The headline of the article was recorded. Headlines, when written correctly, present the most important information in the article. Readers may choose to read an article based on the headline, which may possess a positive or negative tone and presents the angle of the story.
- *Lead paragraph*: The lead paragraph offers the reader a basic summary of the article's content and presents the overall information of the article.
- *Publication date*: The date of the article was noted to ensure that articles were published within a three-week period between 13 March and 4 April 2017.
- *Theme*: The theme of the article was recorded. Themes were chosen based on the headline and lead paragraph of each article. Four themes were found in the articles examined: sex, human rights, Arab history and Arab youth rebellion. Contrasted with Raseef22's mission statement, these themes showcased what the authors' main concerns were.
- *Target audience*: The target audience of the article was recorded. This permits the author to better understand who the journalist and the website intend to engage with and on what topics.
- *Author's biography*: The author and her biography were noted. The biography of the author provides an insight into Raseef22's modus operandi and whether it abides by its mission to target Arab millennials.

At the time of analysis, the format of Raseef22's website allowed the reader to know whom each article is targeting. Indeed, beside each by-line, the target audience is by country or region it belongs to (e.g., 'Tunisia' or 'the 22'), how long it would take the reader to go through the article (e.g., 5 minutes or 7 minutes) and the type of article the reader has chosen (e.g., article, photo essay, blog). In 2019, Raseef22 revamped its website, doing away with the reading duration and target country in the byline. The target country or region, however, still appears on the featured image of the article on the website. Users are also able to filter articles by country of focus or region. My sample included articles meant for Lebanese, Egyptian, Saudi, Iraqi, Palestinian, Syrian, Tunisian, Algerian and overall Arab audiences. The articles sampled were published between 13 March and 4 April 2017. Overwhelmingly, articles that target a certain country were written by young journalists native to the country in question.

Breaking taboos, one story at a time

Young Arab journalists are taking to the Internet – and to Raseef22 – to write about taboo topics that would be censored in the traditional Arab media landscape and on social media platforms. Of the twelve articles chosen, sex was the most contentious theme (Abdel Rahman 2017; Bazzi 2017; Hasab and Hilal 2017; Khalil 2017), followed by expressions of Arab youth rebellion and questions pertaining human rights (Boussalmi 2017; Fathi 2017; Zeitouni 2017) and investigative reporting on phenomena in Arab history (Hasab and Hilal 2017; Hosni 2017). Additionally, four authors had a biography indicating they were either social media activists or young graduates pursuing a profession in journalism (Ali 2017; Bazzi 2017; Belkassem 2017; Fathi 2017), giving rise to the assumption that Raseef22 fashions itself as a millennial platform written by the millennial Arab for the millennial Arab, wherever they may be.

Saudi women are reclaiming their voice by producing, editing, publishing, distributing a magazine that casts a glimpse into the inner workings of their lives (Raseef22 2017). Arab women struggle to get legal abortions due to social stigma and criminalization, and turn towards dangerous solutions (Abdel Rahman 2017). Beirut, an anachronistic bastion of progress and tradition, once saw a thriving prostitution industry during the Civil War (Bazzi 2017). These three examples provide an interesting, if fleeting, outlook into the hidden lives and interests of Arab millennials, their priorities, their issues, their small rebellions, that would not make it onto Arab television – whether local or satellite. Without the burden of political money or advertising revenues, Sakka's patronage of Raseef22, alongside funding from foreign philanthropic organizations and individual donations from readers, has enabled the website to push the envelope on topics that are usually spoken about in hushed tones, even behind closed doors.

Overwhelmingly, Arab media systems are under government licensing and laws that have failed to adapt to the spread of the Internet (Duffy 2014). Indeed, Arab states' archaic press laws provide legal authority to pressure journalists to report on certain topics and ignore others for fear of repercussion (Duffy 2014; Rugh 2014). Duffy's examination of Gulf states' media laws has shown them to be the most restrictive on freedom of speech while prescribing severe penalties to journalists on the basis of vague defamation legal clauses. Indeed, accusations of defamation have been used by Arab governments as a tactic to silence journalists and stifle public debate (Duffy 2014; Duffy and Alkazemi 2017; Pintak 2010). Given this reality, Gulf states' media systems do not do well in international press freedom rankings. The World Press Freedom Index published by Reporters Without Borders ranks 180 countries on their press freedom, based on polling of media experts – journalists, scholars and legal professionals – and a database of press freedom abuses. In 2017, among the Gulf countries, Saudi Arabia fared the worst at a ranking of 168 and Kuwait the best at 104 (Reporters without Borders 2017). While the Arab Spring has helped make progress in the media landscape in the Maghreb, particularly in Tunisia – it ranked highest in the Arab world at 97 on the World Press Freedom Index in 2017 and ranked 72 in 2020 – government control of broadcasting systems and political pressures still hinder journalists' work (Marthoz 2012).

That Raseef22 is headquartered in Beirut, Lebanon, is not arbitrary in this sense. Indeed, Lebanon enjoys a pluralistic media landscape that is reflective of its fractured sectarian consociational democracy.

Although Lebanon still has a Ministry of Information and scrutinizes its press under a publications law that harkens back to 1962, its media landscape, made up of privately owned newspapers and television stations, makes it unique in the Arab world. In 1994, then-premier Rafiq Hariri introduced the first law of its kind in the Arab world to regulate television and radio stations that had burgeoned during a brutal fifteen-year civil war (Salloukh et al. 2015). Moreover, Lebanese journalists have historically been employed around the Arab world for their professional and hard-hitting journalism (Kraidy 2012) and Lebanese newspapers have had a longstanding pan-Arab readership. Indeed, it is common knowledge that Egyptian President Gamal Abdel Nasser read Lebanese newspapers every morning before reading Egyptian ones (ibid.). As for television viewing, it has seen an exponential increase in the last few years, and more than 75 per cent of Lebanese are connected to the Internet (Dennis et al. 2017). In 2019, Internet use jumped to 94 per cent in Lebanon (Dennis et al. 2019), likely due to the proliferation of web-based independent news organizations such as Megaphone, which became instrumental during the October 2019 uprising (Azhari 2019). Indeed, as trust for mainstream news organizations – television outlets – plummeted, young Lebanese turned to independent media organizations and grassroots initiatives that delivered unique on-the-ground reporting and independent coverage targeting the ruling class' corruption and negligence.

Gulf countries such as the United Arab Emirates and Qatar have almost achieved full connectivity at 90.6 per cent and 94.1 per cent Internet penetration in 2017 and 96.4 per cent and 99.6 per cent in 2020, respectively (Internet World Statistics 2020), but continue to exert restrictive control on traditional media and Internet use by enforcing stringent but vague defamation and libel laws that extend to cyberspace (Duffy 2014). In Syria, Tunisia and Jordan, legislation was passed to force the registration of online independent news sites under these countries' Press and Publications laws, which contain vague language that prohibits offending religion, the state, or 'the nation' (Pintak 2010). Lebanese regulation, in turn, is perceived as less persecutory because of a failing state whose Cybercrime and Intellectual Property Bureau is more concerned with censoring films and controversial Facebook statuses (Qasqas 2015). Coupled with a 1962 press law that hasn't been updated to include or acknowledge news sites on the Internet, this vacuum has made Lebanon a prime venue for a booming digital media landscape. Additionally, the changing nature of journalism with the advent of the Internet has made it possible for online newspapers to employ journalists from around the world, reforming the notion of a traditional newsroom. The circumvention of these restrictive media laws has then made Raseef22 and other web-based independent media in Lebanon perfect outlets for budding journalists to talk about the subjects that matter most to those like them without fear of censorship.

Hybridity of the Arab public: Towards a new pan-Arab public sphere

Raseef22's unique platform and wide reach in the Arab world provide a unique outlook on Arab urban youth today in the wake of the Arab Spring uprisings and, more importantly, within a globalized world. As previously mentioned, in 2010, the Arab world's low Internet penetration rates were due largely to a lack of Arabic-language cyberspaces for deliberation and political discourse (Rinnawi 2011). At the same time, the uprisings, fuelled by rising youth unemployment and disillusionment, signalled a shift for Arab youths to participate in the political debate. One such example was the Tamarod movement in Egypt, founded to force then-President Mohamad Morsi's ouster. The movement was the brainchild of young activists dissatisfied with an increasingly Islamist government that betrayed the original demands of the people for 'democracy and civilian rule' (Saleh 2014, para. 25). Since then, iron-fisted reign of President Abdel-Fattah al-Sisi, who came to power in a military coup, has systematically cracked down on local human rights organizations, independent media and activists, quashing any remnants of free speech in the country (Freedom House 2020).

Despite failed experiences in the streets, Arabic-language blogs and websites started to appear on the Arab Internet scene, pushing entrepreneurs such as Sakka to invest in online ventures in the Arab world. Although Raseef22 is not the only website that aims to cater to the whole Arab world (e.g., *Mashallah News*), it was the first to do so in Arabic.

Why provide a portal in English if the target audience speaks another language, then? This initial inquiry may seem legitimate to many, especially in the West, but the motivations behind such a decision are purely practical. Meant to be more inclusive and attract young Arabs living outside the Arab world – whether as students, second- or third-generation immigrants abroad – Raseef22 speaks to every Arab millennial at the national, regional or even global levels. In that sense, Raseef22 reflects a hybrid Arab identity performed through a postcolonial understanding of globalization.

According to Kraidy (2008), the conception of 'hybridity' supposes culture at its centre and at the intersection of race, language and ethnicity. In international communication, hybridity is a postcolonial understanding of media texts in a globalized world or, in other words, media texts coming out of cross-cultural encounters and across national borders. Critical media scholars have disputed the meaning of hybridity when the paradigm of cultural imperialism was at its most popular in the 1960s and 1970s (Bhabha 1994; Friedman 1994). Since then, communication theory has welcomed a culturally plural notion of media texts, influenced by theses in film theory and cultural anthropology (Sreberny-Mohammadi 1984). For Mellor (2007), globalization has opened the way for hybridity mainly due to the emergence of a global consciousness on different social issues including human rights and inequality, bolstered by new technologies such as the Internet that have helped do away with spatial and time constraints, facilitating the flow of information across national borders. But more importantly, after the fall of the Soviet Union, the world seemed to embrace capitalism wholeheartedly. For Arab postcolonial states, historically leftist values were traded for an American lifestyle propped up by consumerism and neoliberal policies. Hybridity, then, is typically the result of the movement of cultural commodities, exemplified by media programs. The Westernization (read: Americanization) of Arab postcolonial society has had an impact on Arab media practitioners and journalism scholars, hence new media outlets' valorization of standardized coverage methods. This is aptly illustrated with Raseef22, wherein the cross-cultural encounter occurs on two levels. First, the website's employment of young journalists trained to cover stories in a standardized format, adopted from the professionalization of journalism – fundamentally found in the West. Indeed, all articles are divided by sections or sub-headers in order to paint an overall and structured examination of any topic. For example, Belkassem (2017) tackled the Algerian wine industry through a holistic lens, by talking about its inception, the local and international markets it caters to and the backlash from conservatives in the country. At the same time, Raseef22's accommodation of an English-speaking audience signals a shifting paradigm in journalism in the Arab world as Arab natives attempt to reach out to their compatriots in the diaspora while also recognizing the hybridity of their (young) urban natives who have become avid consumers of Western media programs and texts.

The undeniable dialogism between Western and Arab cultures brought on by a history of colonialism, trade and later globalization, also reflects the format presented by Raseef22 as an independent online platform. Raseef22 purports to find a balance between tradition – symbolized by Arab culture – and modernity – brought on by flows of information and cultural commodities from the Western other.

This dialogical relationship, borrowed from Said (1994), is reflective of an urban Arab youth, whose access to the Internet has been more widespread, and who have learned about the possibilities of a participatory democracy through their consumption of non-Arab media texts. But more importantly, with the continued influence that Arab satellite channels possess, whose political talk shows pitted political opponents against each other in no-holds-barred live segments, pan-Arab audiences witnessed the unfurling of a new public sphere on their screens. Overtly biased coverage of the Arab Spring uprisings and scandals concerning the falsification of sources, however, prompted questions about these channels' independence from their state funders (Kuhn, Reuter and Schmitz 2013), forcing further segmentation along political lines.

Unlike the North American media system, the pan-Arab media system is subject to political pressure due to its reliance on government funding – Al Jazeera from Qatar, Al-Arabiya from Saudi Arabia – more than advertising revenues, thus exerting its own pressures on public opinion (Kraidy 2012; Mellor 2007; Salloukh et al. 2015). This has led to a boom in the Arab blogosphere, opening up the possibility for new spaces of political deliberation on the Internet.

Apart from its dedication to include Arab millennials with different perspectives and backgrounds to tell of their realities, Raseef22's adoption of cyberspace as a deliberative one and its employment of professional journalists and activists to its editorial positions are indicative of a trend that was not born in the Arab world. Indeed, Beers' online news outlet (2004), an experiment that was launched in the early 2000s, offers a tentative debut of regional news websites. In that sense, Raseef22's unique format in the Arab world is supplanted by the knowledge brought from Western examples that have succeeded in providing citizens with a platform for political deliberation. Indeed, Raseef22 has worked to become a space where these discourses come together after the public sphere was squashed in the streets and muted on television.

Yet, the Internet's fragmentation has made it possible for people to seek out content aligned with their world views (Sunstein 2001) and Raseef22's appeal to local, pan-Arab and global audiences has worked to counter that challenge. Boussalmi (2017), for example, interviewed Tunisian singer Emel Mathlouthi, whose music came to symbolize the Tunisian uprising in 2012. Mathlouthi is still seen as an icon of the Jasmine revolution and has lent her voice to sound the demands and struggle of the Tunisian people. On the other hand, Abdel Rahman's feature on abortions takes on a pan-Arab angle by interviewing women and doctors from Egypt and Morocco (2017), revealing practices in such Gulf countries as Saudi Arabia and Kuwait, and introducing legalization campaigns in Egypt and Lebanon. According to data disclosed by Sakka and Raseef22, the independent news site's reach has remained consistent between 2017 (Raseef22 n.d.) and 2019 (Abdel Rahman 2017), reaching over 12 million readers yearly. In contrast, young people between fifteen and twenty-nine years of age constitute 28 per cent or 100.8 million of the overall Arab population.

Raseef22's balance between national, pan-Arab and global audiences further puts the notion of the public sphere as a static entity into question. In that sense, to say that Raseef22 constitutes *one* homogeneous counterpublic would be a hasty conclusion. Raseef22's catering to different cultures that have varying histories, political systems and which have dealt with the Arab Spring uprisings in different ways, along with its use of the English language to appeal to a diaspora around the world, shatters the Western discourse that oftentimes paints the Middle East and North Africa region with a homogeneous brush. Moreover, the hybridity of each of these distinct audiences further invigorates Fraser's initial conceptualization of counterpublics (1990), especially as the Arab world still has the highest youth unemployment rate at 26.7 per cent (ILO 2020) and has been in a state of turmoil since 2010. This seemingly fluid alteration between audience type – and counterpublic – can only be achieved in a computer-mediated setting, certainly.

Conclusion

This chapter has examined the role Raseef22 has played in creating new counterpublics in the Arab world in a computer-mediated environment in 2017. The hybridity of the platform and its catering to urban Arab youths in the wake of failed uprisings have made it unique in its endeavour, especially due to its bilingual format. Despite the rise of new online news sites, satellite television still reigns supreme in the Arab world. This is doubly explained by cripplingly slow Internet connections and access concentrated in urban areas, where non-Arab media texts were more easily accessible. However, the failures of Arab satellite channels such as Al-Jazeera to be the public sphere it once was before the Arab uprisings have turned Arab millennials to the Internet. As Arab states scramble to regulate the Internet, however, Arab youths scramble to find new spaces for political deliberation after the failure of the Arab Spring uprisings. Ten years after the Arab Spring and seven after its launch, Raseef22 has continued to show that it is the premier independent online space, providing an outlet for Arab journalistic talent and dissident voices and in so doing, continues to break taboos by staying true to the Arab Spring's original motto: 'The people want to topple the regime'.

References

Abdel Rahman, A. (2017). 'Seeking an abortion in the Arab World', *Raseef22*, 28 March, updated 11 July. Available at: https://Raseef22.net/article/1069274-extortion-possible-death-seeking-abortion-arab-world [accessed 10 April 2017].

Achcar, G. (2016). *Morbid symptoms: Relapse in the Arab uprisings*. Stanford: Stanford University Press.

Ali, T. (2017). 'Staging the war: Can theatre flourish in Syria', *Raseef22*, 26 March, updated 11 July. Available at: https://Raseef22.net/article/1069254-staging-war-can-theater-flourish-syria [accessed 10 April 2017].

Azhari, T. (2019). 'Megaphone: The voice of Lebanon's uprising', *Al Jazeera*, 8 December. Available at: https://www.aljazeera.com/features/2019/12/8/megaphone-the-voice-of-lebanons-uprising [accessed 30 November 2020].

Bazzi, E. (2017). 'Inside Beirut's most notorious brothels during the "mad years"', *Raseef22*, 4 April. Available at: https://Raseef22.net/article/1069172-inside-beiruts-notorious-brothels-mad-years [accessed 10 April 2017].

Beers, D. (2004). 'The public sphere and online, independent journalism', *Canadian Journal of Education*, 29(1), pp. 109–30.

Belkassem, B. (2017). 'Fakhr al-sinaa'a al-jaza'iriyah: nabithuha allathi kan' ['The pride of the Algerian industry: the wine that once was'], *Raseef22*, 23 March, updated 9 July. Available at: https://goo.gl/gB4Kw7 [accessed 10 April 2017].

Benkler, Y. (2006). *The wealth of networks: How social production transforms markets and freedom*. New Haven, NJ: Yale University Press.

Bhabha, H.K. (1994). *The location of culture*. London: Routledge.

Bohman, J. (2004). 'Expanding dialogue: The internet, the public sphere and prospects for transnational democracy', *The Sociological Review*, 52(1), pp. 131–50.

Boussalmi, D. (2017). '"Omrak ma tqoul fdeyt" toghani Emel Mathlouthi' ['"Never say I will sacrifice myself to you", sings Emel Mathlouthi'], *Raseef22*, 11 April. Available at: https://goo.gl/8bTkU0 [accessed 11 April 2017].

Breese, E.B. (2011). 'Mapping the variety of public spheres', *Communication Theory*, 21(2), pp. 130–49.

Brundidge, J. (2010). 'Encountering "difference" in the contemporary public sphere: The contribution of the internet to the heterogeneity of political discussion networks', *Journal of Communication*, 60(4), pp. 680–700.

Dajani, N. (2012). 'Technology cannot a revolution make: Nas-book not Facebook', *Arab Media and Society*, 5 March. Available at: https://www.arabmediasociety.com/technology-cannot-a-revolution-make-nas-book-not-facebook [accessed 20 March 2017].

Dennis, E.E., Martin, J.D. and Hassan, F. (2019). *Media use in the Middle East, 2019: A seven-nation survey by Northwestern University in Qatar*. Doha Film Institute. Available at: http://www.mideastmedia.org/survey/2019 [accessed 20 November 2020].

Dennis, E.E., Martin, J.D. and Wood, R. (2017). *Media use in the Middle East in 2017: A seven nation survey by Northwestern University in Qatar*. Doha Film Institute. Available at: http://www.mideastmedia.org/survey/2017 [accessed 20 November 2020].

Dhillion, N. (2008). 'Middle East youth bulge: Challenge or opportunity?', *Brookings Institute*, 22 May. Available at: https://www.brookings.edu/on-the-record/middle-east-youth-bulge-challenge-or-opportunity [accessed 20 March 2017].

Downing, J.D.H. (2014). 'Media ownership, concentration, and control: The evolution of debate', in J. Wasko, G. Murdock and H. Sousa (eds.) *The handbook of political economy of communications*, pp. 140–68. Malden, UK: Wiley Blackwell.

Duffy, M.J. (2014). 'Arab media regulations: Identifying restraints on freedom of press in six Arabian Peninsula countries', *Berkeley Journal of Middle Eastern and Islamic Law*, 6. DOI: https://doi.org/10.15779/Z384S3C.

Duffy, M.J. and Alkazemi, M. (2017). 'Arab defamation laws: A comparative analysis of libel and slander in the Middle East', *Communication Law & Policy*, 22(2), pp. 189–211. DOI: https://doi.org/10.1080/10811680.2017.1290984.

Fahim, K. (2011). 'Slap to a man's pride set off tumult in Tunisia', *The New York Times*, 21 January. Available at: https://www.nytimes.com/2011/01/22/world/africa/22sidi.html?pagewanted=1&_r=1&src=twrhp [accessed 20 March 2017].

Fathi, M. (2017). 'Egypt's press syndicate, and the plight of online journalists', *Raseef22*, 4 April. Available at: https://Raseef22.net/article/1069241-egypts-press-syndicate-plight-online-journalists [accessed 10 April 2017].

Fraser, N. (1990). 'Rethinking the public sphere: A contribution to the critique of actually existing democracy', *Social Text*, 25/26, pp. 56–80.

Freedom House. (2020). *Egypt: Freedom on the net 2020 country report*. Freedom House. Available at: https://freedomhouse.org/country/egypt/freedom-net/2020 [accessed 25 December 2020].

Friedman, J. (1994). 'Global crises, the struggle for cultural identity, and intellectual pork barrelling: Cosmopolitans versus locals, ethnics, and nationals in an era of de-hegemonisation', in P. Werbner and T. Moddod (eds.) *Debating cultural hybridity: Multi-cultural identities and the politics of anti-racism*, pp. 70–89. London: Zed.

Galston, W.A. (2003). 'If political fragmentation is the problem, is the internet the solution?', in D.M. Anderson and M. Cornfield (eds.) *The civic web: Online politics and democratic values*, pp. 35–44. Lanham, MD: Rowman & Littlefield.

Habermas, J. (1989). *The structural transformation of the public sphere: An inquiry into a category of bourgeois society*. Cambridge, MA: MIT Press.

Hallin, D.C. and Mancini, P. (2004). *Comparing media systems: Three models of media and politics*. Cambridge: Cambridge University Press.

Harvey, D. (2005). *A brief history of neoliberalism*. Oxford: Oxford University Press.

Hasab, H.A. and Hilal, R. (2017). 'Hasad wa hamal wa jins, limatha kan ajdadouna yaduqoun al-ashwam?' ['Envy, pregnancy and sex, why did our ancestors have tattoos?'], *Raseef22*, 3 April. Available at: https://goo.gl/ZZDsff [accessed 10 April 2017].

Hosni, F. (2017). 'Qosat al-halyoun: dabet al-mukhabarat al-israeiliya allathi dofina seraho maaho fi Ghaza' ['The asparagus story: The Israeli intelligence officer whose secret was buried with him in Gaza'], *Raseef22*, 6 December. Available at: https://goo.gl/mzZuaX [accessed 10 April 2017].

International Labor Organization (ILO). (2020). 'Unemployment, youth total (% of total labor force ages 15–24) (modeled ILO estimate) – Middle East & North Africa',

The World Bank, 20 September. Available at: https://data.worldbank.org/indicator/SL.UEM.1524.ZS?locations=ZQ [accessed 18 December 2020].

International Telecommunication Union (ITU). (2020). *ITU Regional and Global Key ICT indicators. November*. Available at: https://www.itu.int/en/ITU-D/Statistics/Documents/facts/ITU_regional_global_Key_ICT_indicator_aggregates_Nov_2020.xlsx [accessed 1 December 2020].

Internet World Statistics. (2020). *Internet usage in the Middle East: Middle East internet usage and population statistics*. Miniwatts Marketing Group. Available at: https://www.internetworldstats.com/stats5.htm [accessed 30 November 2020].

Khalil, A. (2017). 'Kayf yalja'a al-rajul al-sharqi 'ila iilaj doofehi al-jinsi?' ['How does the Oriental man treat his sexual dysfunction?'], *Raseef22*, 30 March. Available at: https://goo.gl/0L0Fgc [accessed 10 April 2017].

Khamis, S. and Vaughn, K. (2011). 'Cyberactivism in the Egyptian revolution: How civic engagement and citizen journalism tilted the balance', *Arab Media & Society*, 29 May. Available at: https://www.arabmediasociety.com/cyberactivism-in-the-egyptian-revolution-how-civic-engagement-and-citizen-journalism-tilted-the-balance [accessed 20 March 2017].

Kraidy, M.M. (2008). *Hybridity: The cultural logic of globalization*. Philadelphia, PA: Temple University Press.

Kraidy, M.M. (2012). 'The rise of transnational media systems: Implications of pan-Arab media for comparative research', in D.C. Hallin and P. Mancini (eds.) *Comparing media systems beyond the western world*, pp. 177–200. New York: Cambridge University Press.

Kuhn, A., Reuter, C. and Schmitz, G.P. (2013). 'Al Jazeera losing battle for independence', *Spiegel Online*, 15 February. Available at: http://www.spiegel.de/international/world/al-jazeera-criticized-for-lack-of-independence-after-arab-spring-a-883343.html#ref=rss [accessed 10 April 2017].

Marthoz, J.-P. (2012). *The media and freedom of expression in the Arab world*. Norwegian Peacebuilding Resource Centre, NOREF Policy Brief, May. Available at: https://www.files.ethz.ch/isn/143430/ec2878cbfbf2a2eb7eca67710f630430.pdf [accessed 10 April 2017].

McChesney, R.W. (2004). *The problem of the media: U.S. communication politics in the 21st century*. New York: Monthly Review Press.

Mellor, N. (2007). *Modern Arab journalism: Problems and prospects*. Edinburgh: Edinburgh University Press.

Papacharissi, Z. (2009). 'The virtual sphere 2.0. The internet, the public sphere, and beyond', in A. Chadwick and P.N. Howard (eds.) *Routledge handbook of internet politics*, pp. 230–45. New York: Routledge.

Pintak, L. (2010). *The new Arab journalist: Mission and identity in a time of turmoil*. London: Bloomsbury.

Qasqas, O. (2015). 'Fighting cybercrime in Lebanon', *The New Arab*, 21 January. Available at: https://english.alaraby.co.uk/english/features/2015/1/21/fighting-cybercrime-in-lebanon [accessed 10 April 2017].

Raseef22. (n.d.). 'Man nahnu' ['About us']. Available at: https://Raseef22.net/%D9%85%D9%86-%D9%86%D8%AD%D9%86 [accessed 12 April 2017].

Raseef22. (2017). 'Jahanamiya: A unique perspective through Saudi women's eyes', 20 March. Available at: https://Raseef22.net/article/1069088-jahanamiya-unique-perspective-saudi-womens-eyes [accessed 10 April 2017].

Reporters without Borders. (2017). '2017 Press Freedom Index – Ever darker world map'. Available at: https://rsf.org/en/2017-press-freedom-index-ever-darker-world-map [accessed 20 April 2021].

Rinnawi, K. (2011). 'Arab internet: Schizophrenic trilogy', in N. Mellor, K. Rinnawi., N. Dajani and M.I. Ayish (eds.) *Arab media: Globalization and emerging media industries*, pp. 123–48. Cambridge, UK: Polity Press.

Rugh, W.A. (2014). *Arab mass media: Newspapers, radio, and television in Arab politics.* Westport, CT: Praeger.

Said, E. (1994). *Culture and imperialism.* New York: Knopf.

Sakka, K. (2019). 'Opinion: At Raseef22, we gave Khashoggi a platform. After his death, Saudi Arabia is blocking us', *The Washington Post*, 2 January. Available at: https://www.washingtonpost.com/opinions/2019/01/02/raseef-we-gave-khashoggi-platform-after-his-death-saudi-arabia-is-blocking-us [accessed 1 December 2020].

Sakr, N. (2001). *Satellite realms: Transnational television, globalization and the Middle East.* London: I.B. Tauris.

Saleh, Y. (2014). 'Activists who backed Mursi's fall turn against military', *Reuters*, 20 February. Available at: https://www.reuters.com/article/us-egypt-politics-tamarud-idUSBREA1J1E420140220 [accessed 10 April 2017].

Salloukh, B., Barakat, R., Al-Habbal, J.S., Khattab, L.W. and Mikaelian, S. (2015). *The politics of sectarianism in postwar Lebanon.* Chicago: Pluto Press.

Schulz, W. (1997). 'Changes of mass media and the public sphere', *Javnost – The Public*, 4(2), pp. 57–69.

Sreberny-Mohammadi, A. (1984). 'The "World of the News" study', *Journal of Communication*, 34(1), pp. 121–34.

Sunstein, C.R. (2001). *Republic.com.* Princeton: Princeton University Press.

The Economist. (2016). 'Arab youth: Look forward in anger', 6 August. Available at: https://www.economist.com/briefing/2016/08/06/look-forward-in-anger [accessed 20 March 2017].

Vargas, J.A. (2012). 'Spring awakening', *The New York Times*, 17 February. Available at: https://www.nytimes.com/2012/02/19/books/review/how-an-egyptian-revolution-began-on-facebook.html [accessed 20 March 2017].

Zeitouni, S. (2017). 'Tunisia's street musicians lead new wave of rebellion', *Raseef22*, 9 April. Available at: https://Raseef22.net/article/1069317-tunisias-street-musicians-lead-new-wave-rebellion [accessed 10 April 2017].

Chapter 8

PROMOTING LIBYAN NATIONALISM CONCEPTS VIA FACEBOOK: A CRITICAL DISCOURSE ANALYSIS

Safa Elnaili

Introduction

The aftermath of the Arab Spring is troubling. Whether in the Middle East or North Africa, the revolutions have taken a drastic turn off course and dictatorship governments have been replaced with more corrupt ones. Political analysts and experts argue that this deviation is due to the lack of substantial civil and political institutions in these countries (Meltz 2016). There are disparities and differences between Arab Spring countries' changes, and the factors behind these disparities vary, according to each country's history and sociopolitical structure. As a state located between Tunisia and Egypt, Libya may have caught the 'fever' of the Arab Spring right after the success of the former states and may have had the same goals and demands; however, its course was different and its aftermath much more severe.

Libya's social structure is tribal, which makes any political change complex and challenging. According to political researchers, such as Ellison (2015), the lack of powerful state and civil institutions in Libya is one of the strong reasons behind the country's chaotic situation after the revolution. As a result, the political vacuum has empowered tribalism, and religious and sectarian cleavages in the country's political development, thus affecting the formation of Libyan nationalism after the downfall of Qaddafi. The 17 February 2011 revolution in Libya was a public uprising for freedom against dictatorship. Unlike the revolutions in Tunisia and Egypt, Libyans faced a brutal war to gain that freedom.

The twenty-first century is a digital era, an era where the internet is essential to every aspect of life. Social media played an undeniable role in the Arab Spring. In Libya, Facebook led the first calls for revolution and was the leading platform for organizing the public's movement. While rebels fought Qaddafi's forces in the streets of the cities, citizens fought a different kind of war online. Libyans led a digital revolution on social media platforms – an intellectual one. One of the most critical issues discussed on Facebook pages was nationalism and the political values the new state should stand for. The public was divided due to the division in war and the emergence of political parties for the first time in the country's history, in addition to the strong presence of radical groups and those who opposed them from the liberal and moderate groups.

This chapter demonstrates how Libyans discussed and promoted nationalism on Facebook pages after the downfall of Qaddafi's regime in 2011. The study investigates one of Libyan's most popularly used social media platforms – Facebook – that represented two different political orientations in the county: Islamists and Nationalists. It examines, through critical discourse analysis, how the authors of these Facebook pages used language to promote nationalism to their followers and supporters, while resisting nationalistic ideologies from the opposite party.

Libya: An unsettling nation

Libya has suffered under colonization and dictatorship for over a hundred years, leading to sociopolitical turbulence and insecurity in Libyan society. Libya's strategic location has played an essential role in shaping its historical development throughout the centuries. Its location as a North African, Mediterranean country that connects the African and European continents has put the Saharan country in a constant state of occupation.

The Ottoman Empire failed to develop the Libyan state economically (1551–1911) and the Italian occupation governed the underdeveloped state with cruelty (1911–51). After independence, the monarchy was aborted early by a military coup, which prevented King Idris from forming a stable and prosperous country (1951–69). After the coup, Qaddafi's regime and socialism dragged the country into more political and economic collapse (1969–2011) (Pargeter 2012) and finally, there was the Libyan 2011 uprising and its tumultuous and destructive aftermath (2011–). Libyans continued to carry the heavy weight and painful legacy of their early and modern history, and their disturbing present and uncertain future.

Shedding light on Libya's history reflects the negative effects of such occupations and dogmatic rule, especially on the state's modern history, briefly explained in the next section, with both the Italian occupation and Qaddafi's regime. In my opinion, these two periods were the most damaging to modern Libyan society and culture.

Italy strongly believed that it had a historical right to rule Libya and revive its Roman Empire legacy; therefore, it landed its troops on Libyan soil and declared war in 1911. Their three-decade colonization was brutal. Libyans suffered great poverty for many years. The invaders forced them to resist and fight bloody battles to reclaim their lands and restore power. One form of rebellion was refraining from sending their children to Italian schools, to instead school them at the local mosques and teach them the Holy Qur'an (Fagih 2008). The long years of foreign occupation exhausted the locals and kept them continually occupied with fighting and 'martyrdom'.

As a result, this unsettled environment inhibited Libyan citizens from building their community and keeping pace with the socio-economic developments happening in neighbouring countries such as Egypt. The country remained ruined by wars, physically and culturally, until its independence in 1951. After independence, the Libyan monarchy's sixteen years were fragile for the Libyan community because it marked an era of transition from a Bedouin/underdeveloped society to an oil state urging sociopolitical and socio-economic change. Unfortunately, growth was soon interrupted by the 1969 coup by Qaddafi (Chivvis 2014). With the coup came dictatorship and social injustice. Libyan citizens faced cruelty and economic inequality once again. Qaddafi ruled with great power and imposed political censorship on politicians, activists and journalists, restricting their freedom to build the civil society that Libya desperately needed (Chorin 2012). As a result, the regime prohibited political parties and Libyan opposition was banned from the country, placing the Libyan community in isolation from the political and democratic global mainstream. In short, Libya has not witnessed a settled, freely practiced political environment in its modern history (Elnaili 2014).

Libyan uprising in 2011: A digital revolution

Following in the footsteps of Tunisia and Egypt, Libyans marched in the streets in February 2011 to overthrow Qaddafi's rule and call for a new democratic Libya. Unfortunately, the peaceful rallies soon turned into bloodshed in the streets of most Libyan cities. Libyans, once more, faced war for freedom. After months of heavy artillery battles, with the international community's assistance, Libyans finally ended the four decades of dictatorship. They were at the threshold of a new era in the country's history. The transition, however, was problematic; conflict continued among Libyans, leading to a civil war. The aftermath of the Libyan Arab Spring led also to political division and competition to control the oil-rich state.

While fighters fought in the streets and politicians fought in parliamentary hallways, the public fought cyber battles on the Internet. The political void in Libya forced Libyans to form their fronts to advocate and defend their perspectives on how Libya's new political system should be. Libyan diversity surfaced after decades of suppression; this in turn caused clashes in thought due to their lack of democratic experience. Subcultures were formed, leading to political divisions on all levels, especially on social media platforms. Facebook occupied the leading role in calling for the revolution, advertising and introducing political concepts, providing up-to-date news (whether facts or rumours for political purposes) and creating new sociopolitical identities (Oishi 2008). Facebook became Libyans' primary cyber environment for forming a national identity.

National identity in Libya

There is no doubt that the Internet in the twenty-first century is gradually replacing printed newspapers, journals and history books to contribute to the sense of national identity and national sentiments in our modern world. People are expressing their cultural and political opinions in a broader global community.

More than ever, Libyans have also been digitally interacting on Facebook and exchanging their thoughts and opinions on Libya's national identity after Qaddafi. However, political discussions on the Internet have shown some intolerance among opposite political groups. This intolerance has probably been due to the fact that 'Libyan's trust in their government, and in one another, eroded, and they took refuge in the solace of tribe and family. Libyan society … is divided by the cleavages of kinship and region' (Anderson 2011, p. 6).

Stability requires a state of strong national sentiments, a condition that Libya still needs to achieve. Nationalism is based on 'a historical narration of material events, beliefs and values in such a way that a (seemingly) coherent consistency and continuity over time is rendered' (Khosravinik and Zia 2014, p. 759). According to Ellison (2015, p. 7), 'nationalism requires national unity and identity'. The heavy heritage of instability from the Italian occupation and regional/sectarian loyalty from Qaddafi's legacy, in addition to the lack of strong civil institutions, have all been obstacles to having a clear and solid foundation for Libyan national identity. Such a failure of nationalism in countries such as Libya 'The failure of nationalism in a country can be seen in the politicization of tribalism or the persistence of ethnic, religious, or sectarian cleavages – especially in the political or military arenas – at the expense of a cohesive national identity' (p. 8) and these fissures, adds Ellison, harmed the peaceful transition in Libya since the beginning of the Arab Spring in the region.

Tribalism, war and division

Besides understanding Libya's history and politics, it is crucial to shed light on one of the most influential factors in its struggle – tribalism. Libya has approximately 140 tribes with strong political influence and which play a central role in the political arena. Libyans cherish their tribes with pride and their identities are mostly tied to their tribal groups. With the lack of strong civil institutions, tribes became social organizations. They function as the administration that sub-tribes turn to in social conflict rather than to law forces or the courts. Tribalism is not only a social organization for some, but it is an ideology that has developed over time, from Ottoman and Italian occupation to the King Idris monarchy, to Qaddafi's stateless Libya, to the lack of a unified modern state in the post Qaddafi era.

With constant failures to create a strong nation with a unified identity, tribalism became rooted more deeply in Libya`s sociocultural structure as the main political administration. Qaddafi's four-decade rule also fed tribalism, especially in the early 1990s, with foreign sanctions. Qaddafi sought tribal support in internal politics to maintain stability for his administration against Western pressure, making it impossible to constitute a state with a strong national sentiment.

It is also worth mentioning that Qaddafi's failed Libyan state caused divisions among tribes and regions (i.e., cities). As the country leader, his tribe was systematically the most powerful and even feared tribe in Libya. As a result, this caused resentment from other prominent tribes. His 'tribal favoritism' and the inclusion of powerful tribes from his home town of Sirt and other cities in western

Libya led to marginalization among the eastern tribes. All this was in addition to the Berber and Saharan tribes feeling profoundly marginalized and culturally consumed by the more significant majority of Libyan tribes.

As the war erupted in 2011, Libyans were divided based on their tribal loyalty and their cities. Social division supported by tribal conflict created political friction in control of the Libyan state's political steering wheel.

Libyan political fractions

After passing from Italian colonialism, Libya gained its independence, with the aid of Western powers, becoming a federal monarchy in 1951. This independence was sudden and unexpected. There was no clear vision of a unified ideology that shared the goals of the country's three regions at the time – Tripolitania, Cyrenaica and Fazzan. In 1963, the constitution was revised to reflect the change from a federal to a unitary state. With the new state's reliance on Western expertise and Arab socialism in neighbouring countries, Libya was incapable of drawing or defining its political boundaries between East and West (Vandewalle 2012). The country's rapid change in economic growth, as a newly discovered oil state, and the rise of divided loyalties, made the monarchy weak and unable to sustain momentum. Political parties were abolished in the constitution and prohibited from participating in the first-ever elections because the country could not afford political division as a newly born state.

When Qaddafi overthrew the king with his military coup, he too banished political parties and banned direct elections in the country. Qaddafi considered political parties to be dictators and accused those who claimed political assembly to be traitors. Those who opposed his regime were either arrested, executed or fled the country for political asylum. The only political front in the state for four decades was Qaddafi's socialism.

Libyan political parties: Nationalists vs. Islamists

After the rebels overthrew Qaddafi's rule in October 2011, the country was preparing for its very first democratic election in decades. Approximately 130 new political entities were competing for parliamentary seats in the 2012 elections. The nature of these political entities was mainly local and only represented the agendas of their towns and villages. They mostly had short-sighted political visions. Only ten of these entities were considered national political movements, having candidates across all of Libya's constituencies.

Two main political parties stood out in this historic election and were considered the most powerful ones: the Justice and Construction Party and the National Forces Alliance Party (*Al Jazeera* 2012). Many Libyans believed the first party to be a Muslim Brotherhood branch in Libya, calling for founding the country on Islamic grounds, whereas the latter presented itself as a liberal movement, calling for a democratic state. Both parties gained immense popularity and support from citizens around the country, which divided most Libyans into two opposite fronts: nationalists vs. Islamists. Conflict rose between the two ideologies. The nationalists (or sometimes called Arab nationalists) accused Islamists of abusing religion for political gain and serving foreign powers. At the same time, Islamists pointed the finger at nationalists for plotting against Islam and its sacred laws. The nature or history of these two political ideologies is not the focus of this chapter, but needs to be pointed out briefly as the backbone for Libya's ideological/political conflict and how it mirrored the divisions in promoting nationalism.

As a conservative Muslim country, Libyans consider Islam the base for their state's structure, constitution, culture and social traditions. Sharia law is key, thus making religion a very sensitive discussion on social media platforms. Islamists called for the necessity of creating a state based on Sharia law; therefore, their national sentiment was religiously based. On the other hand, although they supported Islam as the foundation of the state, nationalists defined their nationalistic views more with loyalty to state in parallel with religion. Islamists believed in a more significant Islamic state that unites all Muslim nations as one; they did not believe in borders and socio-economic boundaries. In contrast, nationalists believed in the nation as a clear and defined state, independent from any broader ideological ties (Nafi 2008).

Nationalistic scales on Facebook

Hundreds of thousands of Libyans considered Facebook their leading source for updated news of their broken nation, especially during the post-Qaddafi war. They followed posts by political figures and political commentaries on daily issues to show support for and solidarity with their ideological groups. Nationalism was among the important topics discussed by most political groups on Facebook. Authors of such political Facebook groups/pages discussed and advertised national sentiments in their daily posts to gain their followers' trust and form a united front against the political groups they opposed. This chapter looks at these Facebook pages through a critical discourse analysis (CDA) lens to help map the strategy/ ies used to present Libyan nationalism to their followers. It also examines how this cyber conflict affected the progress of sociopolitical and cultural harmony in Libyan society after the revolution. The next two sections discuss the two main ideological strategies (in this chapter, they are called 'scales') that underlined the promoting of nationalism on most Libyan Facebook pages.

Van Dijk (2001, p. 352) defines critical discourse analysis as 'a type of discourse analytical research that primarily studies the way social power abuse, dominance and inequality are enacted, reproduced and resisted by text and talk in the social and political context.' He argues that social and political conflicts can be reproduced by representing the Other in a negative and demonized image. The main focus of CDA is to understand how 'discourse structures enact, confirm, legitimize, reproduce, or challenge relations of power ... in society' (p. 353). Van Dijk uses lexical descriptions and text structure as analytical tools to investigate and underline these representations. It is, therefore, convenient for this study to implement CDA in analysing how nationalism was discussed among Libyans on Facebook (Rahimi and Riasati 2011). The analysis will help understand how nationalism was advocated through political differences and social injustice on Facebook using language.

The scale of treachery and loyalty

With the absence of strong civil institutions and good education to enlighten the public, Libyans struggled to understand their political stand and how to identify themselves with the concepts of 'nation' and 'nationalism'. As social media invaded the culture, political discussions on social media platforms were led by politicians, activists and even regular citizens as the public's primary source for sociopolitical input.

Most Facebook pages fed their followers with political ideologies to form nationalistic sentiments according to their own political views. Unfortunately, such political opinions were based on associating betrayal with the opposite side and loyalty with their own political party. Such concepts and practices can be traced back to Libya's long history of war against an 'Other' or 'Anti-Westerization' (Huang 2002, p. 71), in addition to the political traditions of Qaddafi's regime for the past forty years. Qaddafi used the 'Fear the Other' strategy, feeding the public with hate and fear of the West and any entity that stood against his political views. Such entities or oppositions, according to Qaddafi's Green Book and political perspectives, were traitors and conspirators against the nation. Therefore, Libyans, for many years, were fed with fear as the main base to form nationalism. When the people rose up in 2011, they were still chained by the cultural concept of being suspicious of treason and conspiracy. This concept resurfaced on social media platforms when pro-revolution members dominated the sociopolitical sphere and occupied headlines in social media space. After the end of Qaddafi's era, public disappointment overshadowed the country as the goals of the revolution – equal rights, economic growth, democracy, etc. – were unfulfilled, and revolutionaries were getting off track. After fighting their dictator's iron fist rule as one, Libyans were once again divided. The public's division could also be seen as a result of political division in the parliament and new government, along with the struggle by the newly born political parties to co-exist together democratically. As these entities lacked experience, politics post-Qaddafi was based on two principal grounds: religion and region.

This conflict was carried out through language on Facebook; nationalist sentiments were fed to followers, first, by romanticizing oneself and second, by demonizing the Other, by promoting hate and fear of treason. For example, nationalists always associated nationalism with support of the army and the national military forces; they used such words as 'أبطال' (heroes) and 'حماة الوطن'

(protectors of the homeland) to describe the army and to raise the sense of the need for military forces in their followers. One of the significant army groups supported by most nationalists was the one leading 'عملية الكرامة' (Operation Dignity) in eastern Libya. Led by Libyan military officer and head of the Libyan national army, Khalifa Haftar, this operation was launched to regain control over Libya's second-largest city, Benghazi. The city had been taken over by Al-Qaida militias and other extremist groups who had mounted a campaign of assassinations and bombings, targeting political and military figures. 'Dignity', according to nationalists, represented the dignity of the Libyan people. The mission was to regain control of Benghazi; that is, basing their political views on connecting nationalism and love of the nation with full support of the national army. They strongly believed that only a national army could restore peace. Operation Dignity took two years to push the extremist groups out of Benghazi. When the military took control of the city, nationalists commemorated this victory by posting celebratory words on Facebook pages with the hashtag '# بنغازي_ روحت' ('#Benghazi_ is _home'), indicating that the city had been freed from the grip and rule of the Islamists and was finally back under the control of the national army. On the other hand, Islamists fought the nationalists' concept of nationalism and refused to call Operation Dignity forces a 'National Army', instead referring to them as 'Haftar's forces', thereby stripping that operation of any power or authority to control the country. To Islamists, this authority should have been given to the rebels who had defended Sharia law and Islam from military dictators such as Haftar and his officers. The most common word used by nationalists on Facebook to describe members of the Islamist parties and their followers was 'ارهابيين'. They associated them with terrorism and ISIS as a way to strengthen their own nationalistic concepts. This word connoted accusations of being a foreign agent and hence, a traitor. An example can be seen in a post from one of the Facebook pages supporting Operation Dignity: the post described how the army struggled to remove the land mines planted by the Islamist forces. The post described the mines as 'ألغام الأخوان المسلمين' ('the mines of the Muslim Brotherhood'). Associating these weapons with the political group is a way to categorize them as enemies of the state. Islamists, on the other hand, mocked the use of the word 'تحرير بنغازي' (meaning 'Liberation of Benghazi') by nationalists and considered the military operations carried out by Operation Dignity forces an act of treachery and destruction of the city. Therefore, they use the word 'تدمير بنغازي' (destruction of Benghazi) in their posts to fight back the call to support the military forces led by Haftar as a national duty.

The scale of inclusion vs. exclusion

When political figures, parties and groups were labelled as either loyal or disloyal, the second scale of nationalism came into use in Facebook's digital sphere: inclusion and exclusion. The war in Libya negatively affected the country's social fabric and this in turn, created more divisions among regions, cities and tribes.

Among these divisions was the conflict between eastern and western Libya, particularly over government control of oil fields. This political fight began long before Qaddafi's coup in 1969. The tribes of the eastern region claimed the right to control the oil output and the economy since many of the oil fields were in the east. Still, after Qaddafi took control of the country, his central government put all administrations, including oil administration, under the authority of the western region, where the capital city Tripoli is located. As a result, this put political reconciliations at risk between the country's rival fractions. The fight for oil control continued even after the 2011 revolution, especially after the downfall of Qaddafi's regime in October of the same year and the transitional government's move from Benghazi (the stronghold of nationalists and Operation Dignity), where it was first formed, to Tripoli. This transition, of course, created tension in the tribes of the east, who refused the continuation of the central government system. In 2012, they demanded the formation of a federal state as the only solution to protect the region's economic rights. During the rise of the eastern region's federal system demands, tension was rising on Facebook pages as well; supporters of the federal state of Libya accused tribes of the western region of hampering their economic interests and the region's future. This sociopolitical conflict forced the eastern tribes and supporters of the federal state to develop their nationalistic sentiments. Their nationalism was mostly based on tribalism and region (the Barqa/Cyreaica region). Some more extreme views even demanded the exclusion of western tribes in the east, particularly in Benghazi, from being part of the region's political structure. Some groups even demanded the independence of eastern Libya (Barqa) from the Libyan state. On Facebook, political fronts were created with a sense of inclusion of those from the east and exclusion of those from the west. Some of these posts were, for example, describing themselves as 'أهل برقة الأصليين ' ('برقة (' true people') to only include eastern tribes in their call for nationalism and reject those who were originally from the western region. Facebook followers from the west, on the other hand, considered the eastern demands for oil control and/or independence as treachery, and referred to them as 'الإنفصاليين' ('The Separatists') to show, from their perspective, exclusion from Libya's nationalism.

Another sociopolitical controversy on Facebook was the social wound that cut through the social fabric between two cities in western Libya: Misurata (the only city whose votes for the Muslim Brotherhood exceeded those for any other political party in 2012) and Tawergha. During the bloody war against Qaddafi, many Qaddafi supporters, specifically military supporters in the city of Tawergha, invaded their neighbouring city, Misurata. Orders were given to crush the rebels in Misurata and end the demonstrations. The city's occupation left behind many deep wounds in the people of Misurata: citizens were killed, properties were destroyed, houses were robbed and there were even claims and accusations of rape. The conflict between both cities continued, especially after citizens of Tawergha fled their city in fear of Misuratans' anger. Their request for peace and reconciliation to return home was in vain. Tawerghans were displaced in refugee camps all over the country for years. Their accusations that Misurata was obstructing their return generated heated discussions on Facebook pages. Both sides had supporters who either sympathized with Misurata and rejected the return of the Tawerghans to their city or those who condemned the obstruction and considered it social injustice. For a city that fought fiercely against Qaddafi's regime and lost many souls, Misurata supporters based their political stand against Tawergha on the betrayal of a neighbouring city and betrayal of the revolution, excluding by that Tawerghans' right to be part of their nationalist sentiment. They used, for example, words such as 'مطرودين' (kicked out/unwanted) as a way to express feelings of being physically and emotionally unwelcome in the new Libya. Those who stood by the Tawerghans' right to return home, on the other hand, refused the term 'kicked out' and use instead the word 'مهجّرين' (forced out), to underline social injustice and the need to include them as Libyan citizens with full rights in the new Libya.

Conclusion

From the discussions above, Libyan nationalism views on Facebook were, unfortunately, based on negative concepts. This may be due to the country's long history of unrest, conflict, foreign occupation, dictatorship and civil war. Libya's tribal structure has also been a strong factor in hindering the existence of a more inclusive and democratic state. The lack of a coherent nationalist sentiment that would bring all Libyans under one umbrella could be seen, according to Anderson (2011), as the result of a lack of social and governmental cohesion. She argues that Libya is still in a chaotic state due to the absence of strong political alliances and national organizations. Libyan nationalism on Facebook pages is, therefore, undefined and of an incoherent nature; in other words, Libyan nationalism on digital platforms is as unsettled as the state itself. Nationalism requires democracy and the inclusion of all, democracy and inclusion comes through sociopolitical education, education comes through strong civil institutions and civil institutions come through a strong state.

References

Al Jazeera. (2012). 'Libya's political parties: A brief look at some of the main political forces competing in the July 7 vote for the General National Congress', *News*, 3 July. Available at: http://www.aljazeera.com/news/africa/2012/06/2012626224516206109. html [accessed 3 July 2012].

Anderson, L. (2011). 'Demystifying the Arab Spring: Praising the differences between Tunisia, Egypt, and Libya', *Foreign Affairs*, 90(3), pp. 2–7.

Chivvis, C. (2014). *Toppling Qaddafi: Libya and the limits of liberal intervention*. New York: Cambridge University Press.

Chorin, E. (2012). *Exit the colonel: The hidden history of the Libyan revolution*. New York: Public Affairs.

Ellison, D.B. (2015). *Nationalism in the Arab Spring: Expression, effects on transitions, and implications for the Middle East State: A comparative analysis of Egypt and Libya*, Senior

Essay. Yale University. Available at: https://politicalscience.yale.edu/sites/default/files/files/Ellison_Danielle.pdf [accessed 16 February 2017].

Elnaili, S. (2014) 'Adjectives of colour in Libyan short stories: A stylistic analysis', in A.E. Arua, T. Abioye and K.A. Ayoola (eds.) *Language, literature and style in Africa*, pp. 131–41. Newcastle upon Tyne, UK: Cambridge Scholars Publishing.

Fagih, A. (2008). *The Libyan short story: A research and anthology*. Bloomington, IN: Xlibiris Publishing.

Huang, Y. (2002). 'Approaching "Pareto Optimality"? A critical analysis of media-orchestrated Chinese nationalism', *Intercultural Communication Studies*, 9(2), pp. 69–87.

Khosravinik, M. and Zia, M. (2014). 'Persian nationalism, identity and anti-Arab sentiments in Iranian Facebook discourses: Critical discourse and social media communication', *Journal of Language and Politics*, 13(4), pp. 755–80.

Meltz, D. (2016). *Civil society in the Arab Spring: Tunisia, Egypt and Libya*. Honors Thesis. University of Colorado.

Nafi, B. (2008). 'Nationalism vs Islam: Islamists and nationalists have had a tense relationship since the 1920s', *Al-Jazeera News*, 19 February. Available at: http://www.aljazeera.com/focus/arabunity/2008/02/200852519420197834.html [accessed 1 April 2020].

Oishi, Y. (2008). 'A consideration of media-nationalism: A case study of Japan after the Second World War', *Keio Communication Review*, 30, pp. 5–17.

Pargeter, A. (2012). *Libya: The rise and fall of Qaddafi*. New Haven, CT: Yale University Press.

Rahimi, F. and Riasati, M.J. (2011). 'Critical discourse analysis: Scrutinizing ideologically-driven discourses', *International Journal of Humanities and Social Science*, 1(16), pp. 107–12.

Van Dijk, T.A. (2001). 'Critical discourse analysis', in D. Schiffrin, D. Tannen and H.E. Hamilton (eds.) *The handbook of discourse analysis*, pp. 352–71. Oxford: Blackwell.

Vandewalle, D. (2012). *A history of modern Libya*. New York: Cambridge University Press.

Chapter 9

MARRIAGE AND POLITICS IN HANAN ABDALLAH'S DOCUMENTARY *IN THE SHADOW OF A MAN*

Touria Khannous

'Better the shadow of a man than the shadow of a wall'. Wafaa recalls her mother's words when she learnt of her daughter's impending divorce. Hanan Abdallah's documentary *In the Shadow of a Man* (2013) forces the viewer to explore not only the formal elements of the film but also its historical context, as it encompasses elements of the national at the time of Egypt's most urgent contemporary crisis during its 2011 revolution. This time of transition is highlighted through the representation of marriage and social relations along the axes of gender, class, sexuality and geographic region, as well as religious and political beliefs. At the crux of the documentary is the desire to advocate for women's rights as integral to a new democratic post-dictatorial order. The film focuses on four different Egyptian women, namely Wafaa, Badreya, Suzanne and Shahinda, whose marriages and love stories are interestingly framed in the context of the post-Arab spring transition. As it surveys these four women's lives, the documentary zooms in on their lived realities. This chapter links the stories of these women to the academic literature, thus offering an analysis of how and why their lives took these different forms and developed through these paths, by explaining the social, political and economic context in Egypt. By looking at the film's relationship to gender and revolution, the chapter examines the film within the context of a feminist perspective with respect to marriage and politics. Marriage is just one of the details associated with women's struggles as their problems manifest not only at home but also in the workplace, in schools, etc. The reworking of women's roles through the film's characters familiarizes viewers with how gender is positioned in Egyptian society. By examining the turmoil women in contemporary Egypt still experience as they try to negotiate gender roles, the film embarks on making a nation, on the brink of revolution, aware of the challenges still facing its women. The political struggles for Egyptian women are different from other women's struggles in the Arab world. Thus, the film is not applicable to other contexts, such as Tunisia or Morocco, where feminism was tied to national liberation movements and the political elite (Charrad 2001).

In the case of Egypt, the situation is different. Feminist activists are often poor, working at the grassroots level and claiming the public sphere from within their positions in the private sphere as wives and mothers. Their activism challenges elite feminists who have often claimed the label 'feminist' yet excluded other women's movements. What makes the film solely Egyptian is that, through women's lived realities, it reflects the unique character and history of the struggle for women's rights in Egypt. Also, in its focus on the revolution, the film explores the intersection between female characters' ideas about marriage and the revolution, thus portraying women as having a growing public presence aside from their marital lives and families.

The film represents shifts in film discourse regarding the representation of women's roles since it integrates a diverse range of feminisms from a multidimensional perspective, including Islamic feminism. Arab scholar Khamis blames 'the exclusionary policies of the state' (2010, p. 241) for 'the birth of political, fundamentalist Islamic movements, which could be seen ... as an attempt to resist state suppression, as well as to assert indigenous religious and cultural values and beliefs' (2010, p. 241). Through her feminist script, the filmmaker evokes different female character types, from the conservative Islamist to the liberal woman. Drawing on multiple views from Egyptian women, the film highlights women's diversity and refuses to choose between women of leftist or conservative political and cultural camps. The camera simply ignores boundaries between women who are different from one another. While not all women portrayed in the film necessarily view themselves as feminists, they all embody different strains of diverse Egyptian feminisms: traditional, liberal, socialist and religious. The film proves Badran's argument that the story of Egyptian feminism is 'a story about disjunctures between different types of feminisms' (1995, p. 223).

Transnational filmmaking

Such disjuncture can first be seen in the transnational production of the film itself. Abdallah achieved international success at both the Berlin International Film Festival (2012) and the Doha Tribeca Film Festival (2012), where she won the award for Best Documentary Director. Born in London, where she is also professionally located, Abdallah returned to Egypt to document the lives of women on the eve of the 2011 revolution. Rather than being specifically an Egyptian director, Abdallah is a transnational director, whose documentary film was commissioned by the group UN Women.[1] The fact that the documentary is produced by UN Women attests to its transnational parameters, as well as to the political context of the revolution in which this production was made. UN women's sponsoring of the documentary at a crucial time in Egyptian history needs to be put within the context of the other activities by UN Women in Egypt and, more broadly, the potential impact of such activities on Egyptian women. The question is how filming such a documentary can be helpful to women who are struggling in Egypt. The film raises questions regarding representation, production and reception, as well as social class, since it is a question of who has the means to see the film. The UN has obviously funded this movie to be shown primarily to

Western audiences, which raises questions about its reception and production for the Western versus how it would be viewed in Egypt, and whether it would have been different were it made mainly for Egyptians. By sponsoring such a film, UN Women wanted to raise awareness about gender inequality in Egypt, especially in light of the Convention on the Elimination of All Forms of Discrimination against Women (CEDAW) adopted by the UN Women. While President Mubarak's wife, Suzanne Mubarak, championed women's rights, established the National Council for Women and helped pass gender reforms, including the *Khula* law (women's right to divorce) dubbed 'Suzanne's Laws', many, on the other hand, believe that women's political rights were suppressed under Mubarak's regime in the years leading up to the revolution.

The authoritarian agenda of women's rights

Different sociocultural and political contexts in Egypt contributed to how women could be enfranchised. Women were discriminated against in the personal status code,[2] and there have been different efforts by successive governments to make changes to the code. In pointing to successive Egyptian regimes and the laws they have passed which affected women's status, it is useful to discuss top-down, cosmetic, state feminism. Under Nasser, Egypt promoted State Feminism as an official strategy to improve women's status, as well as promote its national image as a progressive country. Bier (2011) explores 'the interrelated attempts of political elites' during Nasser's era, 'to fashion a new nation-state and a "new" yet authentically Egyptian womanhood during a particularly formative and turbulent era of modern Egyptian history' (p. 2). Such projects also aimed at 'the nationalization of foreign companies, and eventually the creation of a distinctly Arab Socialist state' (ibid.). State feminism under Nasser benefitted the elite but not working-class and rural women. Further, Nasser's policies were not able to change the patriarchal, traditional mentality prevalent in Egyptian society.

President Sadat, Nasser's successor, also tried to improve women's rights in the areas of education and employment but faced fierce opposition from conservatives when he planned to institute laws to improve women's rights in the personal status code. Sadat, via a presidential decree, passed the law that granted women the right to divorce, even though the Assembly voted against it (Olimat 2014, p. 80). At the same time, in his amendment to the constitution, Sadat made Shari'a 'the principal source of Egyptian legislation' (Karam 1998, p. 101). Because of increasing pressure from religious conservatives, many Egyptian women in the 1980s and 1990s felt that their rights were threatened by the rise of Islamism.

Abdallah's documentary shows how historical progress towards gender equality has reverted to traditional patriarchal patterns that are detrimental to the enfranchisement of women socially and politically. It sheds light on the retreat to gender traditionalism that has occurred during the last three decades under Mubarak's regime. Al-Ali points out that, because of the pressure Islamists put on Mubarak to institute Sharia law, the latter 'implemented more conservative laws and policies towards women' thus limiting 'support for women's political representation' (al-Ali 2000, p. 75). To further appease the Islamists, Mubarak's regime amended the personal status code in 1985, which was often viewed as anti-Islamic, thus stripping women of many of the rights that were part of the earlier version (ibid.). Abouelnaga further articulates the complicated relationship between Mubarak's regime and women by blaming the so-called Suzanne's Laws of depriving women's rights of any legitimacy on the grounds that: '[t]he law was used as a tool for propagating women's rights, in so far as it pertained to the project of modernism, and, at the same time, it was used to enforce patriarchal conservative values that allowed for more social control' (Abouelnaga 2016, p. 16). Since the discourse of women's rights was associated with the First Lady, Suzanne Mubarak, who was part of a corrupt regime, there was even more antagonism towards women's rights following the ouster of Mubarak (ibid.). Khamis and Mili (2018, pp. 12–13) describe 'this second' phase of 'state feminism' as

> mostly characterized by a form of … tokenistic feminism, which was mostly dictated and imposed by the regimes in power. One of the most functions which this type of feminism serves is acting as a political prop, which is used to convey the image of a modern, secular, forward-looking country.

Khamis refers to what she terms 'the first lady syndrome', which means 'the reliance on the image, fame and credibility of the first lady to pass certain legislations or to take certain steps which are perceived to be favorable to women, usually with little trickledown effect to wider segments of the population at large' (2018, p. 13).

Because the concept of women's rights in Egypt was co-opted by the state, it took feminists several decades of activism for reforms pertaining to marriage to begin to take effect. In 2000, the Egyptian government yielded to such demands by drafting a new divorce law, which grants women the right to divorce in a new system called *khula* (Sanja and Breslin 2010, p. 407). Even though *khula* was instituted during Mubarak's era, women's rights were nevertheless dealt a serious blow during his dictatorial rule. Family law favoured men and polygamy was not abolished. The Egyptian Women's Union was officially closed and feminists were imprisoned. Several feminist critics have articulated the contentious relationship between women's movements and the state since independence from the British. Badran (1995) explores the ambiguous relationship between woman and nation. It is true that the nationalist political elite did not acknowledge women's political rights; however, the Egyptian Feminist Union had been active until 1956, when it was shut down by Nasser.

A woman's film

By bringing together women's perspectives on issues that continue to provoke most anger and opposition such as marriage and divorce, the film is a critique of male-centred discourses that have silenced women's voices and restricted their interventions. In this respect, the film brings gender issues into mainstream culture and politics. The film fits within trends in Arab feminism, as well as within recent trends in women's filmmaking in the MENA region, in which women filmmakers explore 'problems defined as female ... revolving around domestic life, the family, children, self-sacrifice' (Doane 1981, p. 3). Looking at marriage in Abdallah's film is important in exemplifying important characteristics of these types of films: the divorced woman, the widow, the overwhelmed mother and the disillusioned unmarried woman. The film pictures women's lives at a time of political transition, corresponding to the anxieties 'linked to the ideological upheaval signaled by a redefinition of sexual roles and the reorganization of the family during the war years' (p. 4). The question is: how did the 2011 revolution change Egyptian women's perceptions, understandings and concepts about marriage, and how have these understandings of domestic relationships influenced how women contributed to the revolution? While the revolution changed domestic paradigms within the private sphere, the changing domestic paradigms and women's feminist activism outside the private sphere also helped contribute to fuelling the revolution. As revealed in particularly compelling ways, the film exposes how women's understandings of marriage intersect with Egyptian politics and highlights links between their domestic lives and the transitional process to democracy in Egypt. The four women protagonists depicted in the film reflect on marital and love relations in Egyptian society, share their perspectives on the revolution and call for gender reforms, in the context of the realities they are living during the post-Mubarak era.

The commitment to listening to women in this film is particularly striking in light of the tendency of earlier feature films to marginalize women in general and render them mute and powerless. The idea of a 'woman's film' is really important, hence the value of women's film production, and women filming other women, thus giving voice to the voiceless. The documentary has enabled women to 'express themselves freely and their voices to be heard by the rest of the world, particularly the global media. This resulted in a multidimensional personal, social, political and communicative revolution' (Radsch and Khamis 2013, p. 881). Egyptian-American journalist Mona Eltahawy rightly states that 'the power of women is in their stories ... they are not theories, they are real lives, that, thanks to social networks, we are able to share and exchange' (quoted in Radsch and Khamis 2013, pp. 881–2).

Abdallah chose four women to articulate the story of Egyptian politics within the framework of their domestic lives. Women's political, social and economic struggles are metaphorically conveyed through marriage in the film, since all four women are shown either reflecting on the end of bad marriages or relationships, reminiscing on loving marriages or complaining about the entrapments of marital life. Through their stories, marriage either signifies a feudal system that is oppressive for women, or a modern one based on choice, love and rights. Suzanne insists in her interviews that it is her right to choose her partner. As she reminisces about her dead husband, Shahinda tells her interviewer that her marriage was based on love and equality. While Shahinda and Suzanne believe that marriage should be based on freedom and personal rights, Wafaa and Badryeya's stories exemplify marriage as a feudal system. The institution of marriage in the film seems to mirror the central dynamics in Egyptian politics regarding the status of citizenship and the meaning of equality. In a sense, marriage reflects the norms and practices of the political regime, as it defines dependent relations and supports hierarchical relationships. The camera follows the characters as they reveal their thoughts and relationships and thus allows us to see women who are either trapped with no escape or those who defy conventions and become the sole arbiters of their lives.

Wafaa's story

In the Shadow of a Man looks through a gendered lens at the political and sociocultural restrictions that act like barriers. The film exposes traditional notions of marriage in its depiction of Wafaa's story from the 1960s, offering a negative attitude towards marriage. The first scene of the film portrays Wafaa as a lonely and poor woman, who is trapped in her situation. One barrier that indicates the impossibility of escape is the narrow, endless street in which she is shown walking with only nothingness at the end of sight. Using the gaze of her camera as it looks at Wafaa's domestic life, Abdallah seems less concerned with framing than with portraying the life of this character within her own context. By breaking through cultural and gender boundaries, the documentary is transgressive, making visible women who live behind walls. For example, in the second sequence of the film, the camera films Wafaa in her small apartment, highlighting her interior trajectory and delving into her previous marriage, thus becoming a meditation on memory. The camera allows viewers fullest access to Wafaa and her traditional context and foregrounds the forces that try to obscure and control her.

Abdallah captures the frustration and despair of women in Wafaa's generation who were trapped in abusive marriages and then divorced, having to work domestic jobs to support themselves. Wafaa's limited freedom of movement due to such pressures is, however, contested on the screen. Subsequent camera shots show her walking along narrow alleys overshadowed by walls. This perspective embodies for the filmmaker an impetus towards a far-reaching drive for the character's mastery over her limiting surroundings. The filmmaker uses Wafaa's walking as a mode of resistance, endowing her with visual mastery over the setting. As Wafaa's story unfolds, the audience becomes more aware of how she conceives 'marriage'. Wafaa sets the tone for the dividing gender lines between the male and female worlds portrayed: 'I do not like men. I like them only as friends. But not for marriage. I am living life like a nun. They do not like me, and I do not like them.' Her proclamation is a transgressive gesture through which she strives to occupy a position other than that imposed by her culture, thus challenging social conventions. She is determined to fight for equality in all aspects of life. Wafaa is not a feminist activist in the traditional sense, nor does she think of herself as someone who acts on behalf of feminism and gender equality. Feminist activism in Egypt – and in the Arab World in general – takes many forms, especially in the aftermath of the Arab Spring, from participation in political campaigns and political protest to civil disobedience. Wafaa is a so-called ordinary woman who has developed an understanding of gender oppression through the experience of her marriage, and the film uses narrative strategies to picture such an awakening. Implicitly challenging the image of the Egyptian woman as submissive to male authority, the film suggests that women's independence depends on willingness to transgress cultural and political assumptions. In refusing to adopt a culture that demonizes women who do not agree with its tenets, Wafaa chooses to divorce her husband and work abroad to earn a living. Her new economic responsibility clearly illustrates a reshaping of gender roles that Egypt's social and political instability permit.

Wafaa wears the traditional veil usually worn by her generation of Egyptian women. The veil is a re-enactment of social, cultural and political boundaries, and the film questions assumptions about the veil. Not all women pictured in the film are veiled, and those who are veiled wear different kinds of veiling. This resonates with Ahmed's observation about the complexity of the veil and its local and global implications (2014). The arguments and perspectives surrounding the issue of the veil are complex and diverse, given the multiple sources offering different explanations, whether religious, cultural, social or economic, and it is therefore impossible to capture all of them within the scope of this study. But through Wafaa's veil and the social conventions that seek to keep her invisible, the filmmaker exposes the culture's attempt to separate between genders. It is a way to guard itself against a presumed threat from beyond the wall that the culture itself has put in place. As a self-proclaimed fighter, Wafaa challenges the gendered and cultural factors that allow such barriers to exist: 'I always fought back .... You have to fight back against the people who do not want you to live the life you want. Divorce is freedom.' In the eyes of society, however, Wafaa's social status is diminished: 'When I got divorced, I was not allowed to go out or to move into a place of my own. I felt I was trapped. That is why I accepted any job offer outside Egypt.'

Through Wafaa's story the film recovers a history of traditional marriage politics in Egypt while also resonating with the early era of women's liberation. During this era, women faced inequality, but they were still outspoken and hardworking. The upper classes in Egypt at this time lived a more western lifestyle, so some women were more emancipated. Early feminists called for reform of laws regarding marriage, divorce and inheritance that hampered women's legal status. Leading figures in this movement included Huda Shaarawi, a member of the upper class, and Amina al-Said, who lived in the segregated world of the harem but who was also a middle-class intellectual and editor of the first women's magazine *Hawwa* ('Eve').[3] Shaarawi draws attention in her book *Harem Years* (1986, p. 84) to the problems of her marriage. She states that her eventual divorce from her husband was a gateway to more independence. Wafaa, too, was married at an early age and divorce gave her a taste of freedom. In one episode she insists to her interviewer that 'divorce is freedom because it frees you from the man who is suffocating you.' While Wafaa's story shares some traits with Shaarawi's life, her experience cannot be assimilated to the upper class experience of Shaarawi. She remarks in one scene that she had to travel to the Gulf for a job and that, while now in Egypt, she works as a maid to support herself. Despite differences in class status, Abdallah's film, like Shaarawi's *Harem Years*, emphasizes women's domestic imprisonment in various ways. Shaarawi grew up in the Harem's society (aristocratic and urban at the end of the nineteenth-century society), but the Harem that is described in her memoirs and in her biography, *Casting off the Veil*, written by her niece Nini (2012), is not the same space of segregation portrayed through Wafaa's visual narrative about marriage oppression. Shaarawi was not secluded, since she had an intense public life, including international networks. Wafaa's story, on the other hand, tells of her imprisonment within walls. The very title, *In the Shadow of a Man* ('في ظل رجل'), might imply women's imprisonment. However, it could also be argued that the title refers to 'a Man' and not culture, and it is not totally obvious that 'in the shadow' refers to imprisonment, or even punishment. It is also speculative whether the audiences who watch Abdallah's documentary would interpret either religion, or patriarchy or Mubarak's regime as most responsible for the condition of women in Egypt.

Abdallah implies, through the narrow alley ways pictured at the beginning of the film, that not only political regimes but also 'culture' imprisons women. The walls, narrow alleys and small spaces show the way culture chastises any transgression of boundaries. Punishment and imprisonment are different from 'chastising', however, and walls or boundaries are all linked in the film. It is obvious that space is used not only as a setting to highlight Wafaa's social condition, but also as metaphors for oppressive marriages and relationships. Abdallah includes walls as both actual settings and psychic spaces in order to highlight the crisis of marriage and gender identity in Egypt as well as critique and subvert power relations between men and women, and the military and the people. Therefore, walls not only signify the current national crisis and tense sociopolitical situation in the post-Mubarak era, but also serve as metaphors for women's entrapment in a society still ruled by traditions and conventional social roles. As Wafaa recalls, 'my husband wanted me to be at home all the time'. He subjected her to constant surveillance in a way that resembles the world of law enforcement imposed by the military on Egyptians. Thus, the film highlights the boundaries that divide Egyptian society from within, and which are not necessarily territorial in form. Failed marriages, administrative barriers, failed political regimes, corruption and social injustice all manifest as physical boundaries in the form of fences and walls.

Badreya

The film also sheds light on the crisis of marriage through the story of Badreya. Here, Abdallah evokes feminists who expanded the conversation beyond marriage to address a range of other issues, including women's access to jobs, reproductive rights and political participation. It hints at feminist issues such as promoting economic equality, reproductive and work rights, and egalitarian marriage. From the very outset, Badreya exhibits a feminist consciousness in that she is aware of her political rights and eager to participate in elections for the new 2012 constitution, in the aftermath of the revolution. She is unable, however, to exercise her equal right to work because of social factors in Upper Egypt, a region which is more patriarchal than other parts of the country. The film advances a radical critique of patriarchal patterns in marriage, as well as discrimination against women in the job market. Badreya is critical of Mubarak's corrupt government and she laments the fact that she has not been able to find a job despite her degree. Her tasks in Saeed (Upper Egypt) are limited to the domestic realm – managing the household during a time of economic crisis. It is obvious, however, that Badreya does not find these tasks rewarding, even if they are normal duties. Hijab (2001), a feminist scholar, has pointed out that Arab women present the worst case of invisibility in terms of work, and their share of earned income is the lowest in the world. She blames social and cultural constraints, Arabs' emphasis on cultural identity and the role women play in preserving this identity. She further explains that women's invisibility is more evident in Upper Egypt where, according to a survey conducted in the mid-80s, 'between 55 and 70 percent [of women] were involved in agricultural production. … and 75 percent were engaged in animal husbandry' (p. 41).

While the film highlights the predicament of Badreya and the pitfalls of marital domesticity, it simultaneously rejects common images of Egyptian women that their culture projects and yet affirms them, a rather daring move in light of the conservative climate of contemporary Egypt. Here, Abdallah aims to give us insight into the dynamics of gender in Upper Egypt and how the nature of the workforce in rural areas is gendered, with women comprising a large percentage of agricultural labour and earning low wages. Badreya is a resourceful agent since she contributes to her family's income and takes on a disproportionate share of unpaid work at home. But she is not able to achieve her full potential because of unequal access to job opportunities in the public sphere, as well as a marriage that restricts her mobility. She acknowledges her awareness of opportunities missed and a life wasted: 'Before I got married, I wanted to go to art school and become a painter. I love painting. But none of that happened. But, after marriage, I felt trapped by the responsibilities of the house and children.' In framing Badreya's regrets and her further thoughts on marriage this way, the film critiques the roles of wife and mother that men impose on women. Out of these regrets has arisen an apprehension about her future that reflects a cultural imperative, both gendered and political, that hinders women's progress.

The film links Badreya's marital experience with the political situation in Egypt. The wide-angle camera shot of the countryside, stretching out from sunlit rooms where Badreya is filmed, is juxtaposed with images of Tahrir Square, which bring the movement of violent civil dissent into sharp focus. Scenes from Badreya's daily life and her surroundings are undercut by shots of the revolution unfolding in the Square. In filming the 2011 revolution, the documentary further juxtaposes the tensions extant in the public and private spaces. Outside of the claustrophobic interior spaces of the domestic sphere, where women like Badreya are besieged, is the expansive public space of Tahrir Square, where women are actively participating in the revolution. The film's critique of the condition of women and the values of traditional gender roles extolled by Egyptian society is brought into sharp relief by images of women chanting slogans during the intensifying uprising. The viewer of subsequent images of the Egyptian military shooting at protesters, including women, and dropping explosives, may help the audience understand the mixture of fear and anger that leave Badreya apprehensive about her future and more determined than ever to participate in politics. She is left hopeful that 'for the first time ever, many women in our village went to vote [and for] that referendum. … That referendum about the new constitution that happened after Mubarak stepped down.' Here the film hints at the referendum after the fall of Mubarak's regime, when the military signalled their intention to share power with civilians and amend the constitution. Even more important, during the time of the uprising in which women's bodies became battlefields upon which the military and male protesters contested, Abdallah's documentary ultimately puts the condition of women within the context of the 2011 revolution and questions patriarchal hegemonic discourses that endanger vulnerable but resolute Egyptian women. Badreya is hopeful that the new constitution is going to promote democracy and gender equality, but Arab feminist scholars such as Khamis and Mili (2018) have lamented the fact that the revolution has not led to democracy in Egypt and that, in fact, there has been no transition. They argue that gender equality does not just rest on constitutions or laws but has more to do with mentalities and 'underlying structures of injustice and cultural practices of discrimination, which negatively impact Arab women and limit their potential for growth, development and advancement politically, socially and legally' (p. 6). It might be true that the revolution will not automatically lead to gender equality, but as a result of it, Badreya changed and became a woman concerned with gender issues. She now refuses to accept her domestic role in life and demands her husband's partnership in their marriage.

Suzanne

The film also engages with marriage politics and the 2011 revolution from the perspective of Suzanne, an Islamic woman who wears a *hijab* but views marriage as consent and individual independence. Suzanne, a socially and politically active young woman who owns a clothing store, is still single at age thirty-five and chooses financial independence because marriage for her should mean freedom and rights. She represents a new kind of Egyptian woman, the aspiring business owner who prides herself on having a job and financial autonomy. Her clothing store becomes a meeting space and refuge for women to express their viewpoints about gender issues. Women's increased presence in the store, even in such a consumer-oriented space, offers new opportunities for them to more publicly express their views about the veil, politics and marriage. In one scene, Suzanne states that she chooses to wear a *hijab* because '[She] felt that the men who were proposing were simply attracted to [her] physically.' The filmmaker uses irony to highlight two conflicting positions towards the veil. Whereas for Westerners, Suzanne's *hijab* constitutes imprisonment and oppression, for her, the veil is a way of achieving autonomy. Such scholars as Accad (1978), for instance, have traditionally looked at Muslim women as suppressed and oppressed, and refer to the veil as a 'symbol of oppression'. The wearing of the veil by politically, socially and intellectually active Egyptian women such as Suzanne challenges Western audiences to look more closely at their stereotypical view of the veil in order to see Muslim women's true identities. Women like Suzanne argue for a religious feminism that recovers women's rights from the current political system, which she views as dictatorial and traditional. Thus, feminism, in her view, is a way to recover rights that Mubarak's regime has confiscated from women.

Suzanne exemplifies such grassroots activism when she participates first-hand in the revolution. There she discovers politics and realizes the importance of women's participation. She states:

> Before the 25th of January, I was not politically active at all. I did not even know anything about the constitution or how the country was being run. But during the revolution, I was among politically active people and I learned a lot about politics and our rights …. I was happy someone initiated the call for change. So that we could start to speak up and break up the barrier of fear.

The crucial barrier she discovers also marks women's exclusion from politics. Thus, her reminiscences about the revolution highlight the crucial role women played: 'When people would clang metals to signal that thugs were approaching, women would run to the frontlines with the men.' Suzanne's presence in Tahrir Square is a kind of defiance to the military's objection to a female presence because it threatens its sense of maleness, as well as its objection to a woman's agency beyond the domestic role that the culture has assigned her. The film flashes back to events that happened in Tahrir Square when the military authorized itself to repress the revolution, thereby revealing that military's support of a patriarchal culture that has always subjugated women. During the protests, women were everywhere, singing songs, chanting 'down, down with Mubarak' and calling for retribution in response to the killing of civilians. Women move freely in the square and close-up camera shots document their participation in the revolution. In one scene, the military responds to protesters with gunfire, as women peer from windows and rooftops. One of the wide-angled shots exposes a woman standing on the roof and chanting: 'He who imprisons his own people is from head to toe a traitor.' Thus, the film reveals a cultural as well as a political edge to the situation these women experience. Not only does the military prevent their free movement but, in line with Egyptian traditions, it imposes curfews that also weigh the women down. Adopting the perspective of its women protagonists, the film suggests the possibility of identifying across gender differences, or at least learning to look at the events unfolding in Egypt from the perspective of women.

Suzanne represents the young generation of the Egyptian youth movement that ignited the revolution. She is the embodiment of young activists such as Esraa Abdel-Fattah, who believe that the end of the Mubarak era is a harbinger of change for women who

> gathered to declare their needs and demands by building their own organizations, coalitions and associations. Women [have] looked for different outlets for activism, from participating in awareness campaigns in the streets and public transportation, to joining political parties and nominating themselves for election to the people's assembly.
>
> (Pederson and Salib 2013, p. 258)

What the film also ultimately makes visible is the cost of exclusionary efforts aimed at women who have internalized their subjugation. It is shocking for Western audiences to hear Suzanne's objection to women's election in parliament, despite her involvement in the revolution:

> In my opinion, a woman has limits. I am not prepared to elect a woman in parliament ... a woman who is pregnant or who has young children. How would she be able to devote herself for the parliament? She will not be up to the job she is doing.

In this way, the film suggests that whatever prevents women from participating in politics also estranges them from one another and precludes connection among them. Suzanne's attitude exemplifies the position of Egyptian women who strongly refute calls for changing women's roles. While she seems concerned with women's issues, whether she can be described as a feminist is quite a different issue. Although she views marriage as based on mutual love and reciprocal rights, she still holds conservative views with regards to women's role in politics. This is in alliance with Islamic feminism which sees men and women not as different in capability but rather in their characteristics and roles in society. While the boundary set by the veil seems to protect the integrity of these women's cultural commitments and performed identities, the film, at the same time, shows that women like Suzanne might pose the greatest dilemma for Egyptian feminism, in that they expose its limitations.

Shahinda Maklad

Abdallah's documentary also adds another perspective on marriage and politics through the life and experience of Shahinda Maklad, a Nasser-era leftist who was active in the 1952 revolution, in student and nationalist movements, as well as the 2011 revolution. The film suggests that women, like Shahinda, who enjoy an equitable partnership with their husbands, and relative freedom in their marriage, are more involved in politics. Shahinda, an activist who is known for her campaigns for peasants' rights, and also participated in the protests in Tahrir Square, admits that, even though she belongs to a religious culture where 'traditions still rule', both her father and her husband nurtured her independence. Side by side with her husband, she played a huge role in the 1952 revolution, which eventually led to her husband's assassination in 1966. She subsequently took up her husband's cause and helped farmers claim land from feudal landowners by redistributing land among small peasants. Shahinda is also featured in Rached's documentary *Four Women of Egypt* (1997), which centres on four women friends whose lives have been affected by the changes which happened during the Nasser era.

The appropriation of the story of a socialist activist who grew up within Nasser's revolutionary culture is far more purposeful at a time of great political transition. In addition to highlighting her involvement in the 1952 revolution, the film shows the role Shahinda played in unionizing farmers after the fall of Mubarak's regime. In one scene, she speaks to the camera about her commitment to the farmers' cause, on a day which happens to be 'the inauguration of the farmers' union. The first independent, democratic union for all Egyptian farmers'. For her, the struggle for farmers' rights and women's rights is one struggle, since, as she states, 'a woman cannot be independent in a country that is not independent. She cannot be effective in a country plagued with inefficiency, and she cannot be free in a country that is enslaved.' Shahinda explains that the most essential form of freedom for her was the right to choose her husband Hussein, with whom she eloped after her mother objected to the marriage. Their marriage also defied traditions because of their involvement in politics. As a female activist, Shahinda, however, has to use rhetoric as a mother and an ex-wife to justify her own place in a public space. While highlighting the position of the vulnerable farmer, her role as protector and moral guardian of farmers' rights is more about creating space for her to participate publicly in a manner that men would deem appropriate. Shahinda was also able to justify her presence in public debates by citing farmers' protection. Abdallah has obviously used the character of Shahinda to demonstrate that fighting for freedom could allow international norms of human rights to override tradition and culture. By noting Shahinda's role in the 1952 peasant uprising and her participation in the 2011 revolution, Abdallah shows how workers' resistance is what leads to revolutions. She therefore invites us to make links between old protests and the new protest movement of subaltern subjects that emerged after January 2011. The film was made in 2012, before El Sisi became president. Thus, it does not address the increasing influence of trade unions and workers' activism under El Sisi's regime, which forced El Sisi[4] to appoint a new minister of manpower. Nasserist leftist Shahinda, however, has not lived to see how the revolution she fought for has led to more authoritarianism under El Sisi's regime, which continues to marginalize and oppress women, and how trade unions under the current regime have not delivered their promises to the Egyptian workers they claim to represent. Pratt (2020) points out that El Sisi's regime supports women's movements as long as they respect the gender hierarchies of the nation-state: 'However, in contrast to previous Egyptian regimes, El Sisi's state formation is embedded within the most repressive and militaristic project of authoritarian restoration seen in the history of modern Egypt' (p. 26).

Conclusion

Asked about why she made such a film within the framework of the 2011 revolution, Abdallah states:

> I have always known that there is a wealth of stories waiting to be told by women in Egypt. But, the truth is that after the revolution I had mixed feelings about making a film that focused on women: I felt that it was a subject matter that was being fetishized. What made me carry on despite my concerns was an overwhelming feeling, or perhaps duty, to make a film that would open up discussion about how gender is constructed in Egypt, and the uncomfortable truth of how this defines the parameters of the freedom that women have.
>
> (UN Women, 2012)

But at the heart of this 'duty' to examine how gender is constructed in Egypt is a portrayal of the film's female characters and their lives. Such a portrayal – wonderful, beautifully made and inspiring as the film is – seems limited on a first viewing of the film. Moreover, it may be true that the documentary mirrors the true situation of Egyptian women; however, the audience is left unsure how women might change the nature of their struggle and the forces that limit their freedom. Abdallah did not tell her audiences how women could change the nature of their struggle, but her commitment to listening to women is helping them find their own voice to empower themselves. This decided shift in the representation of women gives the viewer the sense that Egyptian women are looking past the boundaries constructed to exert control over them. Regardless of their level of political agency, it seems that they have acquired certain tools and resources that might bring change in their status quo in the future. For women such as Suzanne, who have achieved some economic independence, an increasing tendency to refuse marriage may indicate a growing sense of empowerment. The film describes alternatives to marriage such as work and political activism. If Egyptian women view the film, they can recognize in it the nature of their own struggle and empowerment. While they may realize how their culture has constructed walls to exert control of one kind or another over them, they must also grasp the urgency of transgressing these boundaries, and the value of cinematic mediums like Abdallah's film to help them see through those walls.

Working with UN Women, Abdallah's film has now taken just such a message of female empowerment to an international scale. Meanwhile, several questions still must be addressed. For example, by sponsoring this movie, is UN Women trying to impose a Western view of marriage on Egyptian women? It would have made the film more powerful if the filmmaker had included what Egyptian women thought of this film. Did it convince them of the urgency of transgressing boundaries? The question is not even whether people in the audience understand the value of cinematic mediums such as documentaries, but did/would seeing Abdallah's film help women see through their situation? It is unlikely that every woman, even every feminist, who watches the film would have the same response.

Asking different kinds of women about their response to the film would help the audience see how they made meaning of the film and the film's explicit or implied ideas about feminism, marriage and the revolution. Asking audience members who they thought the documentary blames for women's oppression or women's struggles and who they would blame would also be important.

Despite its limitation, Abdallah's film provides a potential space to helps us understand the connections between academic literature and the political, social and economic challenges facing Egyptian women during a time of political transition, as well as the mediated representation of these women's identities and journeys. The documentary contributes to efforts to democratize Egypt by putting visual information about women's stories, the poor and those inhabiting subaltern positions into circulation, in the hope of a democratic structure that recognizes silenced voices so that they can be included in the politics of a new Egypt.

Notes

1   UN Women was created in 2010 by the UN and is short for 'United Nations Entity for Gender Equality and the Empowerment of Women' (Refworld n.d.).

2   The personal status code in Egypt is based on Islamic law and governs issues relating to marriage, divorce and inheritance.

3   Available at: https://brill.com/view/journals/haww/haww-overview.xml.

4   For more information on trade unions in Egypt, see El-Shazli (2019).

References

Abouelnaga, S. (2016). *Women in revolutionary Egypt: Gender and the new geographics of identity*. Cairo: University of Cairo Press.

Accad, E. (1978). *Veil of shame: The role of women in the contemporary fiction of North Africa and the Arab world*. Sherbrooke. QC: Éditions Naaman.

Ahmed, L. (2014). *A quiet revolution: The veil resurgence, from the Middle East to America*. New Haven: Yale University Press.

Al-Ali, N. (2000). *Secularism, gender and the state in the Middle East: The Egyptian women's movement*. Cambridge: Cambridge University Press.

Badran, M. (1995). *Feminism, Islam and nation: Gender and the making of modern Egypt*. Princeton, NJ: Princeton University Press.

Bier, L. (2011). *Revolutionary womanhood: Feminisms, modernity, and the state in Nasser's Egypt*. Stanford: Stanford University Press.

Charrad, M.M. (2001). *States and women's rights: The making of postcolonial Tunisia, Algeria and Morocco*. Berkely: University of California Press.

Dawood, A. (2011). 'Backlash against 'Suzanne Mubarak laws' was inevitable', *Egypt Independent*, 8 November. Available at: https://egyptindependent.com/backlash-against-suzanne-mubarak-laws-was-inevitable/ [accessed 23 April, 2021].

de Silva De Alwis, R. (2013). 'Introduction', in *Women in democratic transitions in the MENA region*, pp. 1–8. Report by the Global Women's Leadership Initiative. Washington, DC: Woodrow Wilson International Center for Scholars. Available at: https://www.wilsoncenter.org/sites/default/files/media/documents/publication/ Women_in_democratic_transitions_in_the_MENA_region_compilation.pdf [accessed 23 April, 2021].

Doane, M.A. (1981). 'Woman's stake: Filming the female body', *The New Talkies*, 17, pp. 22–56.

El-Shazli, H.F. (2019). *Trade unions and Arab revolutions: Challenging The regime in Egypt.* London: Routledge.

Four women of Egypt. (1997). Directed by T. Rached. Ottawa: National Film Board of Canada. Available at: https://www.nfb.ca/film/four_women_egypt/ [accessed 11 November 2018].

Hijab, N. (2001). 'Women and work in the Arab world', in S. Joseph and S. Slyomovics (eds.) *Women and Power in the Middle East*, pp. 41–51. Philadelphia: University of Pennsylvania Press.

In the shadow of a man. (2012). *Directed by Hanan Abdallah.* England: Magic Works Production Company.

Karam, A. (1998). *Women, Islamisms and the state: Contemporary feminisms in Egypt.* London: Palgrave Macmillan.

Khamis, S. (2010). 'Islamic feminism in new Arab media – Platforms for self-expression and sites for multiple resistances', *Journal of Arab & Muslim Media Research*, 3(3), pp. 237–55.

Khamis, S. and Mili, A. (eds.). (2018). *Arab women's activism and socio-political transformation: Unfinished gendered revolutions.* New York: Palgrave Macmillan.

Lanfranchi, S.S. (2020). *Casting off the veil: The life of Huda Shaarawi, Egypt's first feminist.* London: I.B. Tauris.

Mosireen Collective. (2012). 'Shahinda Maklad: Beyhawlou yekamemou sout masr. Mish haye'darou' ['Shahinda Maklad: They are trying to silence Egypt. They won't be able to'], 9 December. Available at: https://www.youtube.com/watch?v=U-MsqcaH9UA [accessed 14 June 2018].

Olimat, M. (ed.). (2014.) *Arab Spring and Arab women: Challenges and opportunities.* New York: Routledge.

Pedersen, J. and Salib, M. (2013). 'Women of the Arab Spring: A conversation with Esraa Abdel-Fattah and Lina Ben Mhenni', *International Feminist Journal of Politics*, 15 (2), pp. 256–66. Available at: http://doi.org10.1080/14616742.2013.796218.

Pratt, N. (2020). *Embodying geopolitics: Generations of women's activism in Egypt, Jordan, and Lebanon.* Oakland: University of California Press.

Radsch, C and Khamis, S. (2013). 'In their own voice: Technologically mediated empowerment and transformation among young Arab women', *Feminist Media Studies*, 13(5), pp. 881–90.

Refworld. (n.d.). 'UN Entity for Gender Equality and the Empowerment of Women (UNWOMEN)'. Available at: https://www.refworld.org/publisher,UNWOMEN,20. html [accessed 23 April 2021].

Sania, Shaarawi Lanfranchi (2012). *Casting off the veil: The biography of Huda Shaarawi.* Edited by John Keith King. London: I.B. Tauris Publishers.

Sanja, K. and Breslin, J. (2010). *Women's rights in the Middle East and North Africa: Progress amid resistance.* New York: Rowman and Littlefield.

Shaarawi, H. (1986). *Harem years: The memoirs of an Egyptian feminist, 1879–1924.* Translated by M. Badran. New York: Feminist Press.

UN Women. (2012). 'Q&A with Hanan Abdalla, director of a new film that explores the lives of Egyptian women since the Arab Spring', *News and Events*, 9 April. Available at: https://www.unwomen.org/en/news/stories/2012/4/q-a-with-hanan-abdalla-director-of-a-new-film-that-explores-the-lives-of-egyptian-women-since-the-a [accessed 23 April 2021].

Chapter 10

#TECHREVOLT IN THE ARAB GULF: GENDERED GRASSROOTS RESISTANCE OR STATE VIOLENCE?

Hasnaa Mokhtar

Technological lenses may lead to a skewed reading of society as they acutely centre on the characteristics and features of the associated technology, overshadowing more complex issues related to culture, politics, and social dynamics. Moreover, they tend to erase historical contexts and, subsequently, render human agency invisible.

(Lim 2018, p. 475)

On 25 October 2018, in a rather theatrical performance, Manal al-Sharif, a Saudi woman, deleted her twitter account live on stage at the SignularityU Nordic Summit, Stockholm. Against a backdrop of a presentation screen entitled 'Digital Liberation Power', which also had a photo of a woman holding a poster sign that read 'Who's afraid of Twitter?!', Al-Sharif announced:

> 'Twitter is really a powerful tool. And it's being used against us. I decided today, in front of everyone here, I'm deleting my Twitter account.'
>
> (@suNordic Oct 25, 2018, 12:35PM)

Her move came less than a month after the murder of journalist Jamal Khashoggi in Saudi Arabia's consulate in Istanbul, Turkey, on 2 October. Khashoggi, a Saudi citizen who went into self-imposed exile in the United States in 2017, utilized his Twitter platform of 1.5 million followers to critique the oppressive policies of Saudi Crown Prince Mohammed bin Salman. He also wrote a monthly column for *The Washington Post* where he expanded on his critique and explained how he had left his family, home and job to raise his voice (Khashoggi 2017). Was Twitter responsible for Khashoggi's death? What did al-Sharif mean when she said that social media is being used against 'us'? The public response to al-Sharif's stunt varied between sympathizing supporters and admirers who commended her bravery, and scornful and sarcastic critics who called her a traitor and a disgrace to Saudi Arabia. 'What a powerful gesture', tweeted SAHAR is me (@ILUVLIT Oct 26, 2018, 7:30AM) in response to al-Sharif deleting her twitter account. In contrast, sara alsudairy (@1SD____ Oct 26, 2018, 5:01AM) tweeted saying, 'You don't want to see Saudi safe. She is a traitor that does not affect Saudi Arabia' (@1SD____ Oct 26, 2018, 5:01AM).

Al-Sharif's public move and the reaction it stirred, as well as her 'activism' legacy, speak to larger issues concerning Arab online communities, their motivations and their role in promoting social change and political engagement in the Arab Gulf region. By online communities or new media, I am referring to social media platforms such as Facebook, Twitter and Instagram, and blogs and news websites. Has their emergence in the Arab Gulf allowed for grassroots resistance to thrive or has it given the states powerful political tools to scrutinize people, hunt them down and maybe murder them? In this chapter, I explore the construction and maintenance of online spaces by individuals and social movements to provide avenues for local grassroots activism in Kuwait and Saudi Arabia. I also examine how the states try to control new media outlets to exert power and control over national public discourses. Further, I caution against adhering uncritically to existing assumptions about the emancipatory capacity of the revolutionary potential of technology.

To push back against the 'exceptionalist discourses [that] are still common about the Arabian Peninsula' (Kanna et al. 2020, p. 3), I specifically analyse 1) the release of the Dutch documentary *Kuwait and the Next Generation* (Tegenlicht 2018) and the backlash it received online and locally – Al Shammari (2019) described as 'an Islamophobic, orientalist documentary'; 2) the emergence of new expressions of local feminist activism online that has given voice to the injustices Bedouins and *Bidūn* (stateless people) experience to challenge elitist and carceral feminisms[1]; and 3) the political role new media – bots or internet robots specifically – have played in targeting and criminalizing Arab Gulf female activists and feminists who try to call out local patriarchal norms. By analysing both bottom-up new media resistance and state-initiated campaigns, my goal is to showcase how new media is a double-edge sword that can serve to create new public spaces but also further gendered state violence.

The whitestream gaze

English-language literature that examines and theorizes sociopolitical issues in the Arab Gulf states is often produced under the influence of the whitestream gaze: state-centric, top-down and gender-blind. Al Shehabi (2019) attests to the similarity between "the language and thoughts of early twentieth-century British colonial officers to many writings in English on the Gulf today" (para. 1). People's (not ruling families, or state heads, or political elites) lived experience and their resistance, as well as minute differentiations of gender, class struggle, racialized division of labour, ethnicity, tribal belonging, education, citizenship status, language, ability and family origin are ignored, if not erased. Here, I call into question the prevailing

Orientalist ideas about the region, its internal coherence, and its inhabitants [that] unfortunately are still deeply held and often prop up state narratives about who can claim rightful national belonging, what forms of rule are natural, and which histories are legitimate.

(Kanna et al. 2020, p. 124)

Hence, theoretical arguments claiming that the '*new* Arab public' (see Lynch 2006), is changing the political scene in the Arab world 'that had long been lacking' (p. 3) because of the flow of information technology, especially post the Arab Spring, fail to acknowledge the histories of grassroots organizing that predated new media and challenged oppression locally in organic ways. Such white-male-centric and "techno-utopian" (Lim 2018, p. 461) frameworks are often imposed on the region in order to shape biased views of events against a backdrop of historical complexities and nuances. Perusing some of the literature, the analysis reads as if Arabs were stuck; they had little intellect and consciousness to fight for better futures and contribute to the Western ideal of 'liberal reforms' (Lynch 2006, p. 5) until the whitestream gaze proposed that new media created public awareness hence a motive for change. Having said that, I do not mean to ignore or undermine the fact that new media has had a substantial influence on supporting collective action and 'gaze pr how people coordinate and mobilize leading to manifestations of collective actions in various forms' (Yuce et al. 2014, p. 4). But organized advocacy in the Arab Gulf cannot be reduced to the effects of modern technology. Because generalized and stereotypical discourses about the region's deficiency, stagnation and backwardness, and the urgent need for catching up with western modernity and *democratization*, date back to when the Arabian Mission (as well as British colonial officers) wrote reports at the beginning of the nineteenth century about Arabs affairs for their superiors back home.

Someway we wanted to bring her [America's] influence more and more over into that neglected gulf and valley … the Arab country of the Persian Gulf and Mesopotamia, of Moslems, yes, and polygamists, 2,000 years behind the times in the march of civilization. A people backward and unprogressive.

(Vlack 1917, p. 21)

To better illustrate my point, I go back to Manal al-Sharif, who became a prominent figure of Saudi women's rights activism. On 21 May 2011, when driving cars was still banned in the country, she was detained for posting a video on YouTube and Facebook of her driving a car in public. After the video went viral (amworldtodaypm 2011; Shubert 2011), authorities got wind of it and the police arrested her, released her, then detained her again the next day. On 30 May, she was released on bail with the promise of neither driving nor discussing what had happened with the media. Within a few days, western media identified al-Sharif as an organizer of the Saudi women's driving movement (MacFarquhar 2011) and attributed her campaigning to the Arab Spring (Associated Press

2011). Eventually #Women2Drive became the official hashtag of the movement, which gave birth to a 'historical moment', with al-Sharif becoming the face of it (Al Omran 2011; Al-Sharif 2018). This simplistic narrative, which has shaped the events surrounding Saudi women's struggle to drive as somehow being all-inclusive and inspired by the Arab uprisings and al-Sharif's 'activism', (1) ignores that driving has been the agenda of Saudi elites because placing a woman behind the wheel is not about changing patriarchal state regulations that put everyday women at a disadvantage (including male guardianship); (2) neglects how the driving ban was championed by western propaganda as the most important issue for Saudi women against other pervasive forms of invisible, structural violence (Abdel-Raheem 2013; Khashoggi 2018); (3) mutes how the Saudi Crown Prince Mohammed bin Salman was hailed as the reformer for lifting the driving ban while Saudi women activists remain jailed and subjected to torture (Ngo 2018; Rothna 2017); and (4) overshadows pre-new media campaigns that existed before al-Sharif's act. For example, on 6 November 1990, forty-seven Saudi women organized a public protest by driving their cars in the streets of Riyadh. They, too, were arrested and released only after pledging not to drive again – except that they had no social media accounts to livestream the protest. In her sharp analysis of the #Women2Drive campaign, Lim (2018) argues that western media and academic discourses have 'misleadingly and ahistorically categorized the Women2Drive campaign' (2018, p. 462) as Twitter and Facebook revolutions, transforming new media users into "symbols of the uprisings" (p. 462).

> The techno-utopian accounts of the Women2Drive campaign resemble much of the early analysis of the Arab uprisings, which proffered an understanding of the MENA movement that was adverse to history and sidelined the region's local knowledges, replacing such knowledges with an assumptions that technology would produce better social or political conditions (Alrasheed 2017). Importantly, these accounts obscured historical resources and material actions while shifting attention away from complexities that inhere within the region.
>
> (Lim 2018, p. 463)

The universality of such technologically utopian frameworks cannot be applied to the Arab Gulf context uncritically (Zayani 2008). There is a need for nuanced and historicized, critical analyses of the relationship between Arab Gulf women's advocacy, organizing and activism, and the impact new media might or might not have on their efforts. I will attempt to demonstrate the complexity of such task in the following few cases.

Kuwait and the 'next generation' documentary

One day in March 2019 as I scrolled through my WhatsApp responding to unread text messages from friends at Worcester, Massachusetts and colleagues I had just met in Kuwait City, a newly acquainted friend messaged me asking, 'as I you heard the buzz? Did you see the documentary?' I wasn't sure what she was referring to. I inquired and a link she shared sent me to a Twitter storm (@VPROTegenlicht 2018) about the documentary they had just released: *Koorddansen in Koeweit* ['Kuwait and the Next Generation'] (*Tegenlicht* 2018). During this time, I was in Kuwait City conducting my doctoral research about gender-based violence, interviewing activists, survivors and advocates. *Tegenlicht*, Dutch for 'Backlight' and a documentary television programme that the Dutch public broadcasting organization VPRO owns, released the documentary and the majority of people in Kuwait were not pleased.

> Behind the shining facades, the fast jet skis, and the mirrored sunglasses of the super wealthy oil state of Kuwait, a young generation of native Kuwaitis know they will be cared for from cradle to grave and they wallow in this prosperity,'
> (*Tegenlicht* 2018)

stated the British narrator, in a dramatic, ostentatious performance at the beginning of the forty-six-minute film. Fareah al-Saqqaf, co-founder of the Kuwaiti youth development organization Loyac, was featured in the documentary and one of her comments in the film stirred strong critique publicly. 'The hijab is okay because it's like a scarf and it's colorful … whatever … but when they are all in black doesn't that scare you?' she said, as images of women in black were playing in the background. The characterization of Kuwaiti women who choose to cover up in black, as scary, when a large segment of Kuwaiti society practices the same for cultural or religious reasons, matches the neoliberal discourse of the need to modernize the savage *others*. Her comments were perceived as an attack against people's belief systems and as proof of her internalized prejudice, racism and elitism (Amer 2019). The documentary rehashed every orientalist and Islamophobic stereotype in the book about Muslims and Arabs: Islamic fundamentalists are terrorists and their women whom they hide in black *abayas* are oppressed. The severe impact of the masculinist and lazy theory of rentierism (Altunışık 2014; Beblawi 2016; Gray 2011) on the documentary's theme is also evident as the language paints all Kuwaitis as wealthy, spoiled, lazy and unmotivated, whose government looks after them extravagantly.

The documentary created an uproar in Kuwait and received varied responses via blogs and social media outlets. People were split between supporters, critics, meditators and those who wanted extreme measures taken against Loyac. The debate was both powerful and impactful. It portrayed the complexity and diversity of Kuwaiti public views. On the one hand, friends of Loyac explained that al-Saqqaf had voiced her opinion and that freedom of speech should be respected. 'It's her personal point of view … Stop judging others! This defines who you are and not who they are', tweeted @AljaziAlsenafi Apr 2, 2019, 5:28AM). On the other hand, people who adhere to wearing the *abaya* unleashed a social media campaign requesting the government shut down Loyac's operations. Text messages circulating on WhatsApp invited individuals, 'especially women and girls', to participate in the Arabic hashtag #قياده_لوياك_تشوه_مجتمعنا# (#Loyac_Leadership_ Distorts_OurSociety). 'If people do not denounce this offensive move, they [Loyac leadership] will continue! Please share', read the text message. It also mentioned how Loyac has a history of rejecting young female participants who wear *abayas* from enrolling in their programs. 'Niqab (face cover) is not an intruder to society; the intruder is your [al-Saqqaf's] thinking', said former parliament member Mubarak al-Dwalia (@AlziadiQ8 Apr 8, 2019, 3:41PM). In a Reddit post discussing the documentary, u/azizboarshed, an anonymous commentator, stated that it was hard to disagree with any of the film's content. To that, another anonymous person commented, saying that there was lots of twisted information in the documentary, geared towards a western audience, to highlight the liberalization of Kuwait.

> Her [al-Saqqaf's] ideas of progressiveness is more of cat fight with the conservatives … the documentary fails to shed light on the sate it self or governmental deep states, Merchants and the conflicting sides of the ruling family.
>
> (u/azizborashed 2019)

In a rather sharp analysis, Kuwaiti-Palestinian activist and researcher Abrar Al Shammari (2019) published a piece on *Medium* breaking down the documentary's 'intentional propaganda'. While she admitted that some of the film's criticism was valid, she also felt that it was poor in quality and problematic:

> I take issue with the one-sided perpetuation of Islamophobic, apolitical, classist propaganda that demonized anything religious, stripped everyone but the wealthy and the powerful of any right to agency and to having a voice, and chose to perpetuate lazy stereotypes of what it means to be a young Kuwaiti instead of trying to learn about our struggles and ambitions and situate them within our social, political, and economic realities.
>
> (Al Shammari 2019, para. 15)

Parliamentary member Mohammed AlDallal said in a video that circulated on Twitter that al-Saqqaf had offended people's religious beliefs and Kuwaiti society's conservative principles. 'She had focused her anger on the manifestations of religiosity in society. With her condescending speech, she excluded the other, spread hatred, defied the concept of coexistence, and gave the wrong information' (@m_h_aldallal Apr 2, 2019, 11:56AM). Some even called for filing a hate crime lawsuit against al-Saqqaf. That was when moderate social media voices intervened to resolve the conflict and analyse her comment in a different light. For example, blogger and influencer Khadeija (@khadeijakw Apr 7, 2019, 2:57PM) said that the reason behind attacking al-Saqqaf was a difference of opinion, because she [al-Saqqaf] saw wearing black as frightening and Khadeija, as well as others, saw it as a normal social phenomenon. She critiqued the calls for cancelling her efforts and closing down Loyac. 'This is called (extremism). Opinion is debated with another option and millions of discussion solutions and viewpoints' (@khadeijakw Apr 7, 2019, 2:57PM). Founder of the Human Rights School in Kuwait, Hadeel BuQrais, tweeted a video of her explaining the difference between an opinion and hate speech. She said that some might take al-Saqqaf's opinion as an open invitation for hate crimes to attack any woman wearing black because she looks scary. 'This stereotypical image might change from an opinion into hate speech. That's why it's important to be cautious when presenting difference of opinion' (@HadeelBuQrais Apr 5, 2019, 1:30PM).

A recent visit to VPRO's *Tegenlicht* website and web page for the documentary's yields the following result when attempting to click on the icon to start viewing the film: 'age uitzending is niet meer beschikbaar', which translates as 'This broadcast is no longer available' (*Tegenlicht* 2018). Did Loyac ask the producers to remove the video? If so, did Loyac finance the production in the first place to have that kind of authority over such decision? Or did the outrage voiced via new media ignite some state officials to pressure Tegnelicht into removing the documentary? Were the producers or al-Saqqaf dreading a lawsuit? I could not come to a definite conclusion or any responses to these questions. But the wide range of opposing reactions as well as the puzzling outcome of the film being removed from the digital world illustrate how 'such developments are making it hard to envisage a single, homogenous or model public sphere' (Zayani 2008, p. 75). It also makes arguments like that of Wheeler, stating matter-of-factly that 'technologies of communication are both symbols of what it means to be Kuwaiti, as well as mechanics through which Kuwaiti identity can be communicated' (2000, p. 436), another form of intentionally generalized short-sighted arguments about technology and Kuwaiti identity.

Bedouin #feminism and Bidūn women

Having grown up in Jeddah, Saudi Arabia to Saudi parents, I was sheltered from many of society's problems, especially those of the marginalized. It was not until I started working as a journalist in *Arab News* (2006–10) that I witnessed the severe conditions foreign or migrant workers who conduct manual labour are subjected to. They come from Indonesia, the Philippines, Bangladesh, Sri Lanka, India, Egypt and other countries in Asia, Africa and the Middle East to suffer extreme forms of labour exploitation, due to the *Kafala* (sponsorship) system, which may be 'comparable to slavery' (Sherry 2004, p. 53). I also came to know about citizenship privilege when I married my non-Saudi husband in 2008 and learned about the inhumane and unjust conditions the *Bidūn* (stateless people) have to bear. Nation-state formation and border control have created systems of nationality and citizenship that embrace some and exclude others. Those on the fringes of society have been denied the right to citizenship and thus forced either to migrate or to remain stuck in complicated living conditions without birth certificates, passports or national identification papers, making it almost impossible to work, marry, receive healthcare and basic human services:

In Kuwait, it has been reported that in Bidoon families, as many as 3, 4 or 5 generations were born consecutively in the Arab Gulf States and that as many as a third of the stateless Bidoon population has a direct link to a female Kuwaiti national through marriage or descent.

(Waas 2010, p. 40)

In 2011, as protests against governments were taking place in different Arab countries, large numbers of stateless *Bidūn* took to the streets of Kuwait, demonstrating peacefully against the discrimination by the government. The protests continued between February and March of 2011 until authorities used gas and water cannons to terminate the gatherings and arrested some of the protestors (Motaparthy 2011). Demands from the *Bidūn* were often met with criminalization and further discrimination. On 5 November 2019, the government proposed a new law aiming to solve the problems of stateless people. The new law came after two stateless young men committed suicide for "feeling humiliated" and being fed up with the injustices committed against them (Albloshi 2019). It was also a response to a hunger strike that a group of detained *Bidūn* embarked on to protest their inhumane living conditions (HRW 2019). International human rights organizations, mainstream media and social media highlighted the plight of stateless people, but the gendered dynamics of the problem were often missing.

Bidūn women face compounded violence at the intersection of their lack of citizenship and their gender, which exposes them to 'heightened risks of abuse and exploitation' (Hanson and Teff 2011, p. 1). Manshoor, an independent website that documents the voices of Arab youth, published a piece in Arabic by Salim (2020) entitled 'The forgotten by feminism: What do *Bidūn* women face?' The author wondered if most feminist figures in Kuwaiti society, who live in a bubble of privileges, knew the suffering *Bidūn* women live through:

I think, as many others think, that our issue is far from their priorities, and completely detached from their reality. Aside from taking all this with extreme sensitivity, I do not undermine the individual efforts of Kuwaiti women who seek to convey the suffering of *Bidūn* women, but these individual scattered voices quickly fade away, like ours.

(Para. 3)

The article discussed in detail the gendered violence *Bidūn* women have been subjected to, which from time to time forces some women to remain silent and not report sexual harassment in the workplace due to fear of losing their source of income. Black feminists (Combahee River Collective 2017) have been at the forefront of calling attention to how 'the experiences of women of color are frequently the product of intersecting pattens of racism and sexism' (Crenshaw 1991, p. 1243). In the Arab Gulf context, institutionalized systems of oppression or structural violence (Galtung 1969) intersect with people's social identities, creating different experiences of oppression for both the *Bidūn* and Bedouin[2] women.

Much of the public feminist discourse and women's rights activism in Kuwait remains dominated by elitist feminists whose advocacy and lobbying efforts are focused on political participation and leadership rights (Albloshi and Alfahad 2009; al-Mughni 2001; Al-Sharekh 2017). But social media outlets have created a space for new voices to emerge, calling attention to the preferably unheard narratives of *Bidūn* and Bedouin women. Around the same time that Salim's (2020) piece was published in *Manshoor*, three women started the account 'bedoon_woomen' on Twitter and Instagram. The Instagram page posted messages in Arabic and English to followers saying:

> Help us celebrate Bedoon women! We are attempting to collect any forms of art, poetry, case studies, movies, documentaries, songs, news, photography that is made by Bedoon women or talks about them.
>
> (bedoon_women 2020b)

Both social media accounts of bedoon_women share content celebrating *Bidūn* women's artistic skills, creativity and invaluable contributions to Kuwaiti society. But they also post many of the multi-layered, invisible, systematic oppression the women face that makes them live a life of imprisonment. While the offline and online activism and organizing of the *Bidūn* in Kuwait are more visible than ever before, broadcasting their daily struggles to the world had little impact on changing the structural violence they face, being treated as 'illegal aliens'. Will persistence in voicing their demands for basic human rights via new media motivate the government to grant them citizenship? Again, I do not have the answer to this question, which brings us back to the argument of the 'new Arab public'. While some argue that 'cyberactivism' by and with oppressed groups can lead to emancipation (Ortiz et al. 2019), this techno-utopian fix does not offer a blueprint for 'democratization' or allow people to become part of decision-making bodies and processes – because the way oppression works is more complicated than internet clicks and video posts. This is not to deny how new technologies have become powerful avenues for people on the margins of society to centre their causes, their lived experiences and their truths. Especially that mainstream media have often downplayed, if not completely turned a deaf ear to, the injustices and needs of such marginalized communities.

Another example of the influential role new media have played in enabling diverse feminist actors in Kuwaiti society to make their voices heard is the Instagram account of @bedouin_acts_of_feminism. Discouraged by the stereotypical image of the Bedouin woman as backward and oppressed, as well as her absence from mainstream feminist activism and discourses in Kuwait, Awaishah Alqahtani created the social media account. Her long-term goal is to write a book based on Bedouin women's lived experiences within three time spans: prior to, during and after the Iraqi invasion of Kuwait. The objective is to uncover feminist roles and acts within the Bedouin culture. Alqahtani felt that 'simple acts of feminism can no longer go unnoticed by the global feminism waves. We need to expand our definition of what feminism means' (2019, personal interview).

Bedouin feminism is the empowerment of Bedouin women within their Bedouin environment, so that the bond between the women and their identities and traditions are not in conflict with their pursuit of achieving their aspirations and goals, making it more adaptable to the nature of the environment. It also refuses the assimilation of the concept of feminism realizing that without the differences in feminist concepts and ideas, there wouldn't be distinguished societies and performances.

(@bedouin_acts_of_feminism 2020)

Pervasive #patriarchy and new media

By the beginning of September 2018, I had already settled in Kuwait City, ready to embark on my research project. A few months prior to landing in the city, I started searching online for Kuwaiti public profiles to follow and to contact locally for discussion and interviews. One of the public personalities I came across on Twitter was a law professor at Kuwait University, Fatima al-Matar. An outspoken activist, feminist and writer, she began appearing in the public domain in May 2012 when she participated in demonstrations in solidarity with the *Bidūn* and was attacked and beaten by authorities (Baraka 2012). She also co-organized protests against censorship of books in Kuwait after which authorities shut down her Twitter account for being 'too vocal in regard to the corruption taking place in the Ministry of Information, and the randomness of books being banned' (al-Matar 2018). My interest in al-Matar's views grew stronger when I landed on her personal blog page and read some of her writings and reflections. Her astute analysis of misogyny and the intersecting systems of oppression that perpetuate different forms of gender-based violence in Kuwait reflected her passion for gender justice. In 2018, she launched a club at Kuwait University called *Noon al-Niswa*[3] to allow students to discuss women's rights, feminisms and oppression in a safe space (Alkhshab 2018).

In October 2018, the Derwaza News website quoted one of al-Matar's tweets, where she voiced her concerns over the number of students who disclosed sexual harassment stories during *Noon al-Niswa* club meetings:

The following topic is sensitive and might cause discomfort to some, but I ask the law association and my law students to help me spread this tweet because the problem is big.

(Derwaza News 2018)

The headline Derwaza News chose for the article zoomed in on part of al-Matar's tweets, where she said that if the way women dressed was the reason they got harassed, then why were queer and modestly dressed students being harassed too. The headline read 'Dr. Fatima al-Matar: Queer students are more exposed to harassment at Kuwait University', which seemed like an intentional effort to stir conservative public opinion against her – especially where the lived experiences of queer and transgender people in Arab Gulf societies remain a taboo.

On 15 October 2018, al-Matar tweeted the following:

Me: Dear God, it's almost my birthday
God: I know!
Me: Can I have a Ferrari?
God: Be reasonable!
Me: Women's rights and gender equality?
God: What colour ferrari?

(Mobasher News 2019)

Everything leading up to this tweet seemed to have created the perfect media storm for those who found al-Matar's views extreme. Her joke provoked a furious backlash from religious conservatives and the government. Cybercrimes at the Ministry of Interior launched an investigation, and she was charged with insulting god, blasphemy and misusing her phone:

They referred me to court because I asked God for a Ferrari, and equal rights to men! I can no longer tolerate this hateful, hypocritical society. I no longer believe in a country that is good at imprisoning its own people.

(al-Matar 2018; Deeb 2019)

Two months later, the news broke that al-Matar had left the country and sought asylum in the United States (Deeb 2019; Nabbout 2019). Public opinion was once again split between proponents and advocates of her decision and vilifiers who thought she had crossed a line and deserved persecution. Other people seized the opportunity to clap back at the unfit governance of parliament members, who weaponized cybercrime laws against talented, critical thinkers in the country. But questions about the hostile local climate toward women, which had pushed al-Matar and other Arab Gulf women to flee their countries (Jaafari 2019; Nasser 2019), sparked a much-needed debate via new media, encouraging people to think about the culture of patriarchy and sexism in cyberspace and everyday life.

Al-Sharekh argues that mass technologies of self-expression did not challenge the powerful grip Arab Gulf states had on communication channels. 'It merely complicated it … it remains to be seen to what extend this [new media influence] will enforce social change' (Al-Sharekh 2017, para. 7). She notes that, when it comes to the rights of women and gender equity debates, patriarchal autocrats view social media as 'a tool for inciting dangerous and deviant behaviour like demands for equality' (Al-Sharekh 2017, para. 5). In reality, the internet has given repressive and patriarchal powers contemporary digital devices to launch smear campaigns against vocal critics, especially feminists. Whether it is the Arab Gulf crisis with Qatar, Khashoggi's murder or the arrest of Saudi women's rights activists in 2018, governments 'can now exploit Twitter as an outlet for political propaganda' (Leber and Abrahams 2019, p. 241). Analysing more than 2.3 million tweets from almost 2,400 accounts (2017–18), Aljazeera reported that internet robots were 'fully or partially automated to amplify certain messages, hashtags or opinions' (Ritzen 2001, para. 6). Al-Matar's case – in addition to the arrest of seven prominent Saudi women's rights activists on 15 May 2018 for campaigning online against the driving ban and the repressive system of male guardianship (al-Qadi 2020) – is evident that the states' patriarchies deploy new media technologies for their own agendas. Pervasive patriarchies have launched smear campaigns against feminists who take a stand against the violence women are subjected to and demand certain patriarchal and oppressive systems currently in place to be abolished, which leads to the women's imprisonment and torture. This formula neither aligns with nor meets the criterion of what has been coined as "liberation technology" (see Diamond and Plattner 2012).

#NoToUniversalism

Using a few case studies from Kuwait and Saudi Arabia, I have attempted to complicate the oversimplified, dominant narratives that glorify the widespread use of technology in the Arab world as a pathway to social justice. Arab Gulf societies are complex. Human life and sociopolitical problems are paradoxical. There is no universal truth that can encompass factors governing, modifying and influencing social behaviour, whether in online or offline public spheres. Additionally, faced with a dual dilemma of (1) a field of social sciences, i.e., communications, that is predominantly white and masculine (Chakravartty et al. 2018) and (2) a severe gap in gender literature that studies the Arab Gulf region, the need for situated knowledge – embodied, relational, personable and inclusive of different worldviews – is a must. Researchers need to consider diverse local voices and lived experiences as legitimate sources for building knowledge that mirrors such plural perspectives and outcomes, as I have illustrated.

In the recently publicized documentary drama, *The Social Dilemma* (Orlowski 2020), a group of male tech experts shared their experiential testimonies regarding the dangerous impact of social networking on our humanity and survival. Comparing social media to drug addiction and the stock market, the consensus in the film is that social media is a tool that has its own agenda and ways of pursing it, and can trade in and manipulate human futures. Therefore, "[u]nderstanding data as a fact, or as zeros and ones, flattens their constructed, situated, and timely aspects" (Luka and Millette 2018, para.1). Similar to Chakravartty et al.'s argument that non-white scholars engage race as an analytical framework yet are significantly under-cited and underrepresented in the field of communication, most of the techno-utopian fixes that research the relationship between the Arab Spring and socio-political activism centre the whitestream male gaze, which allows for 'pitfalls of both essentialism and tokenism' (2018, p. 261). For that reason, further research and discussions on the role new media continues to play in shaping public discourses in the Arab Gulf must take into account 'the complexities of class, gender, sexuality, and transnational histories of racial and ethnic difference' (ibid.).

Notes

1   'Carceral feminism refers' to feminist advocacy efforts that blindly trusts and solely
     relies on state interventions and incarceration to solve issues related to gender
     inequity and gender-based violence.
2   'Bedouin' is often translated as 'Arab nomads who lived in the dessert'. In modern
     times, Bedouin could also mean people who live in urban areas but have nomadic
     ancestry and take pride in their tribal belonging.
3   *Noon al-Niswa* refers to the grammatical use of the letter ن ('n') in Arabic when
     added to words (verbs or pronouns) to change them into the plural form of the
     feminine.

References

@AljaziAlsenafi (Al Jazi Al Senafi). (2019) [Twitter]. Apr 2, 2019, 5:28AM. Available at:
     https://twitter.com/AljaziAlsenafi/status/1113010308854042624 [accessed 9 May 2021].
@AlziadiQ8 (Mubarak Al-Dwalia). (2019) [Twitter]. Apr 8, 2019, 3:41PM. Available at:
     https://twitter.com/alziadiq8/status/1115338773531844611?lang=en [accessed 9 May
     2021].
@bedoon_women. (2020a) [Twitter]. ['Following news related to bidun women and
     shining a light on them'].
@bedoon_women. (2020b) [Instagram]. ['Following news related to bidun women and
     shining a light on them']. Available at: https://www.instagram.com/bedoon_women/
@bedouin_acts_of-feminism (Awaishah Alqahtani). (2020) [Instagram]. [Private
     Instagram account]. Available at: https://www.instagram.com/bedouin_acts_of_
     feminism [accessed 9 May 2021].
@HadeelBuQrais (Hadeel BuQrais). (2019) [Twitter]. Apr 5, 2019, 1:30PM. Available at:
     https://twitter.com/hadeelbuqrais/status/1114218648451911681?lang=en. [accessed
     9 May 2021].
@ILUVLIT (SAHAR is me). (2018) [Twitter]. Oct 26, 2018, 7:30AM. Available at: https://
     twitter.com/ILUVLIT/status/1055783712544223232 [accessed 9 May 2021].
@1SD____ (sara alsudairy). (2018) [Twitter]. Oct 26, 2018, 5:01AM. Available at: https://
     twitter.com/1SD____/status/1055746253869514752 [accessed 9 May 2021].
@khadeijakw (Khadeija). (2019) [Twitter] Apr 7, 2019, 2:57PM. Available at: https://
     twitter.com/khadeijakw/status/1114965523534684161 [accessed 9 May 2021].
@m_h_aldallal (Mohammed Aldallal). (2019) [Twitter]. Apr 2, 2019, 11:56AM. Available
     at: https://twitter.com/m_h_aldallal/status/1113107986631852033 [accessed 9 May
     2021].
@suNordic (SingularityU Nordic Summit). (2018) [Twitter]. Available at: https://twitter.
     com/suNordic/status/1054980491103372352 [accessed 9 May 2021].
@VPROTegenlicht (VPRO Tegenlicht). (2018) [Twitter]. 31 May, 2018, 6:02AM. Available
     at: https://twitter.com/VPROTegenlicht/status/1002128049897259011 [accessed 9 May
     2021].
Abdel-Raheem, A. (2013). 'Word to the West: Many Saudi women oppose lifting the
     driving ban', *The Guardian*, 2 November. Available at: https://www.theguardian.com/
     commentisfree/2013/nov/02/saudi-protest-driving-ban-not-popular [accessed 9 June
     2021].

Albloshi, H.H. (2019). 'Stateless in Kuwait', *The Arab Gulf States Institute in Washington*, 8 November. Available at: https://agsiw.org/stateless-in-kuwait/ [accessed 9 June 2021].

Albloshi, H. and Alfahad, F. (2009). 'The Orange Movement of Kuwait: Civic pressure transforms a political system', in M.J. Stephan (ed.) *Civilian Jihad: Nonviolent struggle, democratization, and governance in the Middle East*, pp. 219–32. New York: Palgrave Macmillan.

Alkhshab, Y. (2018). ['"Noon Alniswa": A club to educate girls about their rights'], *Alqabas*, 19 October. Available at: https://alqabas.com/article/594077 [accessed 9 May 2021].

Al-Matar, F. (2018) [Blogspot]. 'Book ban and censorship in Kuwait', *fatimaalmatar*, 3 October. Available at: http://fatimaalmatar.blogspot.com/2018/10/book-ban-and-censorship-in-kuwait.html [accessed 9 May 2021].

Al-mughni, H. (2001). *Women in Kuwait: The politics of gender*. London: Saqi Books.

Al Omran, A. (2011). '"A historical moment": The Saudi women challenging a government by driving', *NPR*, 19 June. Available at: https://www.npr.org/sections/thetwo-way/2011/06/19/137271964/a-historical-moment-the-sa [accessed 9 May 2021].

Al-qadi, F. (2020). 'Do not forget the jailed Saudi women's rights activists', *Al Jazeera*, 8 March. Available at: https://www.aljazeera.com/opinions/2020/3/8/do-not-forget-the-jailed-saudi-womens-rights-activists/ [accessed 9 May 2021].

Alqahtani, A. (2019). Personal interview, 26 December.

Alrasheed, G. (2017). Tweeting towards utopia: Technological utopianism and academic discourse on political movements in the Middle East and North Africa [Doctoral thesis]. Ottawa, ON: Carleton University.

Al Shammari, A. (2019). '"Kuwait and the next generation": An Islamophobic, orientalist documentary of what it means to be Kuwaiti', *Medium*, 31 March. Available at: https://medium.com/@abrar.alshammari/kuwait-and-the-next-generation-an-islamophobic-orientalist-documentary-of-what-it-means-to-be-8dee7027a74e [accessed 9 May 2021].

Al-Sharekh, A. (2017). 'GCC states and social media disruption in an era of transition', in H. Miles and A. Newton (eds.) *The future of the Middle East*, pp. 256–63 [e-book]. Global Policy and Arab Digest. 8 Available at: https://www.smashwords.com/books/view/755015 [accessed 9 May 2021].

Al-Sharif, M. (2018). 'The uofficial Manal al-Sharif wiki', *oct26driving.com*, 9 March. Available at: https://oct26driving.com/a/ [accessed 9 May 2021].

AlShehabi, O.H. (2019). *Contested modernity: Sectarianism, nationalism, and colonialism in Bahrain*. London: One World Academic.

Altunışık, M.B. (2014). 'Rentier state theory and the Arab Uprisings: An appraisal', *Uluslararası İlişkiler*, 11(42), pp. 75–91.

Amer, M. (2019). ['Extremists attack "Loyac" and freedom protectors of parliamentary members come to the defense'], *Al Jarida*, 5 April. Available at: https://www.aljarida.com/articles/1554396190846779200/ [accessed 9 May 2021].

Amworldtodaypm. (2011). 'Manal Al Sharif driving in Saudi Arabia (with English subtitles)', 27 May. Available at: https://www.youtube.com/watch?v=sowNSH_W2r0 [accessed 9 May 2021].

Associated Press. (2011). 'Five Saudi women drivers arrested, says activist', *The Guardian*, 29 June. Available at: https://www.theguardian.com/world/2011/jun/29/saudi-women-drivers-arrested-jiddah [accessed 9 June 2021].

Baraka. (2012). ['Gathering of the *Bidun* in the Taima area and Dr. Fatima al-Matar gets beaten up'], *Alyaum Channel News*, 7 July. Available at: https://www.youtube.com/watch?v=ELc41mPc25s [accessed 9 May 2021].

Beblawi, H.E. (2016). 'The concept of "rentier states" revisited', in A. Galal and I. Diwan (eds.) *The Middle East economies in times of transition*, pp. 199–212. London: Palgrave and Macmillan.

Chakravartty, P., Kuo, R., Grubbs, V. and Mcllwain, C. (2018). '#CommunicationSoWhite', *Journal of Communication*, 68(2), pp. 254–66. Available at: https://academic.oup.com/joc/article-abstract/68/2/254/4958972?redirectedFrom=fulltext [accessed 9 June 2021].

Combahee River Collective. (2017). 'The Combahee River Collective statement', in K.-Y. Taylor (ed.) *How we get free: Black feminism and the Combahee River Collective*, pp. 5–14. Chicago: Haymarket Books.

Crenshaw, K. (1991). 'Mapping the margins: Intersectionality, identity politics, and violence against women of color', *Stanford Law Review*, 43(6), pp. 1241–99. Available at: http://www.jstor/org/stable/1229039 [accessed 9 June 2021].

Deeb, A.V. (2019). 'A Kuwaiti professor fled to the US after being put on trial for a "joke"', February. Available at: https://me.mashable.com/tech/1728/a-kuwaiti-professor-fled-to-the-us-after-being-put-on-trial-for-a-joke-twitter-post [accessed 9 May 2021].

Derwaza, N. (2018). 'Dr. Fatima Al-Matar: Gay students are more exposed to harassment at Kuwait University', *Derwaza News*, 18 October. Available at: https://derwaza.news/Home/Details/5bc89c6d8c42533b30598f43_2 [accessed 9 June 2021].

Diamond, L. and Plattner, M.F. (eds.). (2012). *Liberation technology: Social media and the struggle for democracy*. Baltimore MD: Johns Hopkins University Press.

Galtung, J. (1969). 'Violence, peace, and peace research', *Journal of Peace Research*, 6(3), pp. 167–91.

Gray, M. (2011). *A theory of "Late Rentierism" in the Arab States of the Gulf*. Occasional Paper No. 7, Center for International and Regional Studies, Washington DC: Georgetown University, School of Foreign Service in Qatar.

Hanson, M. and Teff, M. (2011). *Kuwait: Gender discrimination creates statelessness and endangers families*. Field report, 17 October. Refugees International. Available at: https://www.refworld.org/docid/4eb24a882.html [accessed 9 June 2021].

Human Rights Watch (HRW). (2019). 'Kuwait: Jailed Bidun activists on hunger strike', *Human Rights Watch*, 30 August. Available at: https://www.hrw.org/news/2019/08/30/kuwait-jailed-bidun-activists-hunger-strike [accessed 9 June 2021].

Jaafari, S. (2019). 'How rising numbers of Gulf women are escaping abuse to seek asylum', *The World*, 11 March. Available at: https://www.pri.org/stories/2019-03-11/how-rising-numbers-gulf-women-are-escaping-abuse-seek-asylum [accessed 9 June 2021].

Kanna, A., Renard, A.L. and Vora, N. (2020). 'Introduction: Ethnography from the exceptional to the everyday', in A. Kanna, A.L. Renard and N. Vora (eds.) *Beyond exception: New interpretations of the Arabian Peninsula*, pp. 1–25. Ithaca, NY: Cornell University Press.

Khashoggi, J. (2017). 'Opinion: Saudi Arabia wasn't always this repressive. Now it's unbearable', *The Washington Post*, 18 September. Available at: https://www.washingtonpost.com/news/global-opinions/wp/2017/09/18/saudi-arabia-wasnt-always-this-repressive-now-its-unbearable/ [accessed 9 June 2021].

Khashoggi, J. (2018). 'Saudi Arabia's women can finally drive. but the crown prince needs to do much more', *The Washington Post*, 25 June. Available at: https://www.washingtonpost.com/news/global-opinions/wp/2018/06/25/saudi-arabias-women-can-finally-drive-but-the-crown-prince-needs-to-do-much-more/ [accessed 9 June 2021].

Leber, A. and Abrahams, A. (2019). 'A storm of tweets: Social media manipulation during the Gulf crisis', *Review of Middle East Studies*, 53(2), pp. 241–58.

Lim, M. (2018). 'Unveiling Saudi feminism(s): Historicization, heterogeneity, and corporeality in women's movements', *Canadian Journal of Communication Corporation*, 43(3), pp. 461–79.

Luka, M.E. and Millette, M. (2018). '(Re)framing big data: Activating situated knowledges and a feminist ethics of care in social media research', *Social Media + Society*, 4(2). Available at: https://doi.org/10.1177/2056305118768297

Lynch, M. (2006). *Voices of the new Arab public: Iraq, al-Jazeera, and Middle East politics today*. New York: Columbia University Press.

MacFarquhar, N. (2011). 'Saudis arrest woman leading right-to-drive campaign', *The New York Times*, 24 May. Available at: https://www.nytimes.com/2011/05/24/world/middleeast/24saudi.html [accessed 9 June 2021].

Mobasher News. (2019). ['Dr. Fatima al-Matar, a 'woman's' journey from Taima to the asylum center in America'], 16 January. Available at: https://www.youtube.com/watch?v=RqDuFVyOOqs [accessed 9 June 2021].

Motaparthy, P. (2011). 'Prisoners of the past: Kuwaiti *Bidun* and the burden of statelessness', *Human Rights Watch*, 13 June. Available at: https://www.hrw.org/report/2011/06/13/prisoners-past/kuwaiti-bidun-and-burden-statelessness [accessed 9 June 2021].

Nabbout, M. (2019). 'Kuwaiti law professor was put on trial over joke, so she fled to U.S.', *Step Feed*, 16 January. Available at: https://stepfeed.com/kuwaiti-law-professor-was-put-on-trial-over-joke-so-she-fled-to-u-s-7057 [accessed 9 June 2021].

Nasser, S. (2019). 'Who benefits from rescuing Rahaf? Questions linger after whirlwind story of Saudi teen's asylum', CBC, 14 January. Available at: https://www.cbc.ca/news/canada/toronto/rahaf-al-qunun-canada-saudi-refugee-1.4976735 [accessed 9 June 2021].

Ngo, M. (2018). 'Saudi women are now legally able to drive. But women's rights activists aren't the ones getting credit', *Vox*, 24 June. Available at: https://www.vox.com/world/2018/6/24/17492586/women-saudi-arabia-driving-license-prince-mohammed-bin-salman [accessed 9 June 2021].

Ortiz, J., Young, A., Myers, M.D., Bedeley, R.T., Carbaugh, D., Chughtai, H., Davidson, E., George, J., Gogan, J., Gordon, S., Grimshaw, E., Leidner, D.E., Pulver, M. and Wigdor, A. (2019). 'Giving voice to the voiceless: The use of digital technologies by marginalized groups' [panel report], *Communications of the Association for Information Systems*, 45. Available at: https://doi.org/10.17705/1CAIS.04502

Ritzen, Y. (2019). 'The fake Twitter accounts influencing the Gulf crisis', *Al Jazeera*, 21 July. Available at: https://www.aljazeera.com/news/2019/07/21/the-fake-twitter-accounts-influencing-the-gulf-crisis/ [accessed 9 June 2021].

Rothna, B. (2017). 'The brave female activists who fought to lift Saudi Srabia's driving ban', *Human Rights Watch*, 29 September. Available at: https://www.hrw.org/news/2017/09/29/brave-female-activists-who-fought-lift-saudi-arabias-driving-ban [accessed 9 June 2021].

Salim, D. (2020). ['The forgotten by feminism: What do *Bidūn* women face?'], *Manshoor*, 3 July. Available at: https://manshoor.com/people/bedon-women-forgotten-from-feminism/ [accessed 9 June 2021].

Sherry, V.N. (2004). '"Bad dreams": Exploitation and abuse of migrant workers in Saudi Arabia', *Human Rights Watch*, 13 July. Available at: https://www.hrw.org/report/2004/07/13/bad-dreams-exploitation-and-abuse-migrant-workers-saudi-arabia [accessed 9 June 2021].

Shubert, A. (2011). 'Saudi woman claims she was detained for driving', *CNN World*, 27 May. http://edition.cnn.com/2011/WORLD/meast/05/21/saudi.women.drivers/ [accessed 9 June 2021].

The Social Dilemma. (2020). Directed by J. Orlowski. USA: Exposure Labs. Available from Netflix. *Tegenlicht*. (2018). 'Koorddansen in Koeweit' ['Tightrope walking in Kuwait'], VPRO, 27 May. Available at: https://www.vpro.nl/programmas/tegenlicht/kijk/afleveringen/2017-2018/Koorddansen-in-Koeweit.html [no longer accessible].

u/azizborashed. (2019) [Reddit]. 'Kuwait and the next generation', 13 Sepember. Available at: https://www.reddit.com/r/Kuwait/comments/d3mgmg/kuwait_and_the_next_generation/ [accessed 9 June 2021].

Van Waas, L. (2010). The situation of stateless persons in the Middle East and North Africa. United Nations High Commissioner for Refugees (UNHCR), Division of International Protection (DIP) and the Regional Bureau for the Middle East and North Africa. Available at: https://www.unhcr.org/protection/statelessness/4ce63e079/situation-stateless-persons-middle-east-north-africa-laura-van-waas.html [accessed 9 June 2021].

Vlack, H.G.V. (1917). 'The future in Arabia', *Neglected Arabia: The Arabian mission*, 102 (July – August – September), pp. 21–23.

Wheeler, D. (2000). 'New media, globalization and Kuwaiti national identity', *The Middle East Journal*, 54(3), pp. 432–44.

Yuce, S., Agarwal, N., Wigand, R.T., Lim, M. and Robinson, R.S. (2014). 'Studying the evolution of online collective action: Saudi Arabian women's "oct26driving" Twitter campaign', in W.G. Kennedy, N. Agerwal and S.J. Yang (eds.) *7th International Conference, Social Computing, Behavioral-Cultural Modeling, and Prediction (SBP) 2014*, pp. 413–20. Washington D.C., 1–4 April 2014. New York: Springer International.

Zayani, M. (2008). 'The challenges and limits of universalist concepts: Problematizing public opinion and a mediated Arab public sphere', *Middle East Journal of Culture and Communication*, 1, pp. 60–79.

INDEX

Boldface locators indicate figures and tables; locators followed by "n." indicate endnotes

www.ingramcontent.com/pod-product-compliance
Lightning Source LLC
Chambersburg PA
CBHW050438280326
41932CB00013BA/2156